Teaching Urban and Regional Planning

ELGAR GUIDES TO TEACHING

The Elgar Guides to Teaching series provides a variety of resources for instructors looking for new ways to engage students. Each volume provides a unique set of materials and insights that will help both new and seasoned teachers expand their toolbox in order to teach more effectively. Titles include selections of methods, exercises, games and teaching philosophies suitable for the particular subject featured. Each volume is authored or edited by a seasoned professor. Edited volumes comprise contributions from both established instructors and newer faculty who offer fresh takes on their fields of study.

Titles in the series include:

Teaching the History of Economic Thought
Integrating Historical Perspectives Into Modern Economics
Edited by Daniela Tavasci and Luigi Ventimiglia

Teaching Benefit-Cost Analysis
Tools of the Trade
Edited by Scott Farrow

Teaching Human Resource Management
An Experiential Approach
Edited by Suzanne C. de Janasz and Joanna Crossman

Preparing for High Impact Organizational Change
Experiential Learning and Practice
Edited by Gavin M. Schwarz, Anthony F. Buono and Susan M. Adams

Teaching Cultural Economics
Edited by Trine Bille, Anna Mignosa and Ruth Towse

Teaching Nonprofit Management
Edited by Karabi C. Bezboruah and Heather Carpenter

Teaching the Essentials of Law and Economics
Antony W. Dnes

Teaching Strategic Management
A Hands-on Guide to Teaching Success
Sabine Baumann

Teaching Urban and Regional Planning
Innovative Pedagogies in Practice
Edited by Andrea I. Frank and Artur da Rosa Pires

Teaching Urban and Regional Planning

Innovative Pedagogies in Practice

Edited by

Andrea I. Frank

PhD, Teaching Fellow in Urban Planning, Centre for Urban and Regional Studies, School of Geography, Earth and Environmental Sciences, University of Birmingham, UK

Artur da Rosa Pires

Professor of Spatial Planning, Innovation and Development Policy, Department of Social, Political and Territorial Sciences, University of Aveiro, Portugal

ELGAR GUIDES TO TEACHING

Edward Elgar
PUBLISHING

Cheltenham, UK • Northampton, MA, USA

Cover image: Joshua Rawson-Harris on Unsplash.

Published by
Edward Elgar Publishing Limited
The Lypiatts
15 Lansdown Road
Cheltenham
Glos GL50 2JA
UK

Edward Elgar Publishing, Inc.
William Pratt House
9 Dewey Court
Northampton
Massachusetts 01060
USA

A catalogue record for this book
is available from the British Library

Library of Congress Control Number: 2020950927

This book is available electronically in the **Elgar**online
Geography, Planning and Tourism subject collection
http://dx.doi.org/10.4337/9781788973632

Printed on elemental chlorine free (ECF)
recycled paper containing 30% Post-Consumer Waste

ISBN 978 1 78897 362 5 (cased)
ISBN 978 1 78897 363 2 (eBook)

Printed and bound in the USA

Contents

Figures

Tables

Boxes

Contributors

EDITORS

Andrea I. Frank is a Teaching Fellow in Urban Planning at the University of Birmingham. She has extensively researched and documented the development of planning education and has been awarded Senior Fellow by UK's Advance HE in acknowledgement of her engagement and competencies in pedagogy in Built Environment disciplines. From 2000 to 2011, she was the subject coordinator and later co-director of the Centre for Education of the Built Environment (CEBE) for which she conducted workshops, organized conferences, researched and published on issues like work-based learning, creative problem-solving, internationalization, employability and entrepreneurship amongst others. She also is Chair of the Association of European Schools of Planning's (AESOP) Excellence in Teaching Prize Jury and chaired the council for the Global Planning Education Association Network. Since 2017, she has coordinated the AESOP Thematic Group on Planning Education together with co-editor Artur da Rosa Pires. She has co-edited *Urban Planning Education: Beginnings, Global Movement and Future Prospects* (with C. Silver, Springer 2018) and is a founding co-editor of AESOP's open access, double-blind peer-reviewed journal *Transactions of AESOP*.

Artur da Rosa Pires is Full Professor in Spatial Planning and Innovation Policy at the University of Aveiro. His main research interests are Innovation and Development Policy, Spatial Strategic Planning and Local Government and Sustainable Development. He is a member of the Research Unit on Governance, Competitiveness and Public Policy (GOVCOPP), where he has developed both applied and fundamental research, and participated in and coordinated several national and international projects. He was Adviser for Science and the Environment of the Portuguese President of the Republic (2009–2011), Member of the Portuguese Government as Secretary of State for the Environment and Spatial Planning (2004), Vice President of the Regional Commission for Coordination and Development, Centro Region (2003–2005) charged with the responsibility for Innovation Strategies and Regional Development Policy, and Pro-Rector of the University of Aveiro (2008–2012) with the mission of linking the University and the Region. Recently, he has developed an interest in contemporary educational and pedagogical changes, and coordinates, together with Andrea I. Frank, the AESOP Thematic Group on Planning Education.

CONTRIBUTORS

Nadia Alaily-Mattar is a Research and Teaching Associate at the Chair of Urban Development in the Department of Architecture at the Technical University Munich, Germany.

Iulian Barba Lata is a Lecturer in Spatial Planning at Wageningen University & Research, the Netherlands.

Ronald Barnett is Professor Emeritus of Higher Education at University College London, UK, where he was Pro-Director and Dean of Professional Development. He continues to pursue work in the philosophy of higher education and as a consultant and visiting professor.

Andreas Brück is Senior Researcher and Lecturer, and Managing Director of K LAB (Laboratory for Communication) at the Institute for Urban and Regional Planning – Technical University Berlin, Germany.

Marleen Buizer is Assistant Professor in Strategic Communication in the Department of Social Sciences at Wageningen University & Research, the Netherlands.

Teresa Calix is an Assistant Professor in the Centre for Architecture and Urban Studies (CEAU), Faculty of Architecture at the University of Porto (FAUP), Porto, Portugal.

Duygu Cihanger Ribeiro is an Assistant Professor at Middle East Technical University, City and Regional Planning Department, Ankara, Turkey.

Grazia Concilio is an Associate Professor in the Department of Architecture and Urban Studies at the Politecnico di Milano, Italy.

Paula Custódio de Oliveira is a Researcher in the Housing and Human Settlements Laboratory at the University of São Paulo, Brazil.

Camila D'Ottaviano is Associate Professor in the School of Architecture and Urbanism at the University of São Paulo (FAUUSP), Brazil.

Lukas Gilliard is Assistant to the Executive Directors at HafenCity development corporation in Hamburg, Germany and recently completed his PhD at the Technical University in Munich, Germany.

Anita Grams is a Senior Expert for long-term mobility and spatial development at Swiss Railways SBB and previously was a researcher and director of studies for the MAS in Spatial Planning at the ETH Zurich, Switzerland.

Rachel Kallus is Professor at the Faculty of Architecture and Town Planning, Technion – Israel Institute of Technology, Haifa, Israel.

Terry Lamb is Professor of Languages and Interdisciplinary Pedagogy affiliated with the School of Humanities and the Westminster Centre for Education and Teaching Innovation at the University of Westminster, London, UK.

Angela Million is Professor for Urban Design and Urban Development, and Director of the Institute for Urban and Regional Planning – Technical University Berlin, Germany.

José Carlos Mota is an Assistant Professor in the Department of Social, Political and Territorial Sciences at the University of Aveiro, Aveiro, Portugal.

Mercedes Narciso is an Adjunct Associate Professor in the Graduate Center for Planning and the Environment at Pratt Institute, Brooklyn, New York, USA.

Fernando Nogueira, is Assistant Professor in the Department of Social, Political and Territorial Sciences at the University of Aveiro, Aveiro, Portugal.

Louise O'Kane is a Planner and Engagement Officer at Community Places in Belfast, UK.

Juan Camilo Osorio is an Assistant Professor in the Graduate Center for Planning and the Environment at Pratt Institute, Brooklyn, New York, USA.

Emma Puerari is an Assistant Professor in Urban Design and Planning in the Department of Planning and Environment, Faculty of Spatial Sciences at the University of Groningen, the Netherlands.

Gavan Rafferty is Lecturer in Spatial Planning and Development in the Belfast School of Architecture and the Built Environment at Ulster University, Northern Ireland. He is also Course Director for the MSc in Community Planning and Governance and the MSc Planning Regeneration and Development.

Maria L. Refinetti Martins is a Full Professor in the School of Architecture and Urbanism at the University of São Paulo, and Researcher at the Housing and Human Settlements Laboratory, Brazil.

João Farias Rovati is Full Professor in the Faculty of Architecture at the Federal University of Rio Grande do Sul (UFRGS), Porto Alegre, Brazil.

Adam Sheppard is an Associate Head in the Department of Geography and Environmental Management and a lecturer in urban and rural planning. He is the course director for the Joint Distance Learning Consortium at UWE Bristol, UK.

Alain Thierstein is Professor of Urban Development in the Department of Architecture at the Technical University of Munich, Germany.

Elsa Vivant is an Assistant Professor in the Ecole d'Urbanisme at the Université Paris Est Marne la Vallée, France.

Goran Vodicka is a Lecturer in the Department of the Natural and Built Environment at Sheffield Hallam University, UK.

Ayse Yonder is a Professor in the Graduate Center for Planning and the Environment at Pratt Institute, Brooklyn, New York, USA.

Foreword

Daniel Galland

A few years ago, when preparing a meeting on quality for planning education held under the auspices of the Association of European Schools of Planning, I revisited an insightful chapter on the mission and features of spatial planning written by Raphaël Fischler and Charles Hoch,[1] two acknowledged North American scholars whose work has highly inspired my trajectory as a planning instructor in Scandinavia. Written almost a decade ago, the chapter envisioned what planning students needed to learn to meet the challenges faced by the profession. To attain its raison d'être, it contended that planning education should promote 'an active, searching curiosity in the service of practical judgement' by teaching 'perception, performance and prudence' via reciprocal forms of instruction and practical learning.

While these objectives certainly continue to underpin the field of planning education at the dawn of the 2020s, planning as a field of practice has become increasingly challenged by a myriad of highly disruptive problems characterized by a complex blend of socio-spatial (e.g., rising inequality and differentiation, increased population and migration), economic (e.g., firm strategies, investment decisions, labour dynamics, technological developments) and environmental (e.g., natural resource depletion, epidemics, energy and water demands, food supply, ageing) dimensions and patterns. Far outpacing the capacity of planning to effectively comply with its hallmarks, these wicked issues and their aggravating effects place unprecedented demands on a profession that is once again standing at a crossroads reinventing itself. As John Forester rightly reminds us, planning is 'the organization of hope'.[2] So, if hope is to mobilize planning and its courses of action, then never before has there been greater need for a renewed pedagogical arsenal in planning education – an arsenal capable of endowing university instructors, students and communities with 'co-constructed values, knowledges, skills and competences' to address the pressing challenges of planning.[3]

It is in this spirit that this unique volume not only widens but also enlightens current debates on how planning education and teaching pedagogies can meaningfully contribute to a transformational shift towards urban and regional sustainability as well as a more socially just world in the 21st century. Through a brilliant exposure of contemporary pedagogical trends advanced by educationalists, as well as original and enticing pedagogical accounts developed by planning educators from different parts of the world, the chapters in this book showcase an invigorating journey exhibiting timely cases of teaching and learning for, in and with communities; innovative classroom-based competencies driven by critical engagement and reflexivity skills; and capacity building strategies for further planning education and life-long learning. At the same time, the compilation strongly contributes to bridge a dialogical gap between contemporary debates relating to transformative changes in higher education, and novel pedagogical dimensions in the specific field of planning. Beyond exposing the reader to these trends, an outstanding merit of the book is its portrayal of a new learning landscape in planning which is being gradually consolidated.

At a time when the COVID-19 pandemic has significantly hampered the delivery of co-constructed learning, community-based and other new-fangled, in-class pedagogical practices, the missive and value of interdisciplinary learning and working, and of integrating co-learning, co-designing and co-working with communities unquestionably remains. In this respect, the present volume similarly contributes to provide a better understanding of how planning education endeavours to transcend disciplinary boundaries while interconnecting planning curricula and teaching pedagogies allowing students to undergo committed and fervent action-driven learning. Spatial planning is indeed required to engage with multiple and fluid frames that better acknowledge and respond to the shifting content of the real-world picture.[4] It is in this context that this revealing tome should comprise an essential read for planning educators seeking to foster transformational change through 'radically new pedagogies' aimed at addressing both old and new wicked problems.

Daniel Galland
Copenhagen, Denmark
August 2020

NOTES

1. C. Hoch and R. Fischler (2012). Mission, goals and features of spatial planning. In B. Scholl (ed.), *Higher Education in Spatial Planning: Positions and Reflections* (pp. 16–23). Zurich: vdf Hochschulverlag AG.
2. J. Forester (1989). *Planning in the Face of Power*. Berkeley: University of California Press.
3. T. Lamb and G. Vodicka (2020). Education for 21st century urban and spatial planning: Critical postmodern pedagogies. In A. I. Frank and A. da Rosa Pires (eds.), *Teaching Urban and Regional Planning: Innovative Pedagogies in Practice*. Cheltenham, UK and Northampton, MA, USA: Edward Elgar Publishing.

4. J. Harrison, D. Galland, and M. Tewdwr-Jones (2020). Regional planning is dead: Long live planning regional futures. *Regional Studies.* (pp. 1–13) Accessed September 2020 at https://doi.org/10.1080/00343404.2020.1750580

Acknowledgements

Initial ideas for a book featuring newly emerging pedagogies in the field of urban and regional planning were inspired by animated discussions and lively debates about novel pedagogies used in planning education programmes in Europe and beyond at the 2017 and 2018 Association of European Schools of Planning (AESOP) congresses in Lisbon, Portugal and Gothenborg, Sweden, respectively. As such our thanks goes to those present at these sessions who provided through their presentations, discussions and interest the stimulus to encourage us to embark on this book project.

We are also appreciative for the support from our institutions – the University of Aveiro, Cardiff University and the TU Dortmund. A special word of thanks goes to Professor Karsten Zimmermann, from TU Dortmund, a place that has contributed much throughout the years to the development of the planning field and planning education, who provided to one of the editors generous support, encouragement, and the flexible working arrangements that helped to pull together the manuscript at the end of 2019 and beginning of 2020.

The book would have not been possible without the unwavering support of the team at Edward Elgar – first and foremost, Katy Crossan, who patiently and competently responded to queries and issues we encountered throughout the process from developing the proposal to finalizing the manuscript. We also are grateful for the suggestion of Alexander Pettifer to invite and work together with pedagogical and educational specialists. In turn, these educationalists embraced the opportunity bravely, venturing across disciplinary boundaries, and their insights have greatly enriched this book. The interdisciplinary encounters that emerged have opened new perspectives and lenses through which to interpret the experiments and trends observable in the teaching and pedagogical case studies in planning education that are featured in the book. On a personal level these encounters triggered new learning and insights that enriched us as individuals but also our outlook on the future of education for planning.

There are many more that deserve our thanks, including our colleagues who listened to our ideas and helped us reflect on them, reviewers of the book proposal, and the contributors of the chapters who remained patient and faithful to the project throughout the lengthy process of the production of the volume. The latter were understanding and entertained our repeated requests for changes and edits with speed and efficiency. Finally, our families and friends, who showed support and understanding of this project by considering ways to enhance our and others' capacity to build better, sustainable and resilient living habitats and address the many pressing global challenges in human settlements on a fragile planet which is home to us all.

Andrea I. Frank and Artur R. Pires

1. Introduction: transformational change in planning education pedagogy?

Andrea I. Frank and Artur da Rosa Pires

There may never have been a greater need for spatial planning than at the start of the 21st century with both urban and non-urban space transforming at unprecedented rates due to urbanization, sprawl and human-induced change to natural habitats. It is the task of planning and planners not only to guide communities, companies, and politicians on how to use and manage land based on scientific evidence, but also to build capacity to plan and shape places and spaces through creative vision into liveable, resilient, and sustainable communities. Planning is a relatively young and applied discipline, which has evolved and re-invented itself several times over. The field needs to adjust continuously; just like Engineering or Medicine, its practice is shaped by and reacts to external technological, demographic and societal factors. And, it is our belief that further deep and fundamental change, indeed a transformation, is needed to both how we plan and the requisite education and training so that future generations of planners are as best prepared to confront the contemporary challenges of the Anthropocene such as climate change, intensifying socio-economic inequalities, environmental pollution and decline, and growing resource scarcities. It will mean introducing new knowledge areas but also, more poignantly, new pedagogical approaches. These will be the focus of this volume.

Simply, the aim of this book is to foster and advance the dialogue on contemporary challenges to planning education, focusing particularly on pedagogies. It calls attention to ongoing and – arguably – transformational changes in spatial planning and its education provision by showcasing how educators from around the globe have begun to address emerging gaps in competencies with novel and innovative pedagogies and teaching.

CONTEXT

Education for urban and regional (spatial) planning began about a century ago when academics teaching at universities in Europe and the USA, in related disciplines such as civic engineering, architecture, landscape architecture, and geography, started to introduce courses covering urban issues. These courses, or modules in today's higher education terminology, included topics such as designing town extensions or doing civic surveys to diagnose and understand urban issues before developing 'treatments' and solutions. From such individual modules or courses gradually entire programmes of study emerged, first at postgraduate, and later also at undergraduate level, and nowadays provide education and training in the art and science of city building and design, and spatial planning to a growing cohort of planning professionals (Frank and Silver 2018).

In most countries, education for urban and spatial planning is delivered in higher education settings where it has been and remains closely linked to preparing students for professional practice. As professional profiles and curricula are linked to national contexts and institutional structures, the skills, knowledge and values to which graduates are socialized as part of their education relate, at least nominally, to guidelines produced by professional societies and bodies. This creates a valuable link between professional practice, and student employability (Frank 2020) – although the role of practitioners or professional bodies, in shaping or influencing curricula, varies and is not always clear cut (Poxon 2000). Over time, subject-specific pedagogies emerged and became accepted hallmarks of curricula shaped to instil planning relevant competencies, such as classes requiring project work (in some contexts called studios), various formats of work-based learning integral to the curriculum or extracurricular, group/team work and a range of activities to develop graphic, written and oral communication skills. Having developed from different disciplinary roots and learning traditions (Rodriguez-Bachiller 1988; Frank 2012), planning curricula have often focused on singular typologies of knowing and knowledge creation, leading to a heterogeneous professional profile globally.

Some common trajectories prevail, nevertheless. For example, we note how the focus of planning education changed, often in response to newly emerging needs and changing societal conditions (e.g., Brooks 1988; Hemmens 1988; Dalton 2001; Stiftel et al. 2009; Scholl 2012) and pedagogies and teaching approaches along with it (Lang 1983; Heumann and Wetmore 1984; Krueckeberg 1985). More specifically, these changes have included a move from a strong practice-oriented applied engineering and design tradition and relevant pedagogies like studios, fieldwork and internships to more theory, social science and economy with lectures and tutorials. In newer revisions of curricula, entrepreneurship and management training (Rodwin and Sanyal 2000; Guzzetta and Bollens 2003), with role play or simulations, as well as a re-establishment of studio and group projects (e.g., Neuman 2016) can be noted. Now, at the start of the 21st century, it seems planning education curricula and pedagogies are due for another major shift in response to a collaborative and more recently transformative turn in planning.

Over and over, planning has been identified as one of the professions vital to progressing the sustainability of cities and regions (Briassoulis 1999; Jepson 2001; UN Habitat 2009, 2016), replete with associated issues such as mitigating climate change, urban resiliency, inclusivity and so forth. However, progress towards developing more sustainable cities and places has been hampered by the difficulty of overcoming entrenched ways of doing things (Wolfram et al. 2019), and it is increasingly being argued that traditional approaches may no longer suffice (e.g., Rooij and Frank 2016; Albrechts et al. 2020). Collaborative and more recently transformative practices are being promoted which involve changes to the role and tasks of planning and its rationalities (Rodwin and Sanyal 2000) as well as the tools and the institutions involved in planning. For some, the transformative turn in planning means overcoming neoliberalist urbanism (e.g., Angotti 2020) with calls to adopt greater social, ecological and ethical responsibilities in the spatial planning and design fields (Salama 2015).

One should not underestimate the depth and breadth of these developments, which go beyond merely incorporating a new knowledge area. Frankly, it means that planners are expected to be able to address ever more complex and 'wicked' problems in challenging and fluid institutional settings. Transformative planning is frequently cutting across sectoral and territorial boundaries, engaging a variety of different actors through novel methods, while frequently acting outside the statutory framework. As champions of transitioning places away from unsustainable conditions, planners will need to be action-oriented, able to build alliances and overcome adversity. It requires creativity (Landry 2000; Albrechts 2005), not just in the traditional design sense, but employing creative thinking techniques more broadly (see De Bono 1992; Higgins and Reeves 2006). Success of future plans and the professionals behind them will depend on transparent and clear communication with a diversity of stakeholders including the general public. Peel (2000) forcefully argued that future planners are to be facilitators and coordinators of change – change agents who empower others, co-create and co-shape urban districts, neighbourhoods and spatial development trajectories. There is also a need for more integration and merging of different traditions into single innovative and visionary programmes and developments (see Lamb and Vodicka, Chapter 2), with an openness to work with other fields and disciplines being one of the suggested areas of development. And while interdisciplinary literacies have been part of what planning education is to provide – in reality, pedagogies that foster interdisciplinary team working have been hard to implement in university settings upholding disciplinary silos and learning traditions. Moreover, risk-averse students and institutional efforts to harmonize and streamline educational experiences as a consequence of greater top-down quality assurance processes can stifle uptake of novel and experimental learning experiences where learning outcomes are potentially more unpredictable and variable.

At this point it is worth noting that, in a parallel development pedagogical research and educationalists are engaging in an unprecedented discussion about the challenges of education, and especially of higher education, in a globally changing world. They are suggesting, namely, that future cohorts of students will (a) have different expectations of their learning environment and how they prefer to learn, and (b) that educating for life in the 21st century will require learners to develop different skills and dispositions to remain positive and action-oriented. Visser (2018) has argued, similarly, that the realities of global issues, such as climate change, loss of biodiversity, health endangering pollution and resource shortages which threaten, in fact, the existence of humanity itself, require a different learning landscape altogether. Drawing on Crutzen and Stoermer (2000, p. 18), who emphasized that "a world-wide accepted strategy leading to sustainability of ecosystems against human induced stresses will be one of the great future tasks of mankind, requiring intensive research efforts and *wise* application of the knowledge thus acquired" [emphasis added], Visser (2018, p. 6) suggests it is imperative to focus on emotional competencies (not merely knowledge) as prerequisite to profoundly change "our way of being in the world".

Some suggestions for developing students' transformational competencies necessary to effect transitional change can be gleaned from pedagogies identified as effective by the growing body of research into education for sustainable development (ESD). Studies suggest, for example, that experiential learning and action pedagogies (see e.g., Frisk and Larson 2011; Barth and Michelson 2013), as well as transformational learning spaces affording both physical space and "dedicated time for reflection, dialogue and action" (Moore 2005, p. 337), are valuable in ESD. It is also evident, that many transformational learning experiences occur in informal settings (Visser 2018). Both issues provide impetus when considering curriculum design and pedagogies.

The emerging perspectives on educational changes, and the inherent tensions with broader institutional constraints, are certainly of great relevance to planning education, which obviously unfolds precisely in such context. Nevertheless, the links between the two strands of debate, on wider educational changes and planning education per se, are essentially missing from much of the recent debates and are addressed only sporadically and in a rather fragmented way. There is certainly a need for a closer articulation between these two bodies of thought and this book aims to take a step forward in that direction by bringing together educationalists and planning educators to address and discuss change in the education of planners in contemporary society.

A third strand of thought exists that cannot be dissociated from the two previous ones and that certainly impinges on both of them. It is focused on the discussion about 'the University of the Future' and on how the university, and academia, will adapt to the political, technological, social and environmental drivers of change that will shape the world to come. Here the discussion spans from emerging efforts to counter the ever-increasing bureaucratization of the tertiary sector through to attempts to redesign the student learning experience as well as to redefine universities' missions as engaged universities (e.g., Goddard 2009; Barnett 2009, 2011, 2017). These discussions are, *inter alia*, opening up new avenues to develop collaborative and interactive curricula in which students can experience a meaningful action-oriented learning experience. Expectations are that students should be endowed with up-to-date scientific knowledge, but also basic and transversal skills, as well as with social and civic competencies, in order to engage more actively with communities and to foster the capacity to build innovative, inclusive and sustainable development transitions. Deep learning is facilitated by exposure to different kinds of real-world problems and processes of knowledge creation and development through design or scientific inquiry, which is in turn supported by intermittent reflections and theoretical discussions. All these themes add another layer of educational and pedagogical challenges to those mentioned earlier.

APPROACH

Given the above arguments and context, one of the questions that arises is how could and should a new learning landscape unfold and express itself specifically for the field of spatial planning? A second issue is how far the educational challenges, as well as personal development competencies, could be met with an adaptive evolution of current education traditions and practices or whether more fundamental and radical pedagogical changes would be needed?

Seeking to invoke a deeper and richer debate of these issues, we solicited case examples from planning educators featuring innovative and novel pedagogies in spatial planning, on the one hand, and, on the other, we invited prestigious educationalists to comment on (i) the broader changes that are likely to influence higher education in the years to come, in respect to educational and pedagogical approaches, and (ii) the implications or the challenges that the above trends will raise, in terms of educational approaches, to a specific field of practice that deals with changes in society, such as spatial planning. In order to connect the two types of contribution, a short description of the aims of the book, as well as a summary of each chapter, were made available to the educationalists.

In all, there are 13 case studies from a global set of planning educators spanning from Latin America to the Netherlands and Germany. This said, the collection does not claim to be comprehensive in any respect, as many excellent and noteworthy practices are not part of the volume. It simply would have been impractical. The focus here is on initial planning education, i.e. Bachelor and Master level programmes and to a minor extent continued professional development or advanced studies. We acknowledge that doctoral education for spatial planning will also require attention in future (see e.g., Kehm 2007; Internationales Doktoranden Kolleg 2016) but decided that this is beyond the scope of the present book. Also, as examples were drawn from presentations of the Association of European Schools of Planning (AESOP) congresses, there is a lack of cases from Asia, Africa and Australia/New Zealand.

The teaching case studies are written to enhance accessibility and sharing amongst the growing global community of planning educators. A broad definition of planning was applied to respect and indeed celebrate the diverse conceptions of planning in different national contexts. Thus, pedagogical initiatives are framed in a wider context and beyond the strict disciplinary borders of 'planning'. Although we refrained from using templates to impose format, we worked with the authors to ensure that case studies are written and structured in a manner to not only inspire but also facilitate adaptive use, reuse and evaluation through and by others. For that purpose, authors were asked to:

1. Provide a course description, content, and learning objectives;
2. Detail underlying concepts, rationale, and purpose, as well as links with contemporary planning challenges;
3. Offer a grounded critical analysis of the achievements so far; and
4. Identify main challenges and provide guidance and suggestions for implementation of similar initiatives.

Given the wide range of national contexts and higher education systems, readers should be aware that case studies use the terminology that is customary in the given context. For example, a teaching unit could be referred to as a module or course, while the entirety of a degree scheme might be labelled as a course or programme. For each case what is meant typically becomes clear as part of the context and we refrained from seeking a harmonization for the sake of it.

THE STRUCTURE OF THE BOOK

The book is divided into four parts bookended by this Introduction and a Conclusion. Part I provides an overview of general concepts dominating the pedagogical discourse in knowledge development and learning in and for higher education at the start of the 21st century. Each of the following parts (II, III, IV) addresses a meta theme, in line with key challenges in contemporary planning education. The first theme is 'Teaching and learning in, for and with community', the second 'Developing new classroom-based competencies', and the third 'Further education and life-long capacity building'. While it is not necessary or intended that the book is read in sequence, it is recommended the reader engages with the educationalist commentary in conjunction with the case studies. It is also fruitful to study cases within each section together. In the following, details of the four central sections of the book and the relevant case contributions are introduced.

Part I: Pedagogical Debates

Part I introduces perspectives from the field of education. The two contributions enable a juxtaposition of trends and pedagogical developments in planning with those identified for postmodern education, pedagogy and higher education philosophy. In the chapter titled 'Education for 21st Century Urban and Spatial Planning: Critical Postmodern Pedagogies', Terry Lamb and Goran Vodicka provide an informed view of the growing "debate about how education can provide an appropriate preparation for life in the 21st century" as well as the many educational reforms that have been introduced in many parts of the world since the turn of the millennium. They argue for a critical postmodern perspective, promoting "radically new pedagogies in order to respond to the complexities of a world in which it is impossible even to know what it means to 'know', when knowledge itself, as well as ways of knowing, are constantly shifting" and adding that such educational changes also need to take place in the field of urban planning. The authors endorse the view of "understanding pedagogy as a deeply civic, political, and moral practice" and produce proposals for new "urban planning and design practices and pedagogies", with due consideration to "the challenges and opportunities faced by those committed to innovative pedagogical interventions in higher education".

The next chapter, 'Planning Education and Planning the University: A Becoming-Symbiosis', by Ronald Barnett, provides a fascinating view of contemporary challenges to both planning practice and planning education through an insightful and creative exploration of the difficulties and opportunities associated with the fictional task of planning a university in the 21st century. Approaching the university as more than just a complex organization, recognizing the multiplicity of ways in which it is entangled with the wider world and how it faces competing internal and external interpretations of itself and its becoming, Barnett illustrates convincingly that "planning for such an assemblage as the contemporary university is bound to be thwarted with challenge". He argues that, faced with a multi-discursive world, planners and planning students need to be familiar not only with transdisciplinarity but with the more "ambitious" concept of "trans-spatiality", that "transcend[s] epistemological spaces and move[s] across ontological spaces". In other words, dealing with a multiplicity of discourses in any given planning situation will require students "to stretch themselves, stretch their being, into uncomfortable registers and modes of experience". The argument goes, then, "in such a conception of planning studies, students stand on a precipice and hurl themselves forward, not to their deaths but to their becoming". In this sense, "to involve students in the challenges of planning … is at once a matter of curriculum and of pedagogy. The two cannot be separated: it is not a matter of choosing the what of the curriculum (contents) and then the how of the pedagogical approach. No. The two are interwoven." This is an absolutely remarkable and thought-provoking statement for reshaping planning education and pedagogical practices.

Part II: Teaching and Learning in, for and with Communities

Part II comprises five teaching cases, all of them dealing, in different and illuminating ways, with transdisciplinary issues, community involvement, co-creation and co-production of knowledge and the need to establish stronger links between science and society. Each case describes how educators have framed, facilitated, and managed the inclusion of stakeholders in teaching in particular modules/courses which are part of planning education programmes at different institutions. This reflects the trend in the sector to inclusive, communicative planning practices by introducing students to complex settings of urban politics, opening eyes to the diverse and often contradictory stakeholder interests and views in modern cities. Each chapter focuses on different issues.

A major innovation discussed in Chapter 4, 'Pedagogy Built on Working with Communities: A First Semester Core Course' by Ayse Yonder and colleagues, is a first-year module in a two-year Master's programme. This diverges from standard practices where students are as a norm gradually introduced to greater complexity and more difficult problems as they progress through their educational itinerary. The results are clearly positive and most students reveal a "true sense of enthusiastic learning". However, Yonder and colleagues are very attentive to the importance of adequate pedagogical support and conscious that studio pedagogy has changed over time, "shifting away from physical planning towards an emphasis on social science and research". And they also emphasize the importance of the institutional context, recognizing the Pratt Institute's legacy of studio pedagogy "not just for learning but creating knowledge" and an orientation "to address poverty and top-down government policies". As a consequence, they are sensitive to how the process impacts partner communities as well as to the tensions and frustrations that may occur among students, often associated with the "transformed subjectivities" deriving from students being confronted with residents that do not share their values. The result, in the words of one of the students, is that "the course is not only an introduction to planning but an opportunity to shape your values as an urban planner through practice and learning".

Chapter 5, 'Planning with the Community: Engaged Professional Education in an Ethno-Nationally Contested City', by Rachel Kallus, offers another example of community-based learning at Master level. Its focus is on how planning in an ethno-nationally contested city creates particular challenges and learning opportunities. The author explores the development, among students, of the sense of 'otherness', i.e., the capacity to learn about others, an experience that also leads students to learn about themselves, to face "the gap between their personal and professional identity [and to] undergo a process of identity formation". Such an experience can be as enriching as disturbing for the student, requiring "innovative engagement techniques" and an informed approach to reflexivity and to "critical pedagogy". Kallus highlights the educational challenges of enabling students to establish "a connection between society, knowledge, and context" and pinpoints the need to reflect about the dilemmas and responsibilities for educators of stimulating community engagement in situations where "the distinction between political orientation and political commitment is blurred" – namely, in the context of planning in contested places.

Chapter 6, 'Challenges in Education of Participatory Planning: Collaborating with Patients and Physicians to Plan Mental Health Facilities' by Elsa Vivant, offers a new approach of relating planning to society and community involvement in planning. Students are to consider the conditions of the (re)location of a new mental health care facility. In an insightful way, this project deepens appreciation of the concept of 'otherness' and the associated educational challenges. Working closely with mental health providers and patients, it offers students a new meaning to and understanding of otherness, confronting them in a rather blunt way with the socio-political and ethical implications of planning practice. Indeed, Vivant argues that the "by no means trivial" experience induces reflexivity amongst students, not only about the meaning and purpose of their work but also about their own beliefs, prejudices and values. She also addresses explicitly the challenges and responsibilities for educators, in what concerns students' well-being, since "the emotional burdens and tensions involved in group projects can be exacerbated … when working with a vulnerable population". Considering the rising concern of linking science with society this chapter offers a very original approach that may stimulate educational initiatives of linking planning with society in novel ways.

Chapter 7, 'Beyond the Classroom: New Skills through Community–University Outreach' by Camila D'Ottaviano and João Rovati, explores recent educational interventions at the universities of Porto Alegre and São Paulo. Community Outreach is a longstanding institutional mission of Brazilian universities and is part of the regular curriculum of all undergraduate courses.

Although the interpretation and intensity of its application has varied significantly over time, the authors actively question "consolidated routines" and
suggest outreach could pedagogically support "alternative planning practices".
They argue that outreach should be seen as an "instrument to provide closer
links between universities and society in order to address the deep social
inequalities existent in Brazil", though they acknowledge some ambiguity and
that academia tend to "value especially research and development of 'pure
knowledge' ... [and] when [academics] engage in 'practical' activities they
usually do so to respond to 'market' demands". Assuming a different stance,
the authors endorse Paulo Freire's pedagogical principles and see community
outreach activities as a way to educate the qualified professional not only as the
"technician" but also as the "humanized and socially committed individual".
The learning-teaching methodology adopted, relying heavily on Freire's "pedagogy of autonomy", favours the blending of academic and popular knowledge
and promotes sensitivity to the needs of the more fragile social groups as well
as a "willingness to deliver", thereby stimulating a strong commitment to
transform reality. The authors also address the institutional fragility of these
activities, particularly the thinness of the available support and the limitations
of the respective learning processes.

Chapter 8 by Gavan Rafferty and colleagues, 'Collaborative and Innovative
Participatory Planning Pedagogies', is based on a research and curriculum
enhancement project, involving students and educators from three different
universities located respectively in Ireland, Italy, and Portugal. It was finan-
cially supported by the EU under the Erasmus+ programme and included the
purposeful and coordinated redesign of teaching modules, the engagement
in community-based projects in each location and provided multi-contextual
learning opportunities through 'blended' mobility study exchanges (for students, staff, local practitioners and civic actors). Allowing for participation in
three real-life civic engagement experiences, the project aimed at preparing
students to work in diverse cultural contexts, exploring different "transdisciplinary environments to share challenges, co-create knowledge and co-design
solutions and actions". In addition to the specific pedagogical approach and
learning, the possibilities of "co-designing multi-contextual learning opportunities across modules in multiple academic institutions" are particularly
valuable and revealing.

Part III: Developing New Classroom-Based Competencies

Part III illustrates the development of new competencies (outside the
community–university, participatory action realm). When considering the
novelty of approaches, it is important to remember the contextuality of planning. In their own way, each of the cases shows educators challenging prevail-

ing concepts and traditions and seeking to advance transdisciplinary thinking by perforating the boundaries between professions, teachers and learners.

Chapter 9 by Teresa Calix entitled 'Urban Design Studio as a Critical Learning Space within the Architecture Curriculum' is an account of changes in planning approaches and planning education over time. It is based on the evolving nature of an 'urban design studio', created in the late 1990s, in the final year of a first degree on Architecture. At the time, spatial planning in Portugal was not only experiencing significant changes but was also increasing its relevance (e.g., Rosa Pires 2018). The course was designed to provide "education for planning within an architecture programme [hoping] to contribute to the training of urbanists with a more comprehensive and broader view". Two decades after its creation, there is a need to accommodate changes in the approach to planning and in the characteristics and demands of Portuguese society. Calix shows how the course has been redesigned to incorporate inter- and trans-disciplinarity, to enhance communicative skills and to promote community engagement skills. The chapter illustrates a carefully nurtured process of introducing "changes in both content and pedagogical practices as a response to an evolving historical context".

Chapter 10 by Lukas Gilliard and colleagues, 'Addressing the Interplay of Design-Based Disciplines and Social Sciences in Urban Development Education', is also based in a design studio context, in this case of an inter-disciplinary Master in 'Urbanism, Landscape and the City'. Starting from the premise that contemporary urbanism, and namely the relational conception of space, is questioning traditional planning concepts, such as 'cities as bounded territories', as well as conventional instruments of urban planning, the authors argue that new approaches are needed to guide the evolution of urban societies. Moreover, the argument goes, "the competencies for steering urban development are distributed among various disciplines … [and] under these conditions, spatial planners will rarely work alone on projects". Having in mind that students (and professionals) tend to adopt ways of thinking that are specific to their disciplines, purposeful pedagogies and methodologies are then seen as absolutely necessary to facilitate working across disciplinary boundaries. The chapter describes a studio that aims not only "to provide students with knowledge on the key principles of 21st century planning and development practice", but also to enable them to work collaboratively. This latter goal is achieved through the adoption of Trend Analysis as a methodological tool to effectively combine "the rationalist, scientific, empirical work of social scientists and the more subjective, creative work of architects and planners". The detailed description is punctuated by illuminating insights on the nature of contemporary development processes and the challenges they raise to traditional planning approaches. The failure to adequately address such challenges may lead, the authors argue, to the "political insignificance" of planning.

The chapter by Marleen Buizer and Iulian Lata, 'Using Theatre and Performance for Greater Reflexivity in Planning and Design Education', illustrates the adoption of the same pedagogical approach in two different courses, one at undergraduate and the other at graduate level. In both cases, the aim is to promote reflexivity among students, stimulating them to reflect on their routines and roles as well as to question the rationale of adopting certain theoretical approaches in specific situations. This is facilitated through the adoption of theatre-based approaches as a heuristic tool to capture and understand the complexity, as well as the multiple and alternative interpretations of a given situation (or 'planning space'). The starting point is the need to prepare students "to enter an increasingly complex [networked] and dynamic world in which uncertainty, struggle and conflict are more common than predictability, consensus and straightforward collaboration". In this context, planners are not anymore seen as "gatekeepers to knowledge, those able to understand, provide the evidence and develop interventions accordingly". Rather, a crucial capacity is their "critical engagement" in a given situation, able to capture the subjective, contested, and political dimensions of a given situation and to deliver "transformative planning practices". Reflexivity becomes a key tenet of "context-specific technical rationality" and the theatre-based approach to support-learning processes is shown as an effective tool for this objective. This is a truly inspiring chapter about the pedagogical routes to sensitizing students and planners to their "responsibility for the places and communities in which they operate" – and a timely word of caution in relation to the uncritical ways in which transdisciplinary and participatory methodologies are being adopted.

Chapter 12 by Andreas Brück and Angela Million, 'Mikroakademie: Peer Learning to Enrich the Curriculum and Enhance Participation and Self-Reflection', presents an approach that deliberately aims at reaching "beyond the scope of standard teaching". On one hand, it is seen as a way to address "a very practical need to broaden the scope of the curriculum" in order to meet the content requirements of contemporary planning. On the other hand, it is used to endow students with skills and abilities, like the capacity of autonomous, life-long learning that is seen as fundamental for coping with 21st century challenges. The Mikroakademie consists of interactive sessions where peer-to-peer learning is stimulated, and students are invited to assume the role of educators. The concept was developed initially to respond to the growing need of planners to communicate ideas with multiple audiences by providing students with opportunities to learn a wide variety of communication and representation techniques "within a studio atmosphere". There are important lessons to be learned from how the approach overcame institutional constraints. Over time, as the programme became established, the innovative teaching-learning processes helped to position teaching as learning, as a part of individuals' instinctive behaviour, growth and development while engendering also a "transformation of planning education from the bottom-up".

Part IV: Further Education and Life-Long Capacity Building

Part IV showcases another important aspect of transformation of future planning education given the need to strengthening pathways into the planning profession (e.g., Commonwealth Secretariat 2011) and for continued professional development and life-long learning identified both by professional societies and governments. The four case studies offer not only alternative and non-traditional pathways of becoming a planner and progressing one's competencies in spatial planning but also concepts for short interventionist activities as a means to provide innovative educational experiences in spatial planning.

Chapter 13 by Adam Sheppard, 'Online, but Not Isolated: Addressing a Key Challenge of Digital Distance Learning', reflects on the recent revision to a longstanding distance learning Master's in Planning, which moved from blended learning (online with residential weeks) to fully online delivery. The contribution offers interesting insights into overcoming student isolation – a characteristic of online settings, which could impede learning, the student experience as well as impoverish and hamper the acquisition of soft skills such as collaboration and communication that are vital for the planning field. The difficulty of delivering such competencies remotely has been used in arguments against moving planning degrees to online learning in the past. Remarkable is the close cooperation with students that guided the redesign of the programme architecture. By creating an elaborate hierarchy of different types of virtual spaces and interaction opportunities from formal classrooms and associated activities to casual interactions in coffee shops, the learning environment mirrors (to some degree) the manifold social interactions experienced on university campuses. Akin to the material campus, control over spaces differs, and interactions are variably instigated by the educators or by students or in some cases by both.

The second case in this section likewise provides a programme view. Chapter 14, 'A Problem-Based and Process-Oriented Curriculum in Continuing Education' by Anita Grams, elaborates on a part-time postgraduate degree at the ETH Zurich, specifically designed to upskill experienced and already practising planners through training in particular advanced methodologies and interdisciplinary team working. In fact, a prerequisite of admission to the programme is a prior degree in a spatially related discipline and several years of work experience. The focus throughout the programme is on developing competencies in defining problems and finding solutions for complex real-life, urban, and regional planning tasks in projects at different scales. The study mode is a mix of face-to-face and remote team working. The programme represents an interesting model of advanced higher education where professional practice is informing and at the same time is informed through theory and study experiences in a complex Kolbian cycle of learning (Kolb 1984).

Chapter 15, 'Professional Training for Social Responsibility: Fundamentals and Practice of a Residency Programme in Architecture and Urbanism' by Maria L. Refinetti Martins and Paula Custódio de Oliveira, discusses a collaborative post-degree training programme (aka residency) of one year delivered jointly between the University of São Paulo's Faculty of Architecture and Urbanism and the city of São Paulo. The aim of the residency programme is to train early career planning professionals. It is like the previous case a structured continued education experience. Nevertheless, the interpretation and context of planning is starkly different. Students attend tailor-made classes at university and work in parallel on projects such as developing district plans. By combining 'academic' and 'professional' activities, participants are enabled to conduct broader research while also gaining an understanding of the constraints of public management. Through the residency programme, actors (city administration, universities, and professionals) collaboratively provide important technical assets and construct knowledge which increases the probability of project and plan implementation. The residency programme facilitates engagement of students and university staff in addressing prevailing social issues in the nation's urban areas and as such offers a new type of pedagogical approach embodying Barnett's (2017) engaged university.

Chapter 16, 'A Student Workshop on Tactical Urbanism: One Day to Change the 100th Year Neighbourhood?' by Duygu Cihanger Ribeiro, presents and critically reviews a short extracurricular teaching intervention in form of a four-day event. Expanding on the standardized approaches in Turkish planning curricula that tend to focus on strong technical and design skills conceiving city plans and urban level projects, this event introduces an alternative approach to planning and city making, known as 'tactical urbanism'. This approach promotes the use of temporary, small-scale, action-based interventions that typically involve local users to effect bottom-up change and transformation. Over a few days, participants get to know a place, and in discussion with inhabitants become familiar with issues. Interventions are conceived, created, and implemented in an ad hoc fashion showcasing and testing potential solutions, as well as developing visions for change and creating discussion points. The case features an enriching learning opportunity for students from different universities. However, a transfer to a continued professional development activity for practitioners can easily be imagined.

TOWARD A NEW LEARNING LANDSCAPE FOR EDUCATION IN PLANNING

To recapitulate, then, in this human-dominated era, at the start of the 21st century, there is an urgent need to get better at, i.e. learn, how to interact constructively and ethically with a complex world in flux (Visser 2018). This requires, first, a more inclusive view of learning, a broader view of what counts as valid knowledge (Rooij and Frank 2016) and an ability and disposition to "adapt readily to rapidly changing environments" (Lebler 2007, pp. 206–7). Second, it requires new ways of learning (pedagogies) and learning environments. It may require new worldviews potentially triggered by experiential and/or transformative pedagogies (Mezirow 2009). There is broad consensus amongst education specialists that learning requires and at the same time results from exchange, open-minded interaction and dialogue with much being gained through inter- and trans-disciplinary exchanges. This applies not only for the learner but the educator who is a learner at the same time.

Scholarly meetings and professional congresses of planners and planning educators have traditionally provided forums of exchanges and dialogue on how to develop the field's pedagogies to best suit professional practice needs albeit largely without interdisciplinary exposure. Over the last two decades or so a considerable surge in engagements with pedagogical innovation geared towards improving knowledge and skills acquisition for contemporary planning challenges can be noticed. The diversity of initiatives, with rationalized and clearly defined purpose, creativity and the commitment by planning educators has grown significantly. However, as research in substantive areas is prioritized in many academic settings, the discourse rarely moves beyond congress debates and only occasionally into a journal. This means the debate is far from reaching the in-depth level sought by both the presenters and the audience.

This book, thus, seeks to leverage and create space for this deeper debate by beginning to conceptually interrogate educational philosophy and theory in the spatial planning context. We hope that such a forum will stir the imagination of fellow planning educators to continue to work with other disciplines, and particularly educationalists, to develop appropriate environments for learning and personal development that will prepare planning graduates and practitioners to cope with and shape ethically the unknown futures (Barnett 2004) of our urban and non-urban environments.

Transforming planning education curricula and pedagogies will be an ongoing process. The case studies in this volume illustrate a range of contemporary trends. Still, the picture is partial and incomplete. Other noteworthy examples have recently emerged with planners drawing creatively on methods from other subject areas, such as ethnography. These variably expand the repertoire of research and data collection methods, tap into different fields of knowledge by trying to understand a place through biographical accounts or transversal walks over a week or longer, conducting immersive observations and casually but purposefully talking to locals. Another pedagogy that is more applied and action-oriented, the living labs (Evans et al. 2015), is inspired by science experiments in the broadest sense.

The manuscript for this book was completed as a majority of the world's population was asked to drastically change their lifestyle and behaviour from one day to the next in response to combating a global health pandemic triggered by the COVID-19 virus. The associated strict social distancing measures have stopped abruptly fieldwork, research, collaboration, and joint activities – temporarily at least. In time we believe this will be overcome – but how co-design and action-learning may be transformed to be more flexible and resilient will need to be contemplated so as not to entirely revert to theoretical debate and project work that is disconnected to the many realities on the ground and outside the campus walls. Ironically, socially responsible engagement is perhaps more than ever needed in such disruptive times. A positive of every crisis is that it inevitably sparks creativity and we will reflect on some ideas for hybrid (online and face-to-face) adaptations in our final chapter.

REFERENCES

Angotti, T. (ed.) (2020) *Transformative Planning: Radical Alternatives to Neoliberal Urbanism*. Chicago: University of Chicago Press/Black Rose Books.

Albrechts, L. (2005) Creativity as a driver for change. *Planning Theory* 4(3): 247–269.

Albrechts, L., Brabanente, A. and Monno, V. (2020) Practicing transformative planning: The territory-landscape plan as a catalyst for change. *City, Territory and Architecture* 7(1). https://doi.org/10.1186/s40410-019-0111-2.

Barnett, R. (2004) Learning for an unknown future. *Higher Education Research and Development* 23(3): 247–260.

Barnett, R. (2009) Knowing and becoming in the higher education curriculum. *Studies in Higher Education* 34(4): 429–440.

Barnett, R. (2011) The coming of the ecological university. *Oxford Review of Education* 37(4): 439–455.

Barnett, R. (2017) Constructing the university: Towards a social philosophy of higher education. *Educational Philosophy and Theory* 49(1): 78–88.

Barth, M. and Michelsen, G. (2013) Learning for change: An educational contribution to sustainability science. *Sustainability Science* 8(1): 103–119.

Briassoulis, H. (1999) Who plans whose sustainability? Alternative roles for planners. *Journal of Environmental Planning and Management* 42(6): 889–902.

Brooks, M. (1988) Four critical junctures in the history of the urban planning profession: An exercise in hindsight. *Journal of American Planning Association* 54: 241–248.

Commonwealth Secretariat (2011) *Commonwealth Capacity Building for Planning: Review of Planning Education across the Commonwealth.* London and Edinburgh: UCL Development Planning Unit and Commonwealth Association of Planners.

Crutzen, P. and Stoermer, E. (2000) The 'Anthropocene'. *Global Change Newsletter* 41: 17–18.

Dalton, L. (2001) Weaving the fabric of planning as education. *Journal of Planning Education and Research* 20(4): 423–436.

De Bono, E. (1992) *Serious Creativity: Using the Power of Lateral Thinking to Create New Ideas.* New York: Harper Business.

Evans, J., Jones, R., Karvonen, A. Millard, L. and Wendler, J. (2015) Living labs and co-production: University campuses as platforms for sustainability science. *Current Opinions in Environmental Sustainability* 16: 1–6.

Frank, A. I. (2012) Time to think planning (education): From marginal interface to central opportunity space? In L. Bertolini (ed.), 'Interface: Time to Think, Time to Act'. Special Issue of *Planning Theory & Practice* 13(3): 465–490.

Frank, A. I. (2020) Education and demonstration of professional competence. In N. Green Leigh, S. P. French, S. Guhathakurta and B. Stiftel (eds.), *The Routledge International Handbook of Planning Education* (pp. 12–28). New York: Routledge.

Frank, A. I. and Silver, C. (2018) *Urban Planning Education: Beginning, Global Movement and Future Prospects.* Chams: Springer.

Frisk, E. and Larson, K. L. (2011) Educating for sustainability: Competencies & practices for transformative action. *Journal of Sustainability Education* [Online]. http://www.susted.com/wordpress/content/educating-for-sustainability-competencies -practices-for-transformative-action_2011_03/ [Accessed 29 May 2020].

Goddard, J. (2009) *Reinventing the Civic University.* London: NESTA.

Guzzetta, J. A. and Bollens, S. A. (2003) Urban planners' skills and competencies: Are we different from other professions? Does context matter? Do we evolve? *Journal of Planning Education and Research* 23: 96–106.

Hemmens, G. C. (1988) Thirty years of planning education. *Journal of Planning Education and Research* 7(2): 85–91.

Heumann, L. F. and Wetmore, L. B. (1984) A partial history of planning workshops: The experience of ten schools from 1955 to 1984. *Journal of Planning Education and Research* 4(2): 120–130.

Higgins, M. and Reeves, D. (2006) Creative thinking in planning: How do we climb outside the box? *The Town Planning Review* 77(2): 221–244.

Internationales Doktoranden Kolleg (2016) *Urbane Transformations-landschaften/ Urban Landscape Transformations.* Berlin: Jovis.

Jepson, Jr., E. J. (2001) Sustainability and planning: Diverse concepts and close associations. *Journal of Planning Literature* 15(4): 499–510.

Kehm, B. M. (2007) Quo vadis doctoral education? New European approaches in the context of global changes. *European Journal of Education* 42(3): 307–319.

Kolb, D. A. (1984) *Experiential Learning: Experience as the Source of Learning and Development* (Vol. 1). Englewood Cliffs, NJ: Prentice Hall.

Krueckeberg, D. (1985) The tuition of American planning. *Town Planning Review* 56(4): 421–441.

Landry, C. (2000) *The Creative City: A Toolkit for Urban Innovators.* London: Earthscan.

Lang, J. (1983) Teaching planning to city planning students: An argument for the studio/workshop approach. *Journal of Planning Education and Research* 2(2): 122–129.

Lebler, D. (2007) Student-as-master? Reflection on a learning innovation in population music pedagogy. *International Journal of Music Education* 25: 205–220.

Mezirow, J. (2009) Transformative learning theory. In J. Mezirow and E. W. Taylor (eds.), *Transformative Learning in Practice: Insights from Community, Workplace, and Higher Education* (pp. 18–32). San Francisco, CA: Jossey-Bass.

Moore, J. (2005) Seven recommendations for creating sustainability education at the university level: A guide for change agents. *International Journal of Sustainability in Higher Education* 6(4): 326–339.

Neuman, M. (2016) Teaching collaborative and interdisciplinary service-based urban design and planning studios. *Journal of Urban Design* 21(5): 596–615.

Peel, D. (2000) The teacher and town planner as facilitator. *Innovations in Education and Training International* 37(4): 372–380.

Poxon, J. (2000) Shaping the planning profession of the future: The role of planning education. *Environment and Planning B* 28: 563–580.

Rodriguez-Bachiller, A. (1988) *Town Planning Education: An International Survey*. Aldershot: Avebury.

Rodwin, L. and Sanyal, B. (eds.) (2000) *The Profession of City Planning: Changes, Images, and Challenges 1950–2000*. New Brunswick, NJ: Transaction Publishers.

Rooij, R. and Frank, A. I. (2016) Educating spatial planners for the age of cocreation: The need to risk community, science and practice involvement in planning programmes and curricula. *Planning Practice and Research* 31(5): 473–485.

Rosa Pires, A. (2018) Breaking the ties with the master plan: Spatial strategic plans in Portugal. In L. Albrechts, J. Alden and A. Rosa Pires (eds.), *Changing Institutional Landscape of Planning* (pp. 181–208). New York: Routledge (first published 2001 by Ashgate Publishing).

Salama, A. M. (2015) *Spatial Design Education: New Directions for Pedagogy in Architecture and Beyond*. London and New York: Routledge.

Scholl, B. (ed.) (2012) *HESP – Higher Education in Spatial Planning: Positions and Reflections*. Zürich: Vdf Hochschulverlag.

Stiftel, B. et al. (2009) Planning education. In UN Habitat (United National Human Settlements Programme), *Planning Sustainable Cities* (Chapter 10). London: Earthscan.

UN Habitat (2009) *Planning Sustainable Cities.* London: Earthscan.

UN Habitat (2016) *Urbanization and Development: Emergent Future*. World Cities Report 2016. Nairobi: United Nations Human Settlements Programme.

Visser, J. (2018) The Anthropocene: A different learning landscape for a different world. Lecture delivered at the Universitas Nusa Cendana in Kupang, Indonesia 10 October.

Wolfram, M., Borgstrom, S. and Farrelly, M. (2019) Urban transformative capacity: From concept to practice, *Ambio* 48: 437–448.

PART I

Pedagogical debates

2. Education for 21st century urban and spatial planning: critical postmodern pedagogies

Terry Lamb and Goran Vodicka

INTRODUCTION

Since before the turn of the millennium, debates about education and how it can provide an appropriate preparation for life in the 21st century have gained impetus and led to educational reforms in many parts of the world (Andreotti 2010; Laurillard 2013). This has been stimulated in part by a sense of constant flux and fluidity as globalization impacts at all levels and sectors of society (including higher education), accelerated by ever-evolving technologies, increasingly complex global movements, and the emergence of post-industrialist, neoliberal changes to social, economic and employment patterns, where "mechanisms of the market economy now define both politics and the highest ideals of the nation" (Giroux 2010, p. 189). In relation to the "terrain of the urban", Brenner and Schmid (2015, p. 153) demonstrate how it has been "subjected to a high-intensity, high-impact earthquake through the worldwide social, economic, regulatory and environmental transformations of the post-1980s period", which call into question the spatial specificity of the urban, bringing "fundamental uncertainties regarding the very sites, objects and focal points of urban theory and research" (p. 154).

The extent of such global shifts has inevitably driven debates about what is actually happening, where it is heading and how we can manage to prepare ourselves and stay afloat in its midst, and such debates have affected both education and urban planning practice, the twin foci of this chapter. For example, academic debate has been engendered about whether such shifts constitute a late development, an echo, of modernity and its related hegemonic, colonialist and exclusionary traditions, or in fact something entirely new and *post*modern (Andreotti 2010; Jacquemet 2005). In relation to education, if the 21st century is construed as *late* modern, educational change can be envisaged conservatively, either as a way of making the most of new, ever-developing opportunities to continue to expand the neoliberal free market approach on the global level or, from a more critical perspective, to address the injustices which neoliberalism entails (Bauman 2000). By contrast, a *post*modern perspective, calls for radically new pedagogies in order to respond to the complexities of a world in which it is impossible even to know what it means to 'know', when knowledge itself, as well as ways of knowing, are constantly shifting, old hegemonies are being dissolved and the "grand narrative has lost its credibility" (Lyotard 1984, p. 37).

This chapter will argue that global changes are driving educational and pedagogical change, including in the field of planning. This entails a consideration of ontological questions (such as what might be considered as relevant knowledge when solid, singular, normative reality gives way to multiple, fluid, socially constructed, complex realities), as well as epistemological questions (such as the meaning of learning and teaching when knowledges are multivariate constructions, decentred and fragile). In the midst of such profound and constant change, then, it is no surprise that much of the debate has raised issues as fundamental as, for example, the very nature of the curriculum and the roles of learners and teachers. In parallel, the chapter will acknowledge the urgent need to address power structures that permeate the modernist legacy, rather than them getting lost in the relativism that is often associated with postmodern thinking. In doing so, it will make a case for the construct of critical postmodern pedagogies that embrace both the complex flows associated with *post*modernity and the compelling need to address social injustices associated with late modernity. The centrality of ethical practice will also be emphasized.

The chapters in this volume reflect such questions in regard to the nature of urban planning itself as well as ways of educating urban planners. As rapid and complex globalization goes hand-in-hand with rapid and complex urbanization, urban planners have to find creative new approaches to addressing both the challenges and opportunities for city dwellers. For example, ontologically speaking, urban environments need to be imagined that can be inclusive of (super-)diverse and fluid realities and meaningful to everyone who uses them; if planners are to meet the wide range of often contradictory needs of urban actors and to ensure that the "right to the city" (e.g., Harvey 2008) is a right for everyone, they will need to be able to view the world from different perspectives. Epistemologically, this questions traditional linear planning and design processes led by experts, requiring instead the crossing of borders (Rios and Watkins 2015; Vodicka 2018) to include knowledges from other academic and professional fields as well as the voices of local residents themselves, all of whom bring new perspectives, transnational, transcultural etc., into the iterative process. When inclusive cities are the goal, the planning processes to achieve this also need to be inclusive.

Such changes in the nature of planning have been reflected in the emergence of innovative, sometimes radically so, approaches to the education of urban planners. The following section will explore some of the general pedagogical debates that address the needs of learners in the 21st century and how these relate specifically to urban planning. This will be followed by a consideration of some basic principles for educational approaches to urban planning in higher education, making reference to other chapters in this volume. The chapter will end with a brief consideration of the challenges and opportunities faced by those committed to innovative pedagogical interventions in higher education, before proposing urban planning and design practices and pedagogies as ethical and transformative spaces of resistance.

CHANGING NEEDS OF THE 21ST CENTURY LEARNER: FROM POSTMODERN TO CRITICAL POSTMODERN PEDAGOGIES

Definitions of the needs of the 21st century learner tend to include variations on themes of adaptability, entrepreneurism, self-direction, soft skills, inclusivity and social and cultural awareness, which are often tied into the notion of life-long learning. For Griffin, McGaw and Care (2012), for example, 21st century skills incorporate *ways of thinking* (creativity and innovation; critical thinking; problem solving; decision making; learning to learn; metacognition), *ways of working* (communication and collaboration), *tools for working* (information literacy and ICT literacy) and *living in the world* (local and global citizenship; personal and social responsibility, including cultural awareness and competence). Such skills include cognitive, social and ethical aspects, which are understood both to enable people to find their way through life in our ever-changing world and also to fulfil the needs of the knowledge society, in which 'knowledge' has replaced the former commodities of industrialism.

A key pedagogical proposal for 21st century learning involves the need to shift from teacher-directed to learner-controlled learning, incorporating approaches such as self-directed, collaborative, enquiry-based, task-based or distance learning. Variations of these and other learner-centred approaches can be found both in general education policy and in specific disciplines. In language pedagogy and language-in-education policy; for example, the construct of learner autonomy (as well as teacher autonomy) has been explored intensively since the late 1970s (Lamb 2008, 2017). One example that reflects much of the cross-disciplinary development of self-directed learning, is the Council of Europe's promotion of language teaching methods, which entail "raising the learner's awareness of his or her present state of knowledge; self-setting of feasible and worthwhile objectives; selection of materials; self-assessment" (Council of Europe 2001, Section 1.5). In such approaches, the traditional role of the teacher in setting aims and objectives, planning lessons and finding resources to enable the learners to achieve these, and then assessing learning to measure the extent to which the aims and objectives have been achieved, is shifted to the learner.

Reporting on a music conservatorium in Australia, where music students are able to draw on technologies not only to produce music but also to make it widely available to others through a range of channels and media, Lebler (2007) describes the development of a "self-directed learning community", a "master-less studio" (p. 207). He argues that such pedagogical changes are necessitated by the demands of contemporary living:

> [...] teaching practices that have dominated in the past will need to be rethought, and alternatives considered that are likely to produce graduates with the abilities and attributes necessary to adapt readily to a rapidly changing environment [...]. Put bluntly, the shift is from content delivery to capacity building via more 'user'-friendly pedagogical strategies. This is not to say that teachers have no role to play as instructors. [...] But when the development of self-directed learning ability is an explicit goal, it is necessary for students to do much that has previously been teachers' business, setting the direction of work and at least participating in its assessment. (Lebler 2007, pp. 206–207)

In this pedagogical shift, the teacher is backgrounded though not redundant; instead of 'delivering' content, the focus is on the teacher as guide, supporting the learner to take on greater responsibility and to direct their own learning. In such an approach, knowledge is distributed and emergent, created by the learners individually or collaboratively. Such proposals can also be seen in research into the affordances of digital technologies such as Web 2.0, virtual reality, and mobile devices for learning, where knowledge is available to all without the intermediary role of the teacher, and accessible for the purposes of personalized, self-directed, experiential learning (e.g., Beetham and Sharpe 2013; Dron 2007; McLoughlin and Lee 2010).

When viewed from the perspectives of late modernity and postmodernity, however, the shift from teacher to learner reveals itself as complex, requiring critical analysis. As referred to earlier, for Andreotti (2010), the 'post' in postmodernity can be interpreted as 'after', which, despite acknowledging that the 21st century is different from the 20th century, that knowledge is "partial and contingent" (p. 7), and that the digital age brings epistemological implications which makes 20th century teaching approaches inappropriate and demotivating, nevertheless focuses on the Enlightenment "notion of progress" (p. 8). It assumes that all learners, even those previously excluded, will have opportunities to progress if they focus on their own individual needs, learn how to learn, and take responsibility for their learning throughout the life-course. Andreotti suggests that this interpretation of pedagogy is built on the foundations of modernity, with no fundamental structural change implied, but rather a continuation of the neoliberal market-driven project. Such an orientation is particularly evident in Laurillard's (2013) positioning of the teacher as driver of "productive" progress in the digital learning space:

> Our digital native students may be able to use technologies, but that does not mean they can learn from them. Being able to read and write never meant you could therefore learn from books. Learners need teachers. As learners we cannot know what it is possible to know, or how to make that journey to what we want to become. We need guidance. Pedagogy is about guiding learning, rather than leaving you to find your own way. Pedagogy puts the onus on teachers to guide the learner's journey to a particular and productive end. (Laurillard 2013, p. xvii)

The role of the teacher here in leading the learner of course echoes its etymological roots (the Greek παιδαγωγία (*paidagōgia*), in which παῖς (*pais*, genitive παιδός, *paidos*) means 'child' and ἄγω (*ágō*) means 'lead'), but knowledge is accordingly conceived in modernist ways as predetermined, fixed and progress-oriented.

On the other hand, when Andreotti (2010) interprets the 'post' in postmodernity as 'questioning', she is claiming the rejection of the modernist system, which is seen as colonialist and reproductive, "inherently violent in its (mono)epistemic practices" (p. 8). This requires us to "decolonise the imagination" and to pluralize knowledge to enable "the collective creation of non-hegemonic systems" (p. 9). For this to occur, teachers need to support learners, not by helping them to become more effective at making learning 'progress', but by encouraging them to question assumptions, including the role of technology as a vehicle for constructing "consumer identities" (p. 10), "to learn to unlearn, to see different choices and possibilities and to imagine and to think 'otherwise'" (p. 10). Andreotti is thus proposing a more radical view of postmodern pedagogy than a simple shift from 'other'-direction to 'self'-direction, one which recognizes the multiplicity of possible knowledges whilst acknowledging that in 21st century postmodernity hegemonic practices are maintained, albeit differently. In a similar vein and writing about adult education, Kilgore (2004) acknowledges that the learning context is never depoliticized, even when postmodern ways of 'knowing' question the teacher's authority to decide what should be known, relocate meaning away from texts towards 'emergent' learners, and suggest that there is "more than one way to know something and more than one thing to know about it" (p. 47). For Kilgore, power also exists in "postmodern knowing", though the relationship between knowledge and power relates more to the exercise of power than the possession of power:

> The teacher and the student are the product of a dynamic network of cultural and institutional practices that "increase the power of individuals at the same time as it renders them docile" (Sawicki 1991, p. 22). There lies both the complicity with and resistance to oppression. (Kilgore 2004, p. 48)

In Kilgore's analysis, then, postmodern pedagogy does not involve a shift from teacher to learner (what she calls the "death of the teacher" (p. 48)), as this remains limited by modernistic binaries and merely transfers power from one to the other. In fact, she also asserts that we should "subvert the student", in order to "dissolve the student–teacher divide", acknowledging that being a student is only one of a person's many positions. Drawing on Grace (2001), she argues that what is needed is to "make space for alternative democratic visions and discourses" (Kilgore 2004, p. 49):

> Toward a postmodern pedagogy, we would acknowledge that what unfolds before us in the adult education classroom does so largely at our behest. We would be concerned with naming what makes us submissive and identifying what grants us power. We would move from there to the collective creation of what I think of as powerful knowledge, knowledge that is personally empowering and socially trans-forming. (Kilgore 2004, p. 48)

In acknowledging that postmodernity brings multiple, ever-evolving and socially constructed identities, as well as changing the nature of power from a metanarrative rather than removing it altogether in some apolitical, vacillating, insipid version of postmodernity, Kilgore, like Andreotti (2010) and Bauman (2000), proposes a more critical version. This implies the development of what we are calling critical postmodern pedagogies, which can enable learners and teachers to embrace their multiple, shifting identities, to become aware that previous 'truths' are no longer constant, to be reflexive and open to questioning different perspectives, including their own, and to find ways of negotiating that are resistant to oppression, including oppression of others, oppression by others, and oppression of self.

Turning specifically to the educational needs of urban planners, it is clear that these are intimately connected to the global shifts explored above. Thus, merely transferring control from teacher to learner is insufficient to prepare learners to be able to develop plans for the complex, superdiverse (Vertovec 2007), often fragile and always changing urban environments of today's cities (let alone for the cities of tomorrow). Becoming more learner-centred may be a valuable starting point, acknowledging that learning is constructed by learners rather than it being a process of delivering knowledge from teacher to learner. It nevertheless does not adequately address the complex socio-cultural nature of learning and the fact that many other actors are implicated in the process of city-making; this requires not only dispositions for learning differently, but also a readiness to reconsider the assumptions, beliefs and values that learners bring with them from their previous life experiences. Urban planners therefore need education that nurtures a challenging range of different elements, for example: a capacity for critical questioning of fundamental constructs, such as 'urban', 'urban citizenship' (and how it is formed), 'community', 'partnership', 'inclusion' and 'planning/design', as well as the dynamic interrelationships between place and space (e.g., Casey 2013; De Certeau 1984; Dovey 2010; Lefevbre 1974; Massey 1994; Soja 1996; Tuan 1977); a different understanding of the ongoing nature of learning, the roles of learner and teacher, and the ways in which critical postmodern pedagogical practices reflect the shifts in planning practice; a capacity for reflexivity, to understand how positionality impacts on beliefs and values and to find ways of addressing preconceptions through critical reflection as an ethical commitment; an openness to collaboration, even when very different perspectives may be involved, including those from different disciplines, from diverse local communities and from a range of practitioners; an ability to navigate and negotiate multiple discourses in order to understand and be understood; a readiness to live with complexity, uncertainty and risk and to handle dilemmas and tensions constructively; and a commitment to recognizing and challenging existing and emergent power relations and oppressions.

EDUCATIONAL AND PEDAGOGICAL PRACTICES IN URBAN PLANNING FOR TODAY'S WORLD

The global, societal developments over the first decades of the 21st century have stimulated a paradigm shift not only in educational and pedagogical practices generally, but also specifically in the education of urban planners. As spiralling urbanization is a key feature of globalization, existing urban planning practices are questioned, particularly where there is a commitment to inclusion and social justice.

The chapters in this volume reflect the changing nature of education and pedagogy for urban planning and enable us to identify key elements of pedagogical practice that are appropriate in today's world. We would contend that, taken as a whole, the chapters evidence many aspects of what have been referred to above as critical postmodern pedagogies, the plural being used to reflect that the very nature of *post*modernity means that there are multiple ways in which pedagogy can manifest itself. This section will tease out key elements of pedagogical practice, beginning with a focus on the fundamental need for *learning*-centred learning and greater *(critical)* learner autonomy.

It will argue that this reflects the importance of praxis, in which theory and practice are intertwined, with theory being generated by learners through practical action accompanied by reflection and reflexivity, and knowledge being democratized. Secondly, pedagogies that involve collaboration across the boundaries of academic disciplines, professional traditions, and diverse communities will be explored. Finally, the centrality of ethics will be highlighted as crucial to any pedagogies for urban planning, just as it must underpin urban planning practice.

Learning-Centredness and Critical Learner Autonomy

In his exploration of the development of the construct of learner autonomy in language learning, Lamb (2017) demonstrated how it is located within broader Piagetian and Vygotskian (social) constructivist theories of learning, which argue that learners are not passive vessels waiting to be 'filled' with knowledge from an external source, such as the teacher, but are themselves actively engaged in knowledge construction within a socio-cultural context. Acceptance of such learning theories led to a move away from transmissive forms of teaching to more learner-centred approaches. Such approaches can be found across all disciplines and are increasingly being adopted globally, though they are interpreted in multifarious ways depending on the broader cultural and political context. However, the phenomenon of learner autonomy, which became a focus of interest within the field of language education in the 1970s because of the increase in self-access language learning (Holec 1981), initially focused on the ways in which control is simply transferred from teacher to learner. As argued above, this shift alone may be a useful starting point, but it is essentially modernist in its conception and inadequate in the context of the complex, ever-changing, pluralistic world, in which we live, learn and work, and which entails unacceptable levels of social injustices maintained through existing power structures. Rather than centring learning on teachers or learners, then, the focus needs to be on learning itself and the multiple, collaborative, sometimes messy, sources, which enable it to emerge in learning-centred pedagogical environments.

A more critical conception of autonomy for both learners and teachers in urban contexts (Lamb 2000), inspired by the interventions of Paulo Freire's *Pedagogy of the Oppressed* (1970) and Henry Giroux's work on critical pedagogy (e.g., Giroux 1988), contributed to the development of a framework for a 'pedagogy for autonomy' through a European project (EuroPAL – A European Pedagogy for Autonomous Learning), which argues for a more critical vision of education across all disciplines and for a common definition of autonomy for both learners and teachers, who, through their actions, are able to "develop as a self-determined, socially responsible and critically aware participant in (and beyond) educational environments, within a vision of education as (inter) personal empowerment and social transformation" (Jiménez Raya et al. 2017, p. 17). This pedagogy, which connects to practical and critical aspects of learning and teaching within and outside the traditional learning space of the classroom, school, university etc., necessarily rejects liberal understandings of autonomy as 'freedom', but instead engages actively with notions of power and constraints in transformative ways. In so doing, it also builds on Vieira's (2009) work on pedagogy for autonomy in Portugal, which still brings together networks of schoolteachers, teacher educators and academics, and which she has described as "a collective commitment to a collective struggle" (Vieira 2009, p. 10).

Manifestations of pedagogies for autonomy can be found in most of the chapters in this book. Peer teaching (Buizer and Barba Lata, this volume) and online collaborative learning (Sheppard, this volume) are structured approaches to decentring the learning away from the teacher, by demonstrating that students can learn from each other. Problem-based and process-oriented learning, referred to by Grams (this volume), asks groups to engage with a particular problem, often with little support or guidance, as a way of encouraging them to find ways of addressing not only the problem being considered but also the problem of which processes will enable them to address it; these commonly occur within the educational institution as simulated projects, as in Grams's example. Several chapters in this volume (Calix; Yonder et al.) address the value of design studios, in which students work together, often in the university, to design solutions to issues in urban spaces.

Epistemologically, autonomous learning also involves a shift in relationship between theory and practice and a democratization of knowledge. Rather than theory being transmitted with a view to it being applied in practice, theory is generated *through* practice in a process of praxis (e.g., Freire 1970), which describes a cycle of learning that begins with practice and uses reflection to produce knowledge. Reflection is therefore key to both autonomous and professional learning. Schön's (e.g., 1987) work on the reflective practitioner, in which he draws on the education practices of professionals, such as teachers and architects, in fact calls for an epistemology of practice to describe what it means to know *in practice*:

> An epistemology of practice draws attention to the knowledge generated through reflection in and on practice itself; such an approach views the practitioner as an agent/experiment, and recognizes that through transaction with the situation, the practitioner shapes it and becomes part of it. (Kinsella 2010, p. 568)

In this way, learning through action is iterative and involves improvization, which prepares learners for uncertainty and risk as described by Rafferty and colleagues in this volume.

If education is perceived as a cultural and political project, which involves "(inter)personal empowerment and social transformation" (Jiménez Raya et al. 2017, p. 17), autonomy of both learner and teacher also involves critical awareness of their own preconceptions that constrain them to act in a particular way. By acknowledging, reflecting critically on, and finding ways of addressing their preconceptions, they become autonomous of their own internal constraints (Trebbi 2008) through a process of reflexivity, which involves "a subject considering an object in relation to itself, bending that object back upon itself in a process which includes the self being able to consider itself as its own object" (Archer 2007, p. 72). In relation to the teaching profession, for example, Smyth asks the following questions:

> What do my practices say about my assumptions, values, and beliefs about teaching? Where did these ideas come from? What social practices are expressed in these ideas? What is it that causes me to maintain my theories? What views of power do they embody? Whose interests seem to be served by my practices? What is it that acts to constrain my views of what is possible in teaching? (Smyth 1989, p. 7)

It would seem that such critically reflective questions also offer a useful scaffold for urban planners striving to create just places in complex settings. Vivant (this volume) demonstrates how working in the context of a mental health institution, with exposure to very different voices than those usually heard, enabled students to become reflexive and "question the question". Similarly, Yonder et al. (this volume) draw on the concept of "transformed subjectivities" to describe how working with local communities helped the students to "confront their own values", and Buizer and Barba Lata (this volume) demonstrate how theatre-based approaches to education enabled students to confront the ways in which everyday routine behaviours and interactions are suffused with power and to consider ways of moving towards transformative planning practices.

This section has shown how a shift towards learning-centredness and critical learner autonomy, with the concomitant criticality and reflexivity, enables learners to blur the boundaries of theory and practice through praxis. Through critical postmodern, rather than technicist, pedagogical approaches, knowledges, skills and values can be co-constructed in an integrated way to address the challenges of urban planning for the 21st century. The next section will build on this by considering further ways in which boundaries can be crossed.

Boundary Crossing and Participatory Practices

In their chapter, Gilliard and colleagues (this volume) address the need for interdisciplinary and transdisciplinary approaches to urban development "based on the assumption that the competencies for steering urban development are scattered among various disciplines". They describe the ways in which a first-year design studio in an interdisciplinary Master's programme brings together early career professionals from a range of backgrounds "such as architecture, landscape architecture and planning, town planning, civil engineering, environmental planning, geography, and sociology". This reflects the conviction that, in order to address the complexities of the urban context, urban planning needs to involve creative solutions co-produced by multiple professionals and agencies. A similar case is made by other authors in this volume, including Grams and Calix. By preparing students to collaborate across professional and disciplinary boundaries, Calix argues that her urban design studio within the Architecture course also contributes to "the ability to easily adjust to transformation and disruption, in a world that is undoubtedly changing at a breathtaking pace".

However, disciplines and professions are not the only boundaries to be crossed in socially just urban planning for the 21st century. Design-based, live projects (in this volume referred to explicitly by Rafferty et al. and similar to 'community-engaged learning' in Kallus's chapter) straddle the real-world urban environments and the academy through opportunities to engage collaboratively with local communities and/or agencies in order to address authentic issues; in some ways they are similar to service learning (Lamb et al. 2019; and referred to by Yonder et al., in this volume). The work conducted in participatory live projects is more than preparation for professional practice – it *is* professional practice, as well as being the basis for authentically experiential professional learning:

> Live Projects push students out into the world, instead of letting them remain passively contained within the educational institution, so that they become agents acting both within and between the fields of research, practice, education and civic life. (Cerulli et al. 2011, p. 174)

In live projects, the locus of learning is blurred as learning not only takes place in the educational institution but is also experienced in urban settings. In this way, students engage with real people living in real communities, often from social and ethnic backgrounds that are unfamiliar to them, thus taking the urgency to find acceptable solutions to another level beyond simulations, as well as engaging students with a number of personal and professional dilemmas (Kallus, this volume). Furthermore, Yonder et al. (this volume) describe how working with communities enables students to learn to respect local knowledges and contributes to "transformed subjectivities". As with Kallus's (this volume) work in Haifa, Israel, which involves learning with "underserved communities in conflicted urban arenas", and D'Ottaviano and Rovati's work in São Paulo, Brazil (also in this volume), who argue for the adoption of the guiding principles of a "*close bond* with the local setting and society and the *commitment* to reduce the brutal social and territorial inequalities that characterize Brazil", students learn skills of negotiation in power-saturated, socially unjust settings, whilst un-learning any tendency towards essentialization of the 'other' (see Vivant in this volume for an example of this). As an immersive activity, community-engaged live projects necessarily entail both praxis and reflexivity in order to develop socially just approaches to urban-related design and planning.

The nature of 'participation' in all participatory activities, such as live projects, participatory action research etc., cannot, however, be taken at face value and must be subjected to reflexivity, the "vigilant analysis and revision of the very conceptual and methodological frameworks being used to investigate the urban process" (Brenner and Schmid 2015, p. 159). There can indeed be different degrees of participation, but when the intention is to work *with* communities rather than *for* or *on* communities, then this must entail a commitment both to respecting their voices as experts in their own context and to co-creating the project through all the stages of planning, exploration, analysis, implementation and production. As Kallus (this volume) argues, it requires direct contact with local inhabitants, development of a long-term relationship with and commitment to the community, and completion of the project in the negotiated time period. Just as professional urban designers or planners, students must learn to communicate in meaningful and appropriate ways.

The same is the case with the methodologies to be used in such practitioner research and participatory practices. If the intention is to listen to and privilege the often silenced voices in the communities, then interpretive, ethnographic methods are called for that are inclusive and more able to dismantle existing power relationships between the different actors, to generate richer, more complex data than positivist, hypothesis driven methods, and to facilitate inductive analysing and theorizing. Kallus (this volume) describes how the inclusion of an anthropologist on the teaching team enhanced not only the reflexive pedagogy used to train urban planners, but also the approaches to fieldwork. Throughout the volume, examples of innovative, ethnographic tools and methods can be found, including various observation techniques that engage the use of all the senses, casual conversations, and walking methods, such as guided tours and in-depth meetings. This is just the starting point, however, as increasingly complex urban planning challenges require increasingly innovative tools and methods that can engage diverse, sometimes vulnerable, communities in co-creating urban environments (see Campkin and Duijzings 2017; Frediani 2016).

These issues of how to engage with local communities are, of course, ethical issues. As ethics are fundamental to any work in this field, they are highlighted further in the next section.

The Centrality of Ethics in Urban Planning Pedagogies

The issues in the previous section are saturated with ethical concerns. Vivant (this volume), for example, describing the work her students did in relation to the relocation of a psychiatric hospital, which included the voices of the patients, raises numerous ethical dilemmas related to maintaining the patients' dignity, such as how to observe them and take notes ethically, when they are already regularly subjected to observation and note-taking by health workers. Ethics suffuses all stages of engaged participatory practice and practitioner research and it is indeed crucial that the education of urban planners and designers reflects this. Knowledge production through design-driven, engaged activities that entail the intertwining of practice, research, theory, reflection and reflexivity, whilst involving collaborations with a range of communities and agencies alongside professionals and academics from diverse disciplines, is characteristic of practitioner research, including when it is for educational purposes, and requires the same level of ethical standards as any social science research. The five ethical principles of the Academy of Social Sciences (AcSS), produced in 2015 in consultation with the learned societies that form its membership, are as follows:

a. Social science is fundamental to a democratic society, and should be inclusive of different interests, values, funders, methods and perspectives.
b. All social science should respect the privacy, autonomy, diversity, values and dignity of individuals, groups and communities.
c. All social science should be conducted with integrity throughout, employing the most appropriate methods for the research purpose.
d. All social scientists should act with regard to their social responsibilities in conducting and disseminating their research.
e. All social science should aim to maximize benefit and minimize harm.

A full consideration of these principles and how they might be interpreted in relation to the education of urban planners and designers is beyond the scope of this chapter. What needs to be emphasized, however, is that, given the highly complex nature of today's urban context, the ethical implications and how to address them need to be considered not only before each individual project or intervention, but also throughout the whole process. This means that the same levels of reflexivity referred to earlier need to be applied; ethical issues must be constantly subjected to rigorous criticality and adjusted according to the unpredictable shifts and turns that anyone engaging in urban environments will experience. Generally accepted principles such as gaining informed consent, for example, need to be creatively addressed when it is impossible to know how exactly a project is going to unfurl, such as in the case of participatory action research.

Specific examples of ethical considerations include reflexivity regarding the hybridity of insider-outsider research and the multiple identities of students, teachers, professionals, local residents, agencies etc., all of whom may be engaged actively in the research itself both as researchers and participants and may be insiders or outsiders. This is an added dimension to the usual considerations of power dynamics and tensions between different individuals and groups; when research and practice are meant to be genuinely participatory, the insider–outsider identifications can change according to the setting and throughout the duration of the collaboration.

A related ethical issue specific to engagement with communities for educational/research purposes is the question of benefits. Where the focus is on working *with* rather than *on* communities, consideration needs to be given to reciprocity, the ways in which benefits are shared and everyone gains from the experience. It is clear from a number of contributions (e.g. Yonder et al.) that the benefits for students of learning with communities are significant, stimulating, for example, reflexivity, creative knowledge production and openness to innovative, community-focused planning/design. There is furthermore some recognition of the need for communities also to benefit, such as through products to enable them to make representation to other authorities (Kallus) or through the immediate impact of tactical urbanism (Cihanger Ribeiro). Nevertheless, this is a compelling ethical area for further development. It is also reflected in the dilemma of desiring to create sustained relationships, but then having to exit the community at some point, whilst still leaving it with some sustainable benefits. Ethical and workable solutions need to be found for each different context, a further indication that ethical reflection and formal approval is not just a hoop to be jumped through but needs to be sustained reflexively throughout the life of the project.

One further issue that is raised by some authors in this volume (Vivant, Kallus, for example) is the need to pay attention to the students' safety and well-being. Some of the localities in which they are working are beyond the experience of the early career practitioners, and some of the interactions they face or issues raised may be emotionally challenging and raise dilemmas, doubts, personal insecurities, etc. Consideration therefore needs to be given to providing safe spaces, in which they can debrief, discuss, share reflections, etc. Examples to be found include regular supervision meetings with individuals, group discussions, and reflective/reflexive journals that allow integration of the self in the process of knowledge construction.

CONCLUSION: URBAN PLANNING/DESIGN PRACTICES AND PEDAGOGIES AS SPACES OF RESISTANCE

As referred to earlier, critical postmodern pedagogies require us to identify "what makes us submissive and […] what grants us power" (Kilgore 2004, p. 49). In the transformative and critical pedagogy for autonomy developed in the EuroPAL project, this was echoed in the dynamic tensions between constraints and affordances, through which critically autonomous learners/teachers, rather than "feeling disempowered […] need to empower themselves by finding the spaces and opportunities for manoeuvre" (Jiménez Raya et al. 2017, p. 44).

In relation to constraints in higher education, there are powerful arguments that today's universities are largely permeated by the neoliberal ideologies that bring the ideas of the marketplace into the processes of education and leave them with "little interest in higher education for understanding pedagogy as a deeply civic, political, and moral practice" (Giroux 2010, p. 191). These include structural issues, mentioned by several contributors to this volume: the regimentation of time (e.g. D'Ottaviano and Rovati, Rafferty et al.); the shortage of resources (e.g. Yonder et al.), which includes increasing class sizes, interpreted by Ramírez and Hyslop-Marguson as resulting from "neoliberal-style austerity measures based on the discourse of 'crisis'" (Ramírez and Hyslop-Marguson 2015, p. 171); and a preoccupation with top-down quality assurance involving assessment- and measurement-driven teaching, which can engender risk averse teachers and students. An increasing focus on employability tends to mean a greater orientation towards the role of universities as training providers for employers and a resistance to interdisciplinarity. Instead, knowledge is instrumentalized and the curriculum is fragmented in order to offer specialist routes into work, and competition between disciplinary areas means that silos become entrenched, especially given the privileging of STEM subjects as opposed to, for example, the humanities. The impact of politics on universities comes sharply into focus in D'Ottaviano and Rovati's and Refinetti and de Oliveira's chapters in this volume describing their work in Brazilian cities.

Working within this wider context, it is remarkable that education for urban design and planning is shifting towards more learning-centred, collaborative, design-driven, outward-looking, community-focused pedagogies, described by Cerulli (2017, p. 12) as "multiple models of pedagogical projects attempting to deal with the complexity of the 'real' as well as with the practicalities of the 'applied' and material". Clearly, there are discourses in universities that can be appropriated to create the spaces for manoeuvre referred to above, such as those that recall the civic responsibility of the university, referred to by Rafferty et al. (this volume) as the university's "third mission". The engaged, collaborative pedagogies that are becoming prevalent in the education of urban planners/designers are indeed able to disrupt the overarching narratives in higher education. They offer a way of ensuring that the driving force of Freire's critical pedagogy is kept alive, namely to create a more socially just world through a "pedagogy of hope" (Freire 2014), which recognizes that human life is not determined but conditioned.

Cerulli (2017, p. 14) has, however, pointed to tensions that must be constantly wrestled with for urban planning/design pedagogies to reach and maintain their transformative potential:

> In the context of increasingly neoliberal universities, where academic capitalism is becoming the norm, such projects have the potential to configure themselves as effective pockets of resistance, but they can also become instruments for validating and reinforcing the status quo, depending on how they are initiated, developed, framed and assessed.

This resonates with Kallus's concern in this volume that urban planning students need to be conscious of the need for "structural (political) change" rather than simply settling "for reform that enhances everyday lives of marginalized communities". In the postmodern world, in which power permeates everything in complex, non-binary flows that render marginalization itself multi-directional and intersectional, and where the modernist search for certainty gives way to postmodern struggles to understand shifting contexts and identities, critical postmodern pedagogies must enable urban planners/designers to recognize the still compelling responsibility to dissent (Giroux 2010) and resist in the face of social injustices, and to seek these out even when they are hidden, rather than to get lost in the mires of relativism. How this will be manifested in practice will depend on the context, but it is the responsibility of those working in urban planning/design to ensure that existing social injustices are not reproduced by their actions and that their ethical standards are not only impeccable but also subjected to intense and ongoing interrogation, so that their work may be truly transformative.

REFERENCES

Academy of Social Sciences [AcSS] (2015) 'Five Ethics Principles for Social Science Research'. London. https://www.acss.org.uk/wp-content/uploads/2016/06/5-Ethics-Principles-for-Social-Science-Research-Flyer.pdf.

Andreotti, V. (2010) Global education in the '21st century': Two different perspectives on the 'post-' of postmodernism. *International Journal of Development Education and Global Learning* 2(2): 5–22.

Archer, M. (2007) *Making Our Way through the World: Human Reflexivity and Social Mobility*. Cambridge: Cambridge University Press.

Bauman, Z. (2000) *Liquid Modernity*. Cambridge: Polity Press.

Beetham, H. and Sharpe, R. (eds.) (2013) *Rethinking Pedagogy for a Digital Age: Designing for 21st Century Learning*. London: Routledge.

Brenner, N. and Schmid, C. (2015) Towards a new epistemology of the urban? *City* 19(2–3): 151–182.

Campkin, B. and Duijzings, G. (eds.) (2017) *Engaged Urbanism: Cities and Methodologies*. London: I. B. Tauris.

Casey, E. S. (2013) *The Fate of Place: A Philosophical History*. Berkeley: University of California Press.

Cerulli, C. (2017) Conflux of interest: Revealing multiple value systems in socially motivated collaborative university-based projects. *The Journal of Public Space* 2(3): 11–20.

Cerulli, C., Kossak, F., Petrescu, D. and Schneider, T. (2011) Agencies of live projects. In D. Petrescu, C. Petcou and N. Awan (eds.), *TRANS-LOCAL-ACT: Cultural Practices Within and Across* (pp. 172–209). Paris: Preprav.

Council of Europe (2001) *Common European Framework of Reference for Languages: Learning, Teaching, Assessment (CEFR)*. Cambridge: Press Syndicate of the University of Cambridge.

De Certeau, M. (1984) *The Practice of Everyday Life*. Berkeley, CA: University of California Press.

Dovey, K. (2010) *Becoming Places: Urbanism/Architecture/Identity/Power*. London Routledge.

Dron, J. (2007) Designing the undesignable: Social software and control. *Educational Technology & Society* 10(3): 60–71.

Frediani, A. A. (2016) Re-imagining participatory design: Reflecting on the ASF-UK change by design methodology. *Design Issues* 32(3): 98–111.

Freire, P. (1970) *Pedagogy of the Oppressed*, trans. M. B. Ramos. New York: Seabury Press.

Freire, P. (2014) *Pedagogy of Hope: Reliving Pedagogy of the Oppressed*. London: Bloomsbury.

Giroux, H. A. (1988) *Teachers as Intellectuals: Toward a Critical Pedagogy of Learning*. Westport, CT: Bergin & Garvey.

Giroux, H. A. (2010) Bare pedagogy and the scourge of neoliberalism: Rethinking higher education as a democratic public sphere. *The Educational Forum* 74(3): 184–196.

Grace, A. P. (2001) Using queer cultural studies to transgress adult educational space. In V. Sheared and P. A. Sissel (eds.), *Making Space: Merging Theory and Practice in Adult Education* (pp. 257–270). Westport, CT: Bergin & Garvey.

Griffin, P., McGaw, B., and Care, E. (eds.) (2012) *Assessment and Teaching of 21st Century Skills*. Dordrecht: Springer.

Harvey, D. (2008) The right to the city. *New Left Review* 53: 23–40.

Holec, H. (1981) *Autonomy and Foreign Language Learning*. Oxford: Pergamon.

Jacquemet, M. (2005) Transidiomatic practices: Language and power in the age of globalization. *Language & Communication* 25(3): 257–277.

Jiménez Raya, M., Lamb, T. E. and Vieira, F. (2017) *Mapping Autonomy in Languages Education: A Framework for Learner and Teacher Development.* Frankfurt am Main: Peter Lang.

Kilgore, D. (2004) Toward a postmodern pedagogy. *New Directions for Adult and Continuing Education* (Special issue: 'Promoting Critical Practice in Adult Education') 102: 45–53.

Kinsella, E. A. (2010) The art of reflective practice in health and social care: Reflections on the legacy of Donald Schön. *Reflective Practice* 11(4): 565–575.

Lamb, T. E. (2000) Reconceptualising disaffection: Issues of power, voice and learner autonomy. In G. Walraven, C. Parsons, D. Van Veen and C. Day (eds.), *Combating Social Exclusion through Education* (pp. 99–115). Leuven: Garant.

Lamb, T. E. (2008) Learner autonomy in eight European countries: Opportunities and tensions in education reform and language teaching policy. In M. Jiménez Raya and T. E. Lamb (eds.), *Pedagogy for Autonomy in Modern Languages Education: Theory, Practice, and Teacher Education* (pp. 26–57). Dublin: Authentik.

Lamb, T. E. (2017) Knowledge about language and learner autonomy. In J. Cenoz, D. Gorter and S. May (eds.), *Language Awareness and Multilingualism: Encyclopedia of Language and Education* (3rd ed.) (pp. 173–186). Cham: Springer.

Lamb, T. E., Hatoss, A. and O'Neill, S. (2019) Challenging social injustice in superdiverse contexts through 'activist' languages education. In R. Papa (ed.), *Handbook on Promoting Social Justice in Education*. Cham: Springer.

Laurillard, D. (2013) Preface to the second edition. In H. Beetham and R. Sharpe (eds.), *Rethinking Pedagogy for a Digital Age: Designing for 21st Century Learning* (pp. xvi–xviii). London: Routledge.

Lebler, D. (2007) Student-as-master? Reflections on a learning innovation in popular music pedagogy. *International Journal of Music Education* 25: 205–220.

Lefevbre, H. (1974) *La production de l'espace.* Paris: Anthropos.

Lyotard, L. F. (1984) *The Postmodern Condition: A Report on Knowledge.* Minneapolis: University of Minnesota Press.

Massey, D. (1994) *Space, Place and Gender.* Cambridge: Polity Press.

McLoughlin, C. and Lee, M. J. W. (2010) Personalised and self regulated learning in the Web 2.0 era: International exemplars of innovative pedagogy using social software. *Australasian Journal of Educational Technology* 26(1): 28–43.

Ramírez, A. and Hyslop-Marguson, E. (2015) Neoliberalism, universities and the discourse of crisis. *L2 Journal* 7(3): 167–183.

Rios, M. and Watkins, J. (2015) Beyond 'place': Translocal placemaking of the Hmong diaspora. *Journal of Planning Education and Research* 35(2): 209–219.

Sawicki, J. (1991) *Disciplining Foucault: Feminism, Power, and the Body.* New York: Routledge.

Schön, D. (1987) *Educating the Reflective Practitioner: Towards a New Design for Teaching and Learning across the Professions.* San Francisco, CA: Jossey-Bass.

Smyth, J. (1989) Developing and sustaining critical reflection in teacher education. *Journal of Teacher Education* 40(2): 2–9.

Soja, E. W. (1996) *Thirdspace.* Malden, MA: Blackwell.

Trebbi, T. (2008) Freedom – a prerequisite for learner autonomy? Classroom innovation and language teacher education. In T. Lamb and H. Reinders (eds.), *Learner and Teacher Autonomy: Concepts, Realities, and Responses* (pp. 33–46). Amsterdam: John Benjamins.

Tuan, Y.-F. (1977) *Space and Place: The Perspective of Experience.* Minneapolis: University of Minnesota Press.

Vertovec, S. (2007) Super-diversity and its implications. *Ethnic and Racial Studies* 30(6): 1024–1054.

Vieira, F. (2009) *Struggling for Autonomy in Language Education: Reflecting, Acting and Being*. Frankfurt-am-Main: Peter Lang.

Vodicka, G. (2018) *Everyday Public Spaces in an Ethnically Diverse Neighbourhood: Contextualised Convivialities and Boundary-Crossing Urban Design*. Sheffield: University of Sheffield.

3. Planning education and planning the university: a becoming-symbiosis

Ronald Barnett

INTRODUCTION

What is it to plan a university? Can a university be planned? Is the matter of planning a university much like planning a city, to wit the planning of a set of spaces, movements and buildings that will dynamically interact and change over time? Or is there even more to it than this? What, after all, is a university in the 21st century? These questions are highly practical but are also questions that have prompted, for over two hundred years, a philosophical inquiry into the idea of the university. Planning a university, therefore, has temporal, practical and philosophical components. Ultimately, planning and philosophy have to go together.

Suppose now that a university – undergoing a reworking of its strategic plan – has a department or school of planning, with students taking undergraduate and postgraduate studies in urban and regional planning. Could not that very university itself offer the basis of a case study for such students and their courses? Might that university directly offer a range of educational opportunities to students in planning studies? Might the university not serve as a nice cameo of the challenges of planning in the 21st century? It could just be that students and educators in planning studies have on their doorstep an extraordinary – but largely unnoticed and underused – educational resource. That, at least, is the thesis I shall advance here.

WHAT IS IT TO BE A UNIVERSITY?

The first question here is not 'What is it to plan a university?' but, rather, 'What is it to be a university?' One can only speak of planning a university when one has a sense as to what it is to be a university. As a matter in the literature, what it is to be a university has something over two hundred years of history behind it – from the Germanic origins of reflection on the idea of the university at the end of the 18th century and beginning of the 19th century

– but the matter is far from straightforward, and on three counts. Firstly, there are now around 19,000 universities worldwide, and with profound differences between them: to plan a university is to form a particular trajectory among the fraternity of universities. Particularity among universality is the order of the day. However, and secondly, the very idea of 'university' is controversial. Planning decisions, at least implicitly, will be simultaneously taking up positions on the matter. Thirdly, the university continues to unfold but with little in the way of direction. A single university's trajectory is going to be a melange of competing ideas as it unfolds with increasing velocity.

It is noteworthy that one of the vice-chancellors of the universities established in the United Kingdom in the 1960s gave the prestigious annual Reith Lectures – on BBC radio – precisely on "A University in the Making" (Sloman 1964), arising out of his experience in planning the newly emerging University of Essex. That phrase –'"in the making" – was especially percipient. In the 21st century, a university is always in the making. Whether it is a renowned research-led university or a much more modest teaching-oriented university, any university is entangled with the wider world to some degree. It is necessarily caught up in many zones, including those eight of the economy, society, culture, politics, knowledge, the natural environment, persons and learning; and these entanglements are not only local, regional, national and global but also digital. The university swims in the ethers of the internet even while it is evident in real human practices before one's eyes. Like so many enterprises today, the university is a socio-material-digital assemblage. In the company of the university, the category of space becomes not only multi-dimensional but also multi-worldly.

The university, however, is not merely complex but it is entangled in its complexity. (The classic images in the articles on complexity of intertwined spaghetti or knotted seaweed come to mind.) What is it to plan for a university's entanglement? In his classic text on the university, Clark Kerr spoke of it as a 'Multiversity' (Kerr 1995), with its warring departments held famously together only by 'a common grievance over car-parking'. Perhaps these days, it is not even that: either the planners have accepted the logic of the situation and – in urban universities – have outlawed the prospect that faculty and others can drive onto campus (not least given ecological considerations) or, in entrepreneurially oriented systems, have planned for the building of income-generating car parks. But the entrepreneurial university lives by seizing the chances of the moment. Not only can it be planned to a quite limited degree but this is the way it wants matters: it actively seeks a 'de-regulated' and open environment, free of boundaries and constraints.

Is university planning a matter of confronting and lessening those entanglements or is it to *exacerbate* them? Surely, it is the latter. That is to say, a university is a space that is intended to *compound* its entanglements with the world. As a corporate agent (List and Pettit 2011), it swims across the fluid spaces of the many zones that impinge upon it. However, its entanglements are present in *two modes* of the university's being. Firstly, its entanglements are *systemic* in character: they are evident in the systems in which the university engages with the world but, and secondly, they are also evident in its *discourses,* both internally and with the world. This discursive complexity we may legitimately term 'supercomplexity' (Barnett 1990).

This supercomplexity is a transcendent form of complexity, in which the university is all the time sliding across thin ice. This is the case for all organizations but is especially so for the university. To a very large extent, the university lives through discourses, both in its understandings of itself and its possibilities and also through what the world thinks of it (both any particular university and universities in general) and all of these representations fluctuate continuously. Much like public perceptions of petroleum companies, the esteem in which universities are held has taken something of a fall over recent years as institutions have been subjected to increasing public scrutiny. After all, the university is an institution for which no utterance, no framing of the world, and no claim to understand the world can pass unchallenged. This is a *super*complexity in that any relationship that the university forms, both internally and externally, is inherently contestable. The very categories through which it comprehends itself and its place in the world are disputable and *are* disputed within the university itself.

PLANNING A UNIVERSITY

Planning a university, therefore, is a curious matter. There is a stark materiality that is the university. It has its car parks and its buildings, its roads, its immediate interconnections with its locality, its communication systems, its effect on local housing markets, shopping amenities and so forth. At a deeper level, it has its form as a lightly coupled organization, with its separate parts – its departments, centres and offices – enjoying varying levels of autonomy depending on the type of higher education system and institution therein. It has its multitude of activities, which extend well beyond teaching and research, as it engages with the wider world. And at a yet deeper level, it moves among and adds to – and even disturbs – mysterious discourses, at once global and arcane; conversations of humanity that few can penetrate. The junior professor – who is expert in her field – is invited into a radio studio to comment on the burning of the Amazonian forest in a way denied to the Nobel prize-winner in another field. The world permeates the university and vice versa but in criss-crossing lines of engagement in the orchestration of the conversations (plural) of humanity. The spaces of the university, accordingly, are both material and non-material.

It has been observed that, for a university, there can be no definiteness in any direction. Its future cannot be foretold even for tomorrow, let alone for a couple of decades. And yet, for example, planning its physical estate has to be a medium- to long-term activity. A university in an urban setting, with the challenges that that presents as it seeks new premises to cope with its expansion, might have a thirty-year horizon for its estate planning. Its buildings have to be 'adaptable' not only to changes in the understanding of the physics of buildings but in unforeseen and fundamental changes in a particular university's self-understanding. Moreover, a university is far from being fully evident even in the present. It is not merely the sum of its current objects, technologies and activities, even if they could be fully identified, but, as intimated, the university lives in the ethereal spaces of its 'invisible colleges', which swirl across the world.

The university, then, lives in the here-and-now and in the long-term; it lives locally, nationally and globally; it is 'glonacal' (Marginson 2010). It lives materially, in the fabrics of its buildings and its immediate hinterland, and in the ether of ideas; it lives in the activities of individuals and of collectivities (as papers in the sciences may be 'authored' by over a thousand researchers); and it lives in taken-for-granted cultures – both academic and worldly – and amid fiercely contested ideologies, whether of the state or of culture wars or of indigenous communities. Planning for such an assemblage as the contemporary university is bound to be thwarted with challenge.

The material and the ideational frequently intermingle. Where are the boundaries of the university? At its entrances? But perhaps a university has determined to be 'open' to the world and sees itself as a set of public spaces; and as a civic university, indeed. Its grounds are open to the public, and many of its events are 'public' events. But perhaps, at the same time, the university has resolved to outsource its security arrangements and that firm's representatives not merely patrol the grounds but act officiously to bar members of the public from entering its grounds, even with facial recognition cameras. The university, like so many enterprises these days, lives in a liminal space, neither fully private nor public. Planning and designing any such an organization has to be alert to this lack of clear and definite boundaries between it and the wider society.

What it is to be a university in the 21st century, then, is a contested matter; and it is a changing matter. Of any plan of a university, there will be *legitimate* counter-plans, if held only in the minds of the unconverted. In the liquid world in which a university moves, any plan produced today may be out of place tomorrow. A major corporation, having promised to support the establishment of a new Business School or Pharmaceutical Centre may change its mind. A government on the other side of the world may suddenly decree not to finance students who wish to travel to distant universities to pursue their studies. A new government at home may opt to switch funding for post-compulsory education into technical education or foster the development of private universities and reduce its commitment to public universities. A new Rector or Vice-Chancellor may choose to take a university in a new direction, perhaps giving more prominence to STEM disciplines; or – being seized of the challenges of global warming and ecological crisis – may suddenly look to run the whole university on a carbon-neutral, environmentally sensitive basis.

THE CONTENTIOUSNESS OF PLANNING

It will be said that much of this is common to the wider world and what it is to plan any complex enterprise. *That is exactly so*. Contentiousness, sudden and violent and unforeseeable changes, and living both locally and globally and in fluid spaces, are common manifestations of organizational life; the university is not special in these aspects of collective being. Indeed, that the university is very much like other complex organizations in the world is part of the thesis here, namely that in understanding what it is to plan the university, students enrolled in planning degrees have to hand, in their own university, an invaluable resource for understanding the nature of planning in the 21st century. There are, though, two caveats.

Firstly, what it is to be a university is not given but is *inherently* contentious, such that this contentiousness pervades its very being. Its 'stakeholders' are both within and beyond. The university is an assembly of argumentative spaces; and this is not happenstance but is part of what it is to be a university. Planning a university, therefore, has to plan for an organization in which nothing can be assumed in advance, not even what it is to be a university, which means that building designs should allow easy reconfiguration for different uses.

To address this issue, planning might involve itself in envisioning different 'scenarios' of what it might be to be a university, say, 20 years ahead; and think tanks and management consultants have been engaged in just such a practice for some time. But there is a logical difficulty here (in addition to the empirical difficulty of gauging how the future might turn out). Scenario development itself is the formulation of a particular state of play, when the university – qua university – is, as stated, an open and contested entity; and open and contested within itself. Ever since its modern inception in the Middle Ages, the university has been a disputatious entity. This disputatiousness is reflexive, for it rebounds upon the university itself, affecting its character and its evolution. The university is necessarily a learning organization in the 'double-loop' sense (Argyris and Schön 1974): it not only learns about the world and increasingly shares its learning with the world, but 'learns' about itself. Planning a university, therefore, somehow has to accommodate its inherent *reflexive disputatiousness*.

Secondly, the university bestrides the world. Again, this is not happenstance as from the Middle Ages, the university has been international in its outlook and in its composition. The wandering scholars moved comfortably around the universities of Europe, with Latin as a lingua franca. The 20th and 21st century university has not merely accentuated this dimension with upwards of ten million students being 'international' and academics in research-oriented universities being well-versed in the arts of transnational travel and etiquette, but has moved its worldly presences into a qualitatively new dimension as it has seized and much helped to develop the affordances of the computer and the internet. In communication, in data transactions, in multimedia, and in database construction and uses, the university is now *para passu* with the internet.

The university has become a global city in itself, interacting with all the regions of the world, 24 hours a day. This university is a liquid university, with fluid forms that swim in and out and across each other. This digital fluidity (cf. Hassan 2003) enhances its intertwinedness with the world and disturbs its relationships with its 'customers'. The student in a university-driven MOOC can determine if, when and where to engage in a programme of study. The amateur astronomer can engage with a university department of astronomy and may even have a planetary body named after her or him.

A MULTI-DISCURSIVE WORLD

I have been suggesting that the university exemplifies – albeit with some heightened characteristics – what it is to be an organization in a multi-discursive world and, too, the implications that flow therefrom. In a multi-discursive world, an organization has to be light on its feet, facing at once – its shareholders, its stakeholders (not the same thing), its customers, its creditors and auditors. So too with the university. But, as indicated, the university has explicitly to contend with rival versions as to what it is to be a university. Is it to be a deliverer of high-end skills for the economy, an educator of 'global citizens', to uncover the secrets of the universe in 'blue-skies' research, to assist in producing technological breakthroughs that have practical applications, to be a site of independent critical commentary, to aid public understanding of complex matters, to offer a response to the global problems of the age (for example, to address – as many universities are doing – the United Nations' Sustainable Development Goals), to be an engine of 'cognitive capitalism', to promote the life chances of the dispossessed and enhance social justice and so on.

This list illustrates that what it is to be a university in the 21st century is no longer clear, and so planning a university takes on a heightened level of opaqueness. This lack of clarity arises not only through the uncertainty as to what the future may bring but also through the present and immediate conceptual open-endedness as to what it is to be a university.

Let me clarify the argument here. My argument is not that the university is unique in these aspects of multi-dimensionality (of being entangled in multiple ecosystems), of being beset with multiple clamourings and expectations from different directions (its own staff are vocal and do not speak with the same voice as the industrialists who might collaborate with the university) and of (re)forming itself while being unclear as to what it is to be a university in the 21st century. To some extent, these matters confront all organizations, small or large, in the public or the private sector. They even confront a local family-run enterprise that may have been in existence for decades. In a deregulated market, can the small cheesemaker contemplate becoming an exporter and exporting its cheeses to another continent on the other side of the world? What would that mean for the cheesemaker? How might it adapt to the culture of a faraway land? How is cheese eaten and to what extent in a meat-reliant country (say in South America) or a meat-averse country (say Japan)? In which direction might planning go in such an open and conflictual situation?

Instead, the challenges of a liquid and intertwined world are far more subtle and complex than coping with multiple markets and cultures. The case of BP (the UK petroleum company) is instructive. Out of the blue, BP found itself in the centre of world hostility when through an accident one of its oil rigs polluted the Gulf of Mexico. Being on the receiving end of highly critical commentary from a world increasingly seized of ecological issues was difficult enough, causing the chief executive to issue public statements and apologies. However, matters became more challenging still, for the chief executive was obliged to appear before both a Senate hearing in the United States and before a Parliamentary Committee in the United Kingdom and face a barrage of difficult questions. That event speaks directly to the theme being advanced here, of discursive ambiguity.

Just what is it to be a chief executive of a petroleum company? And is it sufficient, by way of a response to that question to enumerate lists of knowledge domains (Geology? Chemistry? Finance? Organizational management?) and skills (of management, leadership, and decision-making)? The example illustrates precisely that, here, the role of chief executive is not given in any sense but is fluid, always expanding. We can surely assume that the head-hunters and search committee, in seeking a chief executive, did not specify 'ability to defend the company in front of international committees and demonstrate publicly a sensitivity both to environmental issues and to the *public* responsibilities of a major corporation thereto'. At issue here are not knowledge or skills but human qualities and dispositions, for example, the disposition to be open to and to respond to public commentary and the qualities of public candour, integrity, and trustworthiness. In short, we are here faced with a value situation, in which organizations are now being called upon to demonstrate that they are producers of and defenders of moral goods.

I shall return to this matter of value situations and moral goods later, but for now, let us look at another example, that of the Berlin Brandenburg Airport (BBA), which has become notorious in planning circles as an instance of bad planning. The Airport was to be a new airport for Berlin, intended to replace two existing airports (on either side of the former Berlin Wall). Planning commenced after the fall of the Berlin Wall in 1989 and construction was begun in 2006, it being scheduled to open in October 2011, dignitaries having the date in their diaries. However, the airport's opening encountered many delays and cost overruns. Causes of the failure to open are attributed to poor construction planning (escalators were found to be too short, there was a short-age of check-in desks, the flight information monitors have already had to be replaced, the lights could not be switched off), execution, management and even corruption. No future date for an opening could be stated with any assurance. At the same time, maintenance costs – not least to run the escalators and all the other systems at regular intervals – continued to rise. Some considered that the airport may never open.[1]

Again, here we have a nice example of the entanglement of organizations with the wider world. Understandably, the commentaries focus on technical issues, on issues of budget overruns, of systems failures and so forth. But it just might be too that somewhat more elusive factors are at play. The airport was *planned* to replace two airports, one in East Berlin and one in West Berlin. It was in part a political project, intended to help the processes of political and social unification. Further, again in keeping with the conceptual questions being pressed here ('What is a university in the 21st century?'), we may ask: 'What is an airport in the 21st century?', not least amid a climate of ecological trepidation, for airports are notoriously polluting phenomena. And pollution here is not only a matter of the natural environment but also spreads across other ecozones, of social institutions, human habitats, transport, culture, and so on. Airports rival universities as a site of planning pandemonium. The building of a third runway at London's premier airport has been a matter of public debate, inquiry and argument for over sixty years.

INTERLUDE

At this intermediate point, let me re-state my thesis. Planning of any complex institution opens to conceptual and, thereby, philosophical matters. This is so for the university itself, but the university is not special here. It is – as we have seen with other examples of an oil company and an airport – an open and even a contested matter as to what is to count as an x – a university, an oil company, an airport – in the 21st century. The openness that attaches to a complex organization, it will have been observed, takes various forms. Organizations change over time and the temporal factor looms large. What is it to plan even a new building, say in a university, when within the lifespan of the building, its original purpose will have been declared otiose? With the passing of time come new perceptions of the possibilities of the spaces and buildings that form the material presence of organizations.

The openness that attaches to large organizations has, as noted, quite other dimensions. Large organizations are complex in themselves, with multi-layered systems, functions, resources, personnel, activities, technologies, goals (which may be mutually conflicting) and values, and all of which overlap, and interpenetrate with unpredictable outcomes, no matter how tightly they may be planned. A complex organization such as a university is willy-nilly engaged with the wider world in multiple ways, a world that is irredeemably complex, with its own systems, cultures, monetary arrangements, biospheres and so forth. The complexity here is a formal one, that is to say these are open-ended systems, the conjunction of whose elements cannot be foretold with any certainty.

To these matters of systemic complexity has to be added a discursive complexity or, as I term it, supercomplexity. Supercomplexity is that state of affairs in which the very categories through which we understand ourselves and the institutions we inhabit are open, are multiplying and, indeed, are disputed. If complexity is characterized by unpredictability (systems may be disrupted) and challengeability (our predictions about those systems can fairly be challenged), supercomplexity is characterized by uncertainty (one's basic concepts can never be fully cashed out and the world always exceeds them) and contestability (one's concepts and frameworks, as a matter of fact, are all the time contested).

On both grounds – complexity and supercomplexity – the world is a shaky and rocky place (there are continuing tremors and occasional earthquakes). It is misleading to suggest that complexity is real and speaks to matters of the world while supercomplexity is 'all in the mind', for supercomplexity too is real. A better shorthand way of putting it is to observe that complexity stems from postmodernity (that is, upheavals in the material world) while supercomplexity is associated with postmodernism (that is, non-absolutism in the world of ideas).

Large organizations, such as the university, are multiply entangled with this world, in all its complexity. We may term the major zones with which an organization is entangled, ecozones. They are ecozones in that they exhibit many of the attributes of ecosystems in the natural world (Barnett 2018). The major zones with which, say, a university is entangled are at least eight: social institutions, the economy, knowledge, learning, culture, persons, the political sphere, and the natural world. These eight possess six ecological substrates. Each ecozone is at once (i) systemic (each is a set of interconnected nodes or elements), (ii) self-reproducing to an extent (each has a tendency to persist over time), (iii) fragile (each is liable to be massively disrupted), (iv) actually impaired (each is functioning at less than its optimum level), (v) subject to human intervention that contributed to its impairment, and yet (vi) open to improvement through human activity.

In each ecozone, challenges of supercomplexity arise. A university – or any other large organization – swims in and across all eight ecozones and, in each zone, is faced with fundamentally intractable issues. What are its values? Are they the same in the zones of the political, the cultural, the personal, the economic and so on? Perhaps its values conflict across the ecozones. Perhaps a university feels a compulsion to act instrumentally at least in the economic zone but strives, even if with difficulty, to treat its staff – and even those who interact with it – as ends in themselves. It may wish to treat the research and knowledge that it produces as its own intellectual property but also wants to advance the public sphere and so is drawn to matters of open access. A contemporary large institution – such as a university – can never settle, can never be sure of itself and its own identity.

PLACE AND SPACE

Against the background that we have been sketching out (in relation to the challenges of planning in general), let us turn more directly to the matter of planning education. I have been suggesting that the university shares many features with other large organizations in contemporary society. All such organizations move in fluid time and space, and are continually facing the challenges of both complexity and supercomplexity. A specialist postgraduate institution of higher education might be the leading such institution in the world in its discipline(s), and respected as such, and may have enjoyed 100 years or more independence. However, given its readings of its situation in the changing world, it may still be determined that it should 'merge' with the massive local university, despite earlier assertions over decades that such an eventuality could never come to pass. It may also determine that it would be wise to start to include undergraduate courses and so change its public profile. It cannot be sure, at any moment, just what it is to be institution x. And, as stated, in all of this, we can see parallels in the wider world; say, in planning a city.

It follows that a department of planning studies in a university has immediately to hand a rich vein through which its students might pursue their studies. The students' own university possesses many, if not all, of the features that they are likely to find in organizations generally on entering the planning profession. Note that 'organization' is a wholly inclusive term here. It embraces both formal organizations, such as a university or an airport, and more nebulous organizations and constructs, such as a city region with unclear boundaries or a national system – of education or health. All of these organizations generate all of the challenges of complexity and of supercomplexity that we have been unfolding here.

Each challenge immediately provokes the awkward question: 'Just what does it mean to be an x (a university, a city region, a health system) in the 21st century?' And: 'Where lie its boundaries?' Is its footprint to be its actual interlocutors or its potential participants? And what is to be understood as its hinterland? And to each such question, as we have seen, not only will there be multiple answers forthcoming, but they will be proliferating and will be conflictual, wearing on their sleeve and advancing contesting sets of values and perspectives. The boundaries of such organizations – their spatiality – cannot be pinpointed in an absolute way but are *contentious*. And this is the nature of the environment in which planning has to take place.

For example, only relatively recently has there come to be reference to indigenous peoples in the mission statements of some universities. This is markedly the case in Canada, Australia and New Zealand but in other places as well. Forming a sense that an indigenous people might come into the purview of a university extends the university. It extends the university as a place: characteristically, the university is pulled out – or pushes itself – into the physical spaces of such communities. But the university is also stretched as a discursive space, and in its understanding of its possibilities and responsibilities. It is – to put the matter formally – stretched *ontologically*; stretched in its very being.

PLANNING EDUCATION: INTO TRANS-SPATIALITY – A FICTIONAL CASE STUDY

Only now are we in a position to offer some conjectures and suggestions about planning studies as a university discipline. It is surely evident that traditional considerations and distinctions should be given a wide birth. For example, yes, the ideas of interdisciplinarity and transdisciplinarity are preferable to disciplinarity but they now need themselves to be surpassed. We need a much more ambitious term, perhaps that of *trans-spatiality*. In drawing on the university as a resource, students will not only traverse different disciplines but will transcend epistemological spaces and move across ontological spaces.

Imagine that a curriculum includes as a case study – on which the students are asked to work – that of a university establishing a new campus on the edge of a city; imagine that the university is a 'world-leading' university and that the locale is an urban setting of poverty and deprivation. A welter of issues of spaces emerge at once. What are the relationships to be between the spaces of the new campus and areas of the immediate locality? What links might be possible between the two? The two locales, after all, move in different worlds, the very local and the global. Spaces here are not just disciplinary – and so are epistemological – but are geographical, social and cultural. The students, in investigating the possibilities, will have to move across these zones simultaneously.

But the spaces opening here for our planning students are even more demanding, for – as stated – they are ontological as well. In surveying the locality, in engaging with locals, in examining planning regulations, in looking at civic plans, and speaking to local councillors and parliamentary politicians, students will have to stretch themselves, stretch their being, into uncomfortable registers and modes of experience (Latour 2013). Just what possibilities might be envisaged for this new campus? Can its disciplines focus on the problems of the immediate urban communities? Might international students feel energized or daunted in engaging with such problems and peoples? What might 'openness' mean, given the proximity of poor and deprived neighbourhoods?

Note that, in focusing on the challenges and opportunities facing this new university campus, not only do considerations of disciplinarity have to be transcended, and the distinction between epistemology and ontology sidestepped (for disciplinarity now becomes a matter of sheer being), but so too the distinction between curriculum and pedagogy. To involve students in the challenges of planning the new campus is at once a matter of curriculum and of pedagogy. The two cannot be separated: it is not a matter of choosing the what of the curriculum (contents) and then the how of the pedagogical approach. No. The two are interwoven.

Once the university's new campus is placed on the curriculum as a matter of serious study, the pedagogy immediately places its demands upon the students. They are thrown into the new campus, they are required to imagine the campus – not yet even designed, let alone built. They are called upon to address the tortuous and impossible questions facing them: Where are the boundaries of this campus? In the immediate locale or the other side of the earth (for the campus will house world-active scholars and researchers)? Which are the pertinent discourses and just how might they be placed in each other's company? How are the voices of the neighbourhood to be weighed against those of the great corporations prepared to invest in the 'spin-off' companies, to be linked to two of the likely departments coming to the new campus? Just where and of what character are the spaces of this campus? Can the mantra of 'local, national and global' suffice or does not a different vocabulary have to be invented?

In seriously grappling with matters such as these, the students will not just have to give of themselves, but they will have to make themselves. They will form themselves as human beings. They will be called upon to empathize with non-commensurable viewpoints, as they listen to the conflicting stakeholders, in the immediate vicinity and well beyond. The urban and the civic, the national and the global, and tales of lives in the neighbourhood and of international students soon to be present in the vicinity have to be *imagined*. Moreover, if the students are to make quasi-planning decisions, values have to be adopted. 'On the one hand this, and on the other hand, that' will no longer serve. The students have to declare themselves, for the new campus cannot be all things to all peoples. Difficult – and even impossible – choices have to be made.

Of course, in the programme descriptions, many of the conventional tropes of curricula and pedagogy will be seen. Interdisciplinarity, transdisciplinarity, breadth, a liberal education, transferable skills, a general education, practicality and others may all be mentioned. The curriculum, we will be told, will be 'co-created' with the students and will be 'research-led'. And descriptions of the pedagogies, too, will raid the contemporary vocabularies. They will be 'problem-based', the students being required to engage in 'active learning', and take on a significant measure of 'personal responsibility'. It will be a 'skills-rich' experience, with 'learning outcomes' of the most varied kind, including 'digital fluency' (Savin-Baden 2015). But this familiar vocabulary and these tropes cannot do justice to what is to be glimpsed here; for what is in prospect is an education – a *higher* education – of the profoundest kind that cannot be caught by such a terminology.

In such a conception of planning studies, students stand on a precipice and hurl themselves forward, not to their deaths but to their becoming. They come to live with ineradicable uncertainty and gain an elevation from it. They live on the edge – dancing between discourses, across spaces, against and beyond ideologies, in and out of practices, and through imagined options. They travel the globe and they immerse themselves in the immediate vicinity of the campus yet to come. They bring forward utopias, of the here-and-now and the future, of the dispossessed and the powerful, of theoretical sophistication and of down-to-earthness. They become poets of the university. They make their curricula and they make their pedagogies. And they make themselves.

UNIVERSITY DESIGN

More prosaically, some additional possibilities may be envisaged:

1. Planning students could engage with the estates departments of universities to learn about what it is to develop an estates strategy for some years, and even decades ahead, whether in an urban or in a more rural setting. They could be set to assist on a particular project, say the siting of a new department. Should it be close to all the present university functions and amenities or should it be in an entirely new setting, perhaps on the edge

of a city? Which is likely to provoke the least ire from residents and to consume fewer energy resources and to produce more political challenges? Which might be the cost–benefit analyses of the heating, lighting, building maintenance, water supply, and waste disposal implications of either option?

2. Planning students could engage with the Pro-Rector and senior officers responsible for overseeing the formation of the University's Strategic Plan or Corporate Strategy. Again, they could be asked to advise and to assist in its formulation. They could be invited to help in organizing 'town hall' meetings, with the staff and external stakeholders and to sift through the multitude of views – many of which will be both imaginary and will conflict – in devising a new strategy for the university that is feasible, does justice to its values and deploys its resources in an eco-sensitive way. But more than that, in groups, they might role-play the expression of counter-values for the university's future, as between economic survival and growth, civic responsibility, eco-sensitivity, personal well-being, public service and so forth.

3. Planning students could engage with the planning department of the local city council and learn about the city's development of itself as a 'smart city', a 'learning city', or an 'eco-city' *and* its perception of the contribution that the university might make thereto. The students could engage in a 'network analysis' of potential *citizen-learners* and then work as a bridge between the city's planning department and the university to discern new possibilities both for university and city. Often, the university is one if not the largest employer in a town and brings in not just multiple income streams but many cultures as well, with a university's students being attracted from perhaps a hundred nations of the world. What are otherwise rather culturally enclosed settings find themselves a microcosm of the United Nations.

4. The students could attempt to set up a meeting with the Rector or Vice-Chancellor and learn about – and press questions on – what it is to be a complex learning organization in a globalized world. They could hear about the challenges – and indeed the risks of working with partners in other countries, of engaging with disparate political and economic regimes and of being sensitive to a multi-cultural setting. Just what is it to plan in such a situation, with so many strands of consideration and uncertainty, strands that are both systemic and discursive?

5. Against the background of a growing interest in the 'public goods' of the university and in its connections with the public sphere, the students could inquire of the local institutions of civic learning – museums, galleries, local historical societies, women's institutes, branches of professional bodies, adult learning centres – and examine possibilities for the uni-

versity to form a local network of community learning. In the process, important questions – legal and otherwise – will arise as to the meaning of 'public' and 'private' spaces in and around the university. Who is permitted to venture onto any of the sites in question (including the university itself)?

These are but examples of the kinds of ways in which planning students might be enabled to draw upon the university as a pedagogical resource. But note, too, that each such example could spawn multiple strands of inquiry and discernment, and open different paths for the students. A cohort of students could be divided into groups, with different groups tackling paths of physical systems, eco-considerations, culture (and multi-culture), digital technologies, values, ideas, history, and future scenarios. And the images, projections, and proposals with which the groups would emerge would be bound to conflict and ways would have to be found of bringing such disparate envisionings into relationships with each other. Conflict resolution – or, more realistically, conflict maintenance – would become an important pedagogical device.

CONCLUSIONS

Planning studies opens curricula and pedagogical paths that offer a properly broad education for the 21st century, and the university itself offers an extraordinary site in which such hopes can be realized. That has been the double contention of this chapter. The key word in that opening double-barrelled sentence is, of course, 'properly'. The term secretes a set of value judgements as to what constitutes a proper education and several such value judgements have been present here. They include not just that planning studies should look to students to consider systems aspects of planning complex initiatives but should also look to students to develop a concern for the total environment with which initiatives are entangled. This 'concern' is a kind of Heideggerian concern (Heidegger 1998). It is a concern for the entire being of what is in question. Taking the university as a case study for planning brings into view just such a concern, for in very short order the question is posed: 'and what is a university in the 21st century?' (This is akin to corresponding questions of planning elsewhere: 'and what is an airport – or health system, or new town, or communication system – in the 21st century?').

But then that 'properly' has another important facet that goes beyond systems awareness, namely that of the discursive character of matters. What it is to be a university – or airport, or health system or new town   is subject to multiple, proliferating and contending viewpoints. Such matters are now inherently contentious, and planning studies have to be sensitive to this discursive mayhem. One way of depicting such situations is to understand them as instances of supercomplexity. This is precisely the nature of the contemporary university. To plan a university is to enter a site of irredeemable contestation. It cannot be assumed – or pretended – that any issue might be open to some kind of Hegelian resolution. Thesis – say, that the university is a neoliberal project – may lead to an antithesis – that the university is an institution of public good. This in no way opens to a peaceful synthesis but results in only more discursive conflict and even hostilities (as the discursive situation opens to yet more imaginings of the university in the 21st century).

As indicated, both curricula and pedagogies have to be called upon to do justice to such a conception of planning studies. Self-evidently, the curriculum will need to be not only multi-disciplinary and interdisciplinary but also open spaces for new transdisciplinary frameworks to emerge – for example, to include ethics, anthropology, cultural studies and poetry. But such imaginative curricula will be desultory unless backed up by imaginative pedagogies, where the students are placed in testing situations and encouraged to come forward with their own 'solutions' to challenges that test students' own values and capacities for handling discursive conflict. In the university, it has been contended here, students and their professors in the field of planning have to hand an extraordinary site that allows just such challenges to be posed and addressed.

There are, then, opportunities for a symbiosis between planning studies and planning the university. A university with programmes in planning education in its midst is especially fortunate, therefore. Why? Because, any such university, in drawing its planning students into the processes of planning the university, might learn about itself. This would be a genuine symbiosis, in which both students and university learn from each other. It would be a symbiosis of becoming, for both students and university; a becoming-symbiosis, indeed.

This kind of educational venture might even pose questions – possibly troubling questions – as to the nature of 'education for *planning*'. Perhaps, given the reflections of this chapter, the very notion of 'planning' itself is due for critique, not least when design, utopias, travel (both epistemological and ontological), multi-dimensional spaces (ontological, cultural, epistemological, geographical) and valuing are all in play. Surely, there is more sliding, glimpsing, imagining, listening, and choosing than (mere) planning here?

NOTE

1. While the argument remains valid, Berlin Brandenburg Airport did finally open in October 2020 during the COVID-19 pandemic with a delay of 9 years.

REFERENCES

Argyris, C. and Schön, D. (1974) *Theory in Practice: Increasing Professional Effectiveness*. San Francisco, CA: Jossey-Bass.

Barnett, R. (1990) *Realizing the University in an Age of Supercomplexity*. Buckingham: Open University Press/Society for Research into Higher Education.

Barnett, R. (2018) *The Ecological University: A Feasible Utopia*. London and New York: Routledge.

Hassan, R. (2003) *The Chronoscopic Society: Globalization, Time and Knowledge in the Network Economy*. New York: Peter Lang.

Heidegger, M. (1998/1962) *Being and Time*. Oxford: Blackwell.

Kerr, C. (1995/1963) *The Uses of the University* (4th ed.). The Godkin Lectures. Cambridge, MA: Harvard University Press.

Latour, B. (2013) *An Inquiry into Modes of Existence: An Anthropology of the Moderns*. Cambridge, MA: Harvard University Press.

List, C. and Pettit, P. (2011) *Group Agency: The Possibility, Design and Status of Corporate Agents*. Cambridge: Cambridge University Press.

Marginson, S. (2010) University. In P. Murphy, M. A. Peters and S. Marginson, *Imagination: Three Models of Imagination in the Age of the Knowledge Economy* (pp. 167–224). New York: Peter Lang.

Savin-Baden, M. (2015) *Rethinking Learning in an Age of Digital Fluency*. London and New York: Routledge.

Sloman, A. (1964) *A University in the Making*. The BBC Reith Lectures, 1963. London: BBC.

PART II

Teaching and learning in, for and with communities

4. Pedagogy built on working with communities: a first semester core course

Ayse Yonder, Mercedes Narciso and Juan Camilo Osorio

INTRODUCTION

Preparing students for practice is a key challenge in planning education. As a future oriented activity, planning by definition has to deal with uncertainty and complex 'wicked' socio-economic problems. Given the increased complexity and future uncertainties due to climate change, increasing socio-economic polarization, and new technologies, this challenge seems to be greater now than ever before. Over the past two decades, the issue of how to balance theory, methods, skills and practice-oriented courses in the core curriculum has been widely debated. Most planning schools in the United States have by now incorporated practice-oriented courses into their core curriculum (Edwards and Bates 2011). Depending on how each programme defines planning, the strategies for practice-oriented learning range from special seminars and internships, to studios (Lang 1983; Long 2012). Over two thirds of the eighty schools listed in the 2015 Planetizen Guide to Graduate Urban Planning Programmes now have a studio course requirement, but several questions remain on how to define, incorporate and assess the learning outcomes of studios (Long 2012; Vidyarthi et al. 2012).

Since most studio projects involve working with a client, there is also the issue of how community engagement takes place within an academic setting, and how the process impacts partner communities (Angotti et al. 2011; Ferman and Hill 2004; Frank 2008). Especially within the current divisive political context, it is critical for planning programmes to assess how they can work collaboratively with community-based organizations and their coalitions to build local capacity to cope with impacts of climate change, and to link to the broader social and environmental justice movements (Shiffman 2007; Stults and Larsen 2018).

This contribution explores the challenges and benefits of offering a studio that involves working with a community-based client organization during the first semester, rather than at the end as culmination, using the case study of Pratt Institute's City Planning Program in New York. After a brief review of literature on studio pedagogy and service learning, we provide a short description of Pratt's practice and community-oriented pedagogy. We then consider the effectiveness of the first-semester *Fundamentals of Planning* studio/seminar course from both the students' and community clients' perspectives. An online survey, with the participation of 185 students (out of the 233 contacted), was used to measure students' assessment of the learning outcomes. Structured interviews with the community partners focused on some key issues raised in the service-learning literature. In conclusion, we consider the benefits, challenges and conditions necessary to effectively integrate a studio course early in the planning curriculum.

PRACTICE-ORIENTED LEARNING

The attitude towards studio pedagogy has changed over time. As the focus of planning programmes shifted away from physical planning towards an emphasis on social science and research, studio pedagogy was abandoned in most schools, to be revived once again in recent years. While for some, the term 'studio' still implies design-oriented activities, studio pedagogy is equally applicable to social policy analysis and formulation since it involves "designing and evaluating courses of action in response to problems" (Lang 1983, p. 123; Long 2012). 'Synthesis', 'learning-by-doing', and 'reflection-in-action', that aim to expose students to the complexity of 'real-world problems' and to initiate 'professional socialization' are some the most common terms found in the learning outcomes in studio syllabi from different programmes (Németh and Long 2012, p. 479). For Higgins et al. (2009), studio pedagogy is about experiential, problem-based, student-centred and reflective learning.

For others, studio courses do more than just teach practice. They also investigate "new modes of practice with a focus on advocacy and community outreach, as well as meaningful collaboration among disciplines" (Long 2012, p. 432). In addition to developing skills for collaborative and transdisciplinary approaches (between professionals, scientists, communities, public and private sector), the experiential learning format also helps students gain "a disposition and ability to act positively in the face of complexity, uncertainty and unknown futures". These are key competencies for contemporary planning practice, according to Oonk et al. (2016) and Rooij and Frank (2016, p. 476). Forester (2013, p. 5), coming from a critical pragmatic perspective, argues that studio settings can provide students with the opportunity to learn to "think critically about outcomes as well as processes, about institutional and process designs, about power and performance ... [and to] reconstruct possibilities where others might initially perceive or presume impossibilities". Working with a community-based client early in their educational process can help students learn to relate theory to practice, and "can be a transformative experience, forcing them to confront their own values" (Le Gates and Robinson 1998, p. 314).

Although there is broad consensus on the benefits of studios as a key component of practice-oriented learning, there are several challenges. Some research points out the potential tensions that might arise from teamwork and bringing together students with different backgrounds in studios (Arefi and Edelman 2013, p. 72). Moreover, "real projects can be messy and unpredictable, drawing students into complex political realms. They generally require work before and after the semester, setting up relationships and completing products" (Cameron et al. 2001, p. 111).

While the literature on studio pedagogy focuses on how to bring practice into the classroom, service-learning literature discusses issues regarding learning in and with communities (Levkoe et al. 2020). University community service is not new; Angotti et al. (2011) point out that planning approaches, like Advocacy Planning, which link service and learning, emerged as early as the Civil Rights era. Federal government programmes in the 1990s then led to a reassessment of the challenges and benefits of earlier university community partnerships (Baum 2000; Dewar and Isaac 1998; Sletto 2010). Angotti et al. argue that community service learning is not only about "shifting the site of learning from the classroom to the community"; it also requires equal partnership between the academic and community partners based on mutual respect, mutual learning and commitment (2011, p. 2).

CONTEXT MATTERS

"Each school's core is ... inevitably a reflection of the uniqueness of the department and the students and faculty who define it" (Edwards and Bates 2011, p. 173). Pratt Institute's Planning Program is rather unique being located in an Art and Design School, where innovative and creative practice is valued at least as much as academic research and publication, and studio pedagogy is emphasized throughout the Institute as a way of not just learning but creating knowledge. Moreover, the programme's approach to planning has been influenced by the legacy of the Pratt Center for Community Development (PCCD). PCCD is the oldest surviving university-based community planning organization in the US, established in 1963 to address poverty and top-down government policies. Over the past six decades, its 'high quality' technical assistance and policy advocacy for social and environmental justice has built trust with community groups around the city – a key to successful university community partnerships (Vidal et al. 2002). This 'activist planning model' and emphasis on transformative practice has attracted adjunct faculty with similar values and experience, and students interested in participatory planning, social and environmental justice, and sustainability issues (Wolf-Powers 2008, p. 3).

The Planning Program is part of the Graduate Center for Planning and the Environment (GCPE) in the School of Architecture with three other graduate programmes, Sustainable Environmental Systems (SES), Historic Preservation (HP) and Urban Placemaking & Management (UPM). The City and Regional Planning Program's (CRP) goals are: "(1) to utilize studio and team learning to educate students about the importance of collaboration in a multidisciplinary field, and (2) to provide opportunity for focused, specialized or interdisciplinary study and degrees" (2014 GCPE Planning Accreditation Report, p. 33).

The practice-oriented components of Pratt's planning curriculum include three studios, a final thesis or demonstration of professional competence project (DPC), and a range of internship/fellowships that provide opportunities to work embedded in communities to develop action-oriented research skills.

An analysis of the 42 advanced studios offered between 2010 and 2016 reveals that most were client-based (83%), had a community development/advocacy focus (81%), and involved partnerships with community based or citywide non-profit organizations (71%). Most studios stressed a multidisciplinary approach by combining faculty from the different programmes and/or inviting experts from different fields (93%), and brought together students from different programmes, fostering an interdisciplinary environment (71%).

A FIRST SEMESTER CORE COURSE: FUNDAMENTALS OF PLANNING

It was within this context that a first semester core course evolved from a three-credit lecture into a five-credit course with a 'mini-studio' component. Its goal is twofold: "to familiarize students with relevant literature on the principles and practice of planning, and to relate those readings to practice by working for a real client on a current planning issue in a New York City neighbourhood". Student learning objectives include learning to: (1) critically evaluate and reflect on the readings; (2) work collaboratively in teams; (3) work with a community client; (4) gather and analyse data on existing conditions to develop planning recommendations that address the client's concerns; and, (5) prepare and make professional presentations.

The seminar component of the course requires students to prepare short weekly commentaries on the assigned readings that are reorganized each semester to provide relevant background for the studio topic. The purpose is to make sure students stay current with the readings for meaningful class discussion and relate the readings to their own experiences and the studio project.

Due to limited in-class time (two three-hour sessions per week), students are required to set aside additional time for teamwork, as well as site visits, community meetings, stakeholder interviews, etc.

The course is taught by three instructors (one full-time and two adjuncts), who select the studio topic and site from among a few potential ideas proposed to them by community groups they had worked with before or know through their networks, based on both the potential class size and immediacy of the community partner's need. Discussions with the community partner about the focus and scope of the studio project often begin months before the semester, and the deliverables and meeting schedules are confirmed before the semester starts.

Students meet the community partner at the beginning of the term to hear directly about the community and the background of the issues they are asked to work on. To get acquainted with the neighbourhood, they start their existing conditions research with a site visit and survey. Students prepare their existing conditions analysis working in three teams focusing on the social, physical and natural environment, and present their findings to the client around the middle of the term. During the second half of the semester, smaller teams are formed to develop short-, medium- and long-term recommendations, based on the client's feedback and priorities as well as their research findings, conducting additional research as needed. They make a final presentation to the client at the end of the semester and deliver their final report. Often, they are asked to present their findings to community members and/or elected officials. They also present their work and get additional feedback from GCPE faculty and peers at the end of the semester.

Inevitably, tensions arise among students with different backgrounds who are used to working individually in more traditional class and studio settings. To resolve such issues, instructors meet with students individually, as needed, and hold a class session after the mid-semester presentation to reflect on the process and brainstorm about how to resolve issues. At the beginning of each semester, they share with the students the lessons learned from previous semesters about how to divide up the work among themselves within and across teams, as well as how to relate to the client. During the latter part of the semester, as students start to work on their recommendations, collaboration gets easier. The final class session is dedicated to reflections on what they have learned and how to improve the learning process.

Teamwork and good class citizenship carry significant weight in grading. Commentaries and participation in class activities account for 25% of the grade, each, and the studio project accounts for half of the grade based on their individual contribution and the team's overall performance. Given the close coaching during the semester, grading is based on a number of different factors, including each student's performance and progress, as well as feedback from the client and other faculty members during midterm and final presentations.

Student's Assessment of Learning Outcomes

Students' views on learning outcomes of the course were gathered through an online survey sent to those who took the course between the spring of 2010 and 2017. The questionnaire had three open-ended questions that explored how the students remembered and would describe the course; whether the concepts and skills learned were useful in their later work; and how the class could have prepared them better for future academic or professional work. Another question asked whether the experience of working for a community-based client was useful towards becoming a professional planner. The question on the most important concepts/skills learned in this course was adapted from the learning outcomes categories developed by Németh and Long (2012) (Table 4.1). The survey response rate was rather high (79%), considering over a third of the 185 respondents had already graduated, and 6% were either on leave of absence or had transferred to another programme within the GCPE or elsewhere.

Harris and Irazabal Zurita (2011) found that the characteristics of what students described as a High Service – High Learning experience involved: (a) a well-defined significant project with a clear schedule, (b) high level of support and supervision, (c) close connection between the deliverable to the organization and course assignment, and (d) transformed subjectivities. In terms of these criteria, the deliverables of the Fundamentals class to the client organization accounted for over half of the students' grade. In terms of support and supervision, as several students acknowledged in the survey, the faculty spent a lot of time working closely with the students; at times, joining them for weekend meetings to provide support and guidance. Working on a planning project for a real community client was very important for the students. The studio process became more structured over time with specific weekly tasks, and guidelines provided at each phase of the project including tips about how to organize the collaborative process, as well as the reports.

Still, some students found unforeseen changes in the schedule and lack of a single correct answer to the issues at hand frustrating. The steep learning curve and the workload represented also challenges for some students. But as Harris and Irazabal Zurita point out, "while assignment design is important to student learning outcomes, so is the attitude of the individual student" (2011, p. 118). Harris and Irazabal Zurita define "transformed subjectivities" as "gaining an understanding of the challenges and opportunities faced by professionals", developing confidence to view oneself as a professional, and "becoming more informed and sensitized about social responsibility and ethics in the profession" (2011, p. 115). Most Fundamentals students felt the class was a good orientation to the profession and helped them confront their own values: "The course is not only an introduction to planning but an opportunity to shape your values as an urban planner through practice and learning."

Another felt facilitating a visioning workshop with "low income residents who have values far different than my own in terms of public space usage was more challenging than I would have imagined. I really had to listen and was keenly aware of my own discomfort and the difficult task of working in a community that is not my own."

Overall, the survey responses seem to confirm that the course has been rather successful in meeting its primary goal of linking the background readings to practice through the hands-on experience of working with a community partner. Almost all the students felt that working with a community partner was useful, and one of the things a majority said stood out in their mind about the course. They learned, not only how to interact with a client, but also to respect local knowledge and realize the challenges community-based organizations (CBOs) face: "It was about working for people who are more invested than my 40-hours per week; working for people who have to live with my decisions or lack of it, and working for people who may know more than I." Others said the CBO provided them the legitimacy to work in the community:

> Having a real client put an urgency and seriousness to our work that would not have existed with a hypothetical client. Knowing who would see our work led us to want to produce the best product possible so we could see it put to use and see a real response to our work. It was also much more validating at the end of the course to have a community group receive your work and be appreciative of it.

Even though several students described the course as "challenging", "intense", "hitting the ground running", and frequently, as "baptism by fire", they all said they were glad that they experienced the steep learning curve during their first semester of graduate study:

> It is almost overwhelming, but it prepares you for what you will be doing in future, and helps you find the areas of planning you want to learn more about.

They felt that the skills they learned and the experiences of the Fundamentals class prepared them for more advanced studios and later practice:

> I find myself referring back to things I learned from the Fundamentals Studio in classes I have had post-studio.

> I believe this studio helped me get the job I have today.

While there was a relatively equal distribution of responses that relate to the main learning outcome categories, as highlighted in bold in Table 4.1, over

60% of the students felt that **collaboration and teamwork, learning by doing, dealing with complexity and uncertainty in planning process, being creative in designing solutions and processes, and working with a community based client** (recognizing accountability or responsibility to the client, assessing planning outcomes on set of values) were the key learning outcomes of the class. A significant number said they would have liked to have more time with the community partner and more direct interaction with people in the neighbourhood. Others wanted more specific communication and analysis skills, or focus on other specific topics, and more in-class time.

Assessment of Benefits to the Community Partner

The interviews with community partners who worked with the Fundamentals studio from 2010–2017 were based on the evaluation criteria suggested in the community service-learning literature and provided feedback on their experience (Bose and Wilson 2014; Erickson 2014; Frank 2008). Questions explored the client's views on the quality and usefulness of the products; how they were used; the time frame; and ideas on improving university–community collaboration. These findings are in part summarized in Table 4.2 illustrating the use of student work but also mechanisms that introduce more continuity into the university–community collaboration to further improve its value.

Most community partners (64%) had worked with the PCCD before. They felt the students were a great resource, bringing energy, enthusiasm, and new ideas and ways of looking at things. The director of GOLES, who was experienced in working with students from different schools, said it was always a positive experience: "Even if sometimes you don't get everything you want, many times you get things you didn't even ask for. So, it's a trade-off." Similarly, for the NYC-EJA director "it was very useful to have many more eyes looking at issues, as compared to just one staff person analysing them. In addition, this provides the opportunity to take an issue and analyse it in its broader context – which is often difficult for staff to do on a daily basis … And students are eager to learn and get involved in co-creating a greater vision." The MARP director, however, felt students "are a great resource but they are students after all, and so, more idealistic than realistic in approaching issues". Another partner thought that some recommendations could be controversial or too complex to implement in the short run.

About half of the clients referred to their own time and capacity limitations, as discussed in Ferman and Hill (2004). Often being under-resourced and understaffed, it was hard for them to make additional time for the studio group, and sometimes, scheduled presentation or meeting dates had to be changed. It was also important to find out early on about the amount of interaction preferred by each client. One partner pointed out that the amount of time it

Table 4.1   *Student assessment of the most important skills learned in this class*

Skills considered important by students	% of N=185 respondents
COMMUNICATION	
Graphical/visual skills	**64%**
Written skills	42%
Oral presentation	**61%**
Understanding the dynamics among plan's multiple stakeholders	**69%**
PROFESSIONAL EXPERIENCE	
Working in a "real world" work environment	56%
Gain project management skills (workflow, time management, etc.)	**61%**
Understanding quality standards expected in practice	57%
Understand various roles of planner	**67%**
LEARNING BY DOING	
Application of general planning concepts to specific context	**76%**
Learning how to synthesize skills, knowledge, values	**59%**
Understanding the relationship between theory and practice	54%
Acknowledge uncertainty/complexity in planning practice	**72%**
Recognition of planning as iterative, long-term process	**69%**
PROBLEM SOLVING	
Ability to formulate logical, defensible planning decisions	51%
Learn how to evaluate several possible scenarios	**59%**
Negotiate oppositional viewpoints	51%
Recognize importance of flexibility in decision-making process	61%
Seek appropriate assistance and expertise	50%
Being creative in designing solutions and processes	**66%**
Develop critical thinking ability	52%
TEAMWORK	
Role recognition in collaborative work	**76%**
Understanding basic group dynamics	**77%**
Development of leadership qualities	**59%**
Gain vital listening abilities	42%
Development of interpersonal cooperation skills	**72%**
SERVICE/WORKING W/A COMMUNITY BASED CLIENT	
Assess planning outcomes on set of values (justice, sustainability, etc.)	**72%**
Sublimation of personal opinion	46%

Skills considered important by students	% of N=185 respondents
Creation of ethical foundation for future practice	51%
Recognize accountability/responsibility to client group	**71%**
Acknowledge and challenge systemic power imbalances	33%

Source: List adapted from Németh and Long (2012).

takes "to bring students up to speed to carry out the analysis" generally meant time away from their own work. The compressed schedule of the semester "doesn't allow them time to build relationships and trust with community members and stakeholders. So, the client has to broker these relationships, meaning additional work for us." Most partners were aware of the difficulty of synchronizing the academic calendar with how things happen on the ground. As one community partner put it, "You must plan the curriculum in advance but on the ground, things can happen more slowly or faster. An idea may not wait or a process can take too long. Just four months doesn't allow students to see the end result."

All community partners had positive experiences with Pratt students. One emphasized how the students were well prepared and respected their time constraints. Those who had longer-term involvement with the programme through fellowship arrangements felt the students generally brought a more comprehensive perspective, and could grasp the issues at hand more quickly:

> By large, the program tends to attract students that are sympathetic to environmental justice and its values. It's a richer interaction because there are similar political views. You do not have to explain too much in order for them to understand the broad principles of the work. Also, there was some diversity, so some students directly understood the issues discussed … The fact that they work with a client and enjoy that work makes the project a very pleasant experience for everyone. (Director of New York City Environmental Justice Alliance – NYC-EJA)

> Pratt students were well prepared for the task and the organization. They were diverse in their backgrounds. They were serious and idealistic but had a practical approach to problems. They worked with a true sense of enthusiastic learning about the grass roots community they were studying and seemed to grasp the community as unique from others. (Director of Two Bridges Community Development Corporation)

All community partners found both the existing conditions analysis and the final recommendations of the studio useful. An issue that almost all brought up was the lack of time for more interaction and follow-up with the research findings and recommendations. One suggested coming back about a year later to evaluate the results of the studio: "Students should know how the product of their work was used."

Interestingly, no one found the semester schedule to be a problem, but all wanted more continuity, a key challenge in community service learning (Martin et al. 2014). They proposed different ideas about how to continue collaboration with Pratt, ranging from follow-up internship positions to multi-year collaboration agreements (Table 4.2).

CONCLUSION

The purpose of adding a studio component to a first semester introductory class was to enable students to relate readings to practice. Offering a studio during the first semester of a Master's programme was an innovation even in the context of Pratt's studio and community-oriented pedagogy. The student and client surveys indicate that the course has been successful in meeting its learning objectives. Not only did the students learn a range of technical skills in a short time that enabled them to prepare and present a professional planning report, but also a number of critical soft skills that prepared them for the advanced interdisciplinary studios in the programme and later professional work. Learning to work collaboratively in teams was the biggest source of frustration for most students. Working with a real client was also a source of anxiety for some, but most acquired a strong sense of accountability and respect for the community partner. Almost all students reflected that they benefited in a range of ways from the learning process – even if they may not have thought so during the semester.

Working with the Fundamentals students was a positive experience for the community partners, too. They could use the existing conditions analysis for different purposes. The student work highlighted issues they had not considered before, often in relation to the potential impacts of climate change. The recommendations generated new ideas beyond the scope they anticipated. While some initially did not consider these 'low priority, high impact' issues as their immediate priority, it encouraged long-term strategies. After Superstorm Sandy, one community partner requested another studio project to prepare a community disaster preparedness and resilience plan. Two organizations joined the citywide environmental justice coalition, NYC Environmental Justice Alliance. Presentations to the community and visioning workshops not only provided useful information to the client, but also helped bring together stakeholders that often did not work together. The presence of an independent outside party provided a sense of neutrality, and eventually, some of the recommendations were refined and implemented.

Continued engagement and support were the community partners' main concern, reflecting a key challenge in community service-learning.

Table 4.2   List of studio projects, outcomes and continuity

CLIENT/Semester/Project	OUTCOMES: How were the studio products used?	CONTINUITY: interns, follow up studios or other involvement
FA 2009 – **Amsterdam Avenue Business Improvement District (BID)** *Commercial revitalization and community development*	Existing conditions posters on permanent display at BID office. Student reports placed in local public library	Follow up studio in Spring
FA 2011 – **Assemblyman's Office and Amsterdam Avenue BID** *A community Vision for the Future*	Presentations and Visioning Workshops commingled diverse groups. Assemblyman disseminated findings/recommendations	Fall semester students collaborated
FA 2011 – **Good Old Lower East Side (GOLES)** *Gentrification, infrastructure, public health and the environment*	Existing conditions analysis and final recommendations useful in grant applications, etc	Student interns in Spring
SP 2011 – **GOLES** *Gentrification and Economic Justice in Lower East Side*	Focus group meeting findings and existing conditions analysis useful in expanding social justice programs	Student intern in Summer
FA 2012 – **Churches United for Fair Housing (CUFFH)** *Development potential of CUFFH properties for resilient community development*	Existing conditions and final recommendations provided useful facts and ideas	Internship position announced but not filled
FA 2013 – **GOLES and the LES Ready! Coalition** *Community Preparedness and Resilience Plan for the Lower East Side*	Deliverables contributed to LES Community Preparedness and Resilience Plan. GOLES dedicated resources for disaster preparedness. A recommendation incorporated into Rebuild by Design Plan	Student interns in Spring & Summer
SP 2013 – **Hester Street Collaborative (HSC) and Asian Americans for Equality** *Manhattan Open Space Analysis and Recommendations*	Deliverables used in applying for capital funding in Spring 2014	HSC has ongoing Fellowship

CLIENT/Semester/Project	OUTCOMES: How were the studio products used?	CONTINUITY: interns, follow up studios or other involvement
SP 2014 – **Carroll Gardens Association (CGA)** Brooklyn *Affordable Housing in Columbia Waterfront and Red Hook*	Studio report presented to Council Member to acquire a proposed site for mixed development	Internship position announced but not filled
FA 2014 – **Two Bridges Community Development Corporation** *Bridging the Waterfront: Recommendations for TB*	Recommendations incorporated into the mission statement and bylaws of a new CDC created by TB	Student thesis on "Resiliency Improvement Districts"
SP 2015 – **Brownsville Partnership** Brooklyn *Brownsville: Opportunity and Strength in the Heart of Brooklyn*	Food retail and greenway recommendations were most useful. BP learned area is vulnerable to storm surge	
FA 2015 – **Youth Ministries for Peace and Justice (YMPJ) Bronx** *Strategies for affordable housing and economic and environmental justice*	YMPJ used vacant land inventory and analysis in its strategic plan. Some recommendations implemented	A student intern at during and after the studio. YMPJ has ongoing GCPE Fellowship
SP 2016 – **Concrete Safaris** *Open Space Systems, Youth and East in Harlem*	Deliverables helped in developing CS's strategic plan and write grant proposals	
FA 2016 – **Chhaya Community Development Corporation** *Affordability, Resiliency and Access for Jackson Heights*	Research on illegal basement conversions used for citywide BASE advocacy campaign; Chhaya joined the NYC-EJA	A student joined Chhaya staff as ANHD fellow; a student thesis on immigrant businesses in JHeights
SP 2017 – **El Puente** *Open Space and Sustainable Economic Development in Southside Williamsburg*	Deliverables used to campaigns and investments in neighborhood	EP has ongoing GCPE Fellowship

Coordination between some of the studios and the internship course led to the creation of studio-linked internships, enabling students to continue to work with the partner CBOs. However, institutionalized coordination and administrative support is necessary for follow-up studios and continued community relations (Martin et al. 2014). Campus-based community design or development centres, like the PCCD, "help create a more permanent framework for community relations and service" (Cameron et al. 2001, p. 110).

The unique advantages of Pratt's Planning Program due to the legacy of the Pratt Center aside, engaging students early on, during their first semester, with a real client around a plan-making project is not only possible, it is important for introducing them to the challenges of professional practice and collaborative work, and to help confront their values and consider future directions. However, this requires a number of considerations. First, a seminar component is critical to ground students in theory and history, and to link the issues in the study area to broader policy debates. Preparing commentaries on the weekly reading assignments provide a background and an opportunity for individual feedback to international students and those who are not familiar with current policy issues. Second, a structured process with weekly assignments and educator availability are essential to overcome potential anxieties and ensure satisfactory completion of the deliverables on time. Third, close collaboration with additional skills courses helps to make a steep learning curve possible. Finally, the faculty must be willing to spend a lot of time to plan the studio process – from meeting the community partner early on to discuss the goals, expectations, deliverables and schedules, to working closely with students during the semester, and incorporating their feedback/reflections into the syllabus. Without community engagement as well as the establishment of long-term relations and trust with community organizations, however, it is not possible to have effective dialogue and mutual learning experience in communities. (See Box 4.1.)

BOX 4.1   TIPS FOR IMPLEMENTATION – DEALING WITH POTENTIAL CHALLENGES

• **Working with community-based organizations as partners**

Finding a community partner interested in working with students can be a challenge. Their busy schedules may not allow them to explore partnerships beyond their own daily workload. A more institutionalized setting, rather than personal networks, to identify and engage community partners will likely enhance effectiveness. Such an arrangement can also help coordinate long-term university community collaboration.

It is important to meet with the community partner at least a month before the semester starts to agree on the deliverables, meeting schedules, the ways the client wants to communicate with students during the semester and engage community stakeholders.

- **Dealing with student anxiety about uncertainty and steep learning curve**

Having weekly assignments for studio and templates for the reports, as well as examples from previous semesters is useful to give a sense of expectations. Faculty availability and willingness to meet outside class hours also helps.

- **Resolving student teamwork tensions**

Making it clear at the start of the semester that teamwork is part of the grade is critical.

Tensions often arise during the first part of the semester. By the second half of the semester, the whole class starts to work together as a single team.

Requiring clear division of both logistical and thematic tasks and giving guidance and examples of how to work collaboratively using examples of how previous studio groups have done it is useful.

Meeting with students individually and in groups, as necessary, and having midterm reflection sessions is important. Midterm and final peer and self-grading exercises could also be effective.

- **Supporting international students and students new to New York City**

International and out of town students are often advised to wait until the second semester to enrol in this studio. Encouraging students to share current articles from newspapers, journals, and attend lectures/event around the city. Relating weekly reading assignments to the studio project.

- **Class size, student/instructor ratio**

Optimum class size has been around 12 (minimum nine and maximum 15).

REFERENCES

Angotti, T., Doble, C. and Horrigan, P. (2011) At the boundaries: The shifting sites of service-learning in design and planning. In T. Angotti, C. Doble and P. Horrigan (eds.), *Service-Learning in Design and Planning: Educating at the Boundaries* (pp. 1–16). New York: New York University Press.

Arefi, M. and Edelman, D. J. (2013) Morrow tomorrow: Exploring the pedagogical experience of a planning studio involving students with mixed skills. *Current Urban Studies* 1(3): 59–73.

Baum, H. S. (2000) Fantasies and realities in university–community partnerships. *Journal of Planning Education and Research* 20(2): 234–246.

Bose, M. and Wilson, J. (2014) Probing impacts: Voices of community. In M. Bose, P. Horrigan, C. Doble and S. Shipp (eds.), *Community Matters: Service-Learning in Engaged Design and Planning* (pp. 278–298). New York: Routledge.

Cameron, M., Forsyth, A., Green, W. A., Lu, H., McGirr, P., Owens, P. E. and Stoltz, R. (2001) Learning through service: The community design studio. *College Teaching* 49(3): 105–113.

Dewar, M. E. and Isaac, C. B. (1998) Learning from difference: The potentially transforming experience of community–university collaboration. *Journal of Planning Education and Research* 17(4): 334–347.

Edwards, M. M. and Bates, L. K. (2011) Planning's core curriculum: Knowledge, practice, and implementation. *Journal of Planning Education and Research* 31(2): 172–183.

Erickson, S. (2014) Reaching out and reaching in: Investigating community outcomes of a university outreach program. In M. Bose, P. Horrigan, C. Doble and S. Shipp (eds.), *Community Matters: Service-Learning in Engaged Design and Planning* (pp. 257–277). New York: Routledge.

Ferman, B. and Hill, T. L. (2004) The challenges of agenda conflict in higher-education – community research partnerships: Views from the community side. *Journal of Urban Affairs* 26(2): 241–257.

Forester, J. (2013) On the theory and practice of critical pragmatism: Deliberative practice and creative negotiations. *Planning Theory* 12: 5–22.

Frank, N. (2008) Measuring public service: Assessment and accountability – to ourselves and others. *Journal of Planning Education and Research* 27(4): 499–506.

Harris, S. C. and Irazabal Zurita, C. E. (2011) Transforming subjectivities: Service that expands learning in urban planning. In T. Angotti, C. Doble and P. Horrigan (eds.), *Service-Learning in Design and Planning: Educating at the Boundaries* (pp. 107–124). New York: New York University Press.

Higgins, M., Aitken-Rose, E. and Dixon, J. (2009) The pedagogy of the planning studio: A view from down under. *Journal for Education in the Built Environment* 4(1): 8–30.

Lang, J. (1983) Teaching planning to city planning students: An argument for the studio / workshop approach. *Journal of Planning Education and Research* 2(2): 122–129.

LeGates, R. T. and Robinson, G. (1998) Institutionalizing university–community partnerships. *Journal of Planning Education and Research* 17(4): 312–322.

Levkoe, C. Z., Friendly, A. and Daniere, A. (2020) Community service-learning in graduate planning education. *Journal of Planning Education and Research* 40(1): 92–103.

Long, J. G. (2012) Symposium introduction: Studio pedagogy. *Journal of Planning Education and Research* 32(4): 430–448.

Martin, J., Baron, E., Rourk Reyes, A. and Tauber, L. (2014) The semester ends but the community challenges do not: A legacy to continue the work in East Harlem. In M. Bose, P. Horrigan, C. Doble and S. Shipp (eds.), *Community Matters: Service-Learning in Engaged Design and Planning* (pp. 299–314). New York: Routledge.

Németh, J. and Long, J. G. (2012) Assessing learning outcomes in U.S. planning studio courses. *Journal of Planning Education and Research* 32(4): 476–490.

Oonk, C., Gulikers, J. and Mulder, M. (2016) Educating collaborative planners: Strengthening evidence for the learning potential of multi-stakeholder regional learning environments. *Planning Practice & Research* 31(5): 533–551.

Rooij, R. and Frank, A. I. (2016) Educating spatial planners for the age of co-creation: The need to risk community, science and practice involvement in planning programmes and curricula. *Planning Practice & Research* 31(5): 473–485.

Shiffman, R. (2007) Comments: Advocacy and community planning: Past, present and future. *Progressive Planning Magazine*, Spring. http://www.plannersnetwork.org/2007/04/comments-3/.

Sletto, B. (2010) Educating reflective practitioners: Learning to embrace the unexpected through service learning. *Journal of Planning Education and Research* 29(4): 403–415.

Stults, M. and Larsen, L. (2018) Tackling uncertainty in US local climate adaptation planning. *Journal of Planning Education and Research*. https://doi.org/10.1177/0739456x18769134.

Vidal, A., Nye, N., Walker, C., Manjarrez, C. and Romanik, C. (2002) *Lessons from the Community Outreach Partnership Center Program*. Washington, DC: The Urban Institute.

Vidyarthi, S., Winkle, C., Smith, J., Zhang, T., Kawamura, K. and Hoch, C. (2012) Holistic, inclusive and practical: Teaching plan-making at the core. *The Town Planning Review* 83(6): 625–645.

Wolf-Powers, L. (2008) Expanding planning's public sphere: STREET magazine, activist planning, and community development in Brooklyn, New York, 1971–1975. *Journal of Planning Education and Research* 28(2): 180–195.

5. Planning with the community: engaged professional education in ethno-nationally contested city

Rachel Kallus

INTRODUCTION

Planning with the Community, as its name indicates, is a community-engaged course focused on theories and practices that link architecture and planning with community-based knowledge, promoting activism and participation. Like other courses involving students in engaged learning, this course stresses social commitment and encourages students to become socially conscientious and involved citizens (Campus Compact 2000). But, unlike similar courses, it places engaged professional education in a politically charged urban environment of an ethno-nationally contested city. This environment, characterized by diverse communities struggling for their place, is accentuated by conflicting ideologies and politics. Through mutual learning with diverse communities, the course brings to the forefront conflicting agendas ingrained in the everyday lived experience of urban residents. It joins a search for new venues for teaching and learning, indicating the return of academia to its traditional social role as a promoter of democratic values and civic engagement (Butin 2010), reiterating academic commitment to social justice and human rights (Soria and Mitchell 2016; Watson et al. 2011). The increased development of such courses in institutions of higher education marks an international trend driven by social, economic and political processes occurring in the western world, which are reflected in universities rethinking the production and imparting of knowledge. However, although community-engaged programmes thrive, the opportunity of shared learning in professional education is less obvious. This is surprising given a growing unstable political context, multi-cultural challenges (Fincher and Iveson 2008; Landry and Wood 2012) and the conflicting notion of urban and national citizenships (Holston and Appadurai 1996). These demands cannot be left outside the classroom. When faced by community-engaged learning they bring new vitality to professional education, along with new and motivating challenges.

Professional training in architecture and in planning has been using the city all along as a laboratory, mainly in the studio, where theoretical underpinning and spatial analysis are practically replicated to acquire applied knowledge. But, although offering applied skills, learning is not based on knowledge shared with actual users, thus negating the nuanced lived experience of urban communities. Even experiential courses that introduce social understanding of the city do not necessarily include community-based knowledge. They are often "about the community", or "community-oriented", but do not engage students with communities in shared learning (Hefetz and Kallus 2018).

Community-engaged professional education aims to connect academic learning to the world outside the classroom and to prepare students for a socially conscious practice, at the least, and for participatory practice at the most. When these courses involve real communities, the encounter provides students with opportunities to meet the reality of actual places, to engage with local knowledge, and to share their proficiency with others. The indeterminacy of urban spaces, the complexity of the human environment, and the powerful notion of the public, all necessitate engagement around issues of urban citizenship. These issues are especially powerful in the context of an ethno-nationally contested city, where urban spaces are loaded with cultural and political meanings that often conflict with national claims (Greeley 2017). But, while the impact of community-engaged courses in conflict zones has been addressed (Golan and Shalhoub-Kevorkian 2014) its significance in architecture and planning curricula has been minimal.

This chapter presents a critical reflection on the course *Planning with the Community*. Based on data gathered during developing and teaching the course in the past ten years, we ask how the course has contributed to students' awareness of conflictual urban realities, what knowledge has it provided, and what it added to their professional toolbox? To answer these questions, analyses were conducted of students' personal journals, of in-class observations, of discussions with students, and students' presentations, in class, to community partners, and to city officials.

The chapter opens with a short literature review on engaged professional education and the potential of the ethno-nationally contested city as a laboratory of engaged learning. It moves to describe the course, including its location, aims, structure and course of action. The third part, based on analytic reflective teaching notes, draws on examples of topics encountered by students during the course and their implications. The last part highlights pedagogical considerations of a politically charged learning setting.

ENGAGED PROFESSIONAL EDUCATION

Recent calls to rethink professional social obligations (Bandyopadhyay et al. 2010; Bell and Wakeford 2008; Dutton and Mann 1996; Marcos and Weiland 2013; Stohr and Sinclair 2006, 2012) raised the need to reconsider professional education (Reardon and Forester 2015). Community-engaged learning provides opportunities for students to participate in meaningful learning about others, as well as about themselves, and enhances the connection between society, knowledge and context (Astin 1999; Moely et al. 2002; Moore 2010). Such learning becomes a bridge between the university and professional practice and increases the relevance of one for the other. Research shows its impact on academic achievement, leadership and self-confidence (Astin and Astin 2000; Astin and Sax 1998) and notes a positive correlation between students' engagement during their studies and their later commitment to social justice as citizens (Nishishiba et al. 2005).

Community-engaged courses have been integrated into professional programmes to combine meaningful community service with enriched learning experiences (Angotti et al. 2012; Gregory and Heiselt 2014; Hardin et al. 2006). Recent calls plea for reciprocity and shared learning, in which both sides contribute to the process and learn about and from each other, i.e. against a sole emphasis on students' learning outcome (Larsen et al. 2014). Others aim to supplement the pedagogy of service learning with a wider professional competence by going beyond conceptual understanding of knowledge and skills (Winkler 2013). These ethical considerations stress community and professional social responsibility (Roakes and Norris-Tirrell 2000) in which partnership has a transformative impact. Calls for innovative engagement techniques note exposure to unorthodox clients, such as non-profit organizations and low-income populations, and demand new skills, such as flexibility and improvization, interdisciplinary communication and collaboration. These participatory practices include local knowledge to augment professional expertise with insights of the community and inclusion of previously silenced voices (Corburn 2003; Fenster and Yacobi 2005).

This chapter recounts students' experiences of community-engaged learning in conflicted urban environments. It suggests that working in such places requires a reflective learning approach, to enable students to comprehend social situations by making them aware of their self in society and transform on-site experiences into valid knowledge (Roakes and Norris-Tirrell 2000; Sletto 2010). Reflexivity, a process of turning back to mirroring oneself (Robertson 2002), has been an important tool in practice-based professional learning, promoting continuous engagement and evaluation of complex situations (Schön 1983, 1987; Wight et al. 2016). Adopting this approach in community-engaged courses pays attention to practical and theoretical principles that inform every-day actions (Bolton 2010).

Although professional education has recognized the potential of community engagement, little attention has been paid to the political dimension of civic engagement and activism. Writers advocate for a critical reconfiguration of conditions of hegemony and their unavoidable constraints. Projective practice, for example, sees the mechanisms of planning, funding, designing and construction as tools for altering politics (Somol and Whiting 2002). Others suggest shifting from macro to micro politics, to open windows for small-scale activism (Marcos and Weiland 2013). In light of collusion of state and markets, dismissing the agency of professional practice, they call to restructure the individual/community repetition of the political around the "small, technical acts by which we are governed" (Reinhold Martin quoted by Roberts, 2015, p. 2). But the question of how to introduce these suggestions to professional education remains open.

THE ETHNO-NATIONALLY CONTESTED CITY AS A LABORATORY

Cities in conflict zones are contested arenas caught between localism and nationalism (Bollens 2000; Calame and Charlesworth 2009). They embody the ethnic locality – the place of the community – as an entity of multiple histories, and as a possible locus of withdrawal and resistance (Cupers 2005; Dovey 2001). Ethnic identities are formed in them through urban memories and everyday experiences (Boyer 1996) in which the urban space comprises layers of conflicted meanings struggling to expose repressed and misrepresented narratives (Hayden 1995). The urban space, however, is also a product of laws and policies aiming at stability that often clash with freedom of speech and assembly. Community engaged practice navigates between these top-down definitions and bottom-up everyday practices shaped by routines and habits as well as by dreams and desires. Working in conflict zones, especially in divided or 'mixed' cities, is likewise typified by negotiation between opposing aspirations of different groups, and the powerful, often explosive, links between the drive for ethnic control and a conflicted reality (Boal 1996; Bollens 1998). Struggles and political opinions concerning material and symbolic aspects of specific communities help crystallize the notion of urban citizenship and how it is formed in practice. As Holston (2008) insists, it is often within the politics of a place that various claims of citizenship are articulated. But space also constructs forms of subjectivity and orientation, as it frames urban life.

As arenas for learning, contested cities can offer students an opportunity to grasp the meaning of conflictual situations, not in an abstract way, or in the neutral environment of the classroom, but rather through the lived experiences of people and the enduring battles on the ground. The Israeli/ Palestinian geopolitical situation, an ongoing ethno-national battleground, provides a dynamic context to rethink urban professional practice. It serves as a challenging learning experience of community-engaged professional education, which this chapter explores.

COURSE STRUCTURE AND AIMS

The course *Planning with the Community* has been taught five times since 2008. It aims to provide a community-engaged learning experience, grounded in theories and practices that link architecture and planning with community participation and activism. A critical social-science perspective offers a reflexive approach that enables students to understand social situations and gain self- and social awareness by paying attention to the practical and theoretical values that inform everyday actions (Bolton 2010). The course integrates professional skills with local knowledge through its reading materials and class discussions, in its assignments, requiring students' personal reflections, and in its applied projects developed with local communities. However, the course is not a studio, mainly because the strategies it develops extend beyond the design approach. Its structure, the active and engaged learning, the relationships of students with the instructors, on one hand, and with their 'clients', on the other, the definition of problems and the information acquired to handle them, ultimately cohere to service-learning (Bose et al. 2014; Roakes and Norris-Tirrell 2000) and to problem-based learning (Shepherd and Cosgriff 1998).

The course focuses on Haifa, the third largest city in Israel; it is the urban centre for the Galilee, as well as a cultural hub for many Palestinians citizens of the country.[1] While the muncipality seeks to market Haifa with its diverse cultures, ethnicities and religious groups (Jews, Muslims, Christians, Druze and Bahai) as a place of ethnic and cultural coexistence, in reality, the city is more segregated representing a perfect contested locus for the course.

Jews and Arabs mostly live in distinct neighbourhoods and have divided education systems. The segregation is not only between Arabs and Jews, but also between Jewish immigrants from the former USSR and Ethiopia, and a growing ultra-orthodox population. The segregation is also evident in the city's topography. On the upper Carmel ridge are the well-off neighbourhoods. The lower income and Arab neighbourhoods are on the lower slopes of the mountain (Kolodney and Kallus 2008).

This segregation has historical roots as under Ottoman rule (1516–1918) communities were encouraged to develop their neighbourhoods according to religious affiliation; Christians to the west of the Old City, Muslims to the east and Jews up the hill to the south. This pattern was continued by the British Mandate in Palestine (1918–1948). In fact, the term 'mixed city' was coined by the British authorities for cities in which Jewish and Arab communities were under the same jurisdiction (Goren 2008). It is still used to denote officially considered 'mixed' towns, although Arab population in these cities accounts for only 9% of the total Arab citizens of Israel (Falah et al. 2000).[2]

Whether Haifa, with about 30,000 Arab residents, a little over 11% of the city's total population,[3] is in fact a mixed city, remains questionable. The current population structure is the result of a process of Judaization, in which the Palestinian community that remained in the city after the establishment of the State of Israel has become marginalized (Ben-Arie 2016; Segev 1984). Nonetheless, Haifa still represents a socio-demographic reality in which there are shared elements of identity, symbolic traits, and cultural markers (Rabinowitz and Monterescu 2008). For many of Haifa's Israeli–Palestinian residents, the city's history is a daily lived experience and an important aspect of their identity (Kallus, Ben-Arie, Zaatry, 2020; Kallus, 2013). Since the first Palestinian *intifada* (uprising), which began in 1988, their national identity has re-established an edge (Kimmerling and Migdal 2003), and Haifa has regained its position as the centre of Palestinian society, with many social and cultural Palestinian institutions and NGOs (Faier 2005; Karkabi 2018).

Course participants over the years have been graduate and undergraduate students from three programmes: architecture, urban planning and landscape architecture. Of the total 62 students, 23 students were graduate, 15 from urban planning and eight from architecture. Of the 39 undergraduate students five were from landscape architecture and the rest from architecture.[4] The gender division was 72.5% female and 27.5% male. The ethnic background of the students was diverse,[5] with 13% of the students Arabs. Out of the Jewish students 19% were recently arrived immigrants, mostly from the former Soviet Union. Religious affiliation was not directly discussed, but it is assumed that Israeli-Arabs were Muslims and Christians, both secular and religious, as were the Jews.[6]

The instructors have expertise in architecture and in urban planning. Since 2010 an anthropologist has joined the teaching team with the aim of supporting reflexive pedagogy and augmenting fieldwork skills. Reflexivity has enabled students to understand social situations and its practice been politically, socially and even psychologically useful to inform everyday circumstances (Bolton 2010). But, as opposed to its instrumental aspects in architecture and planning (Schön 1987), reflexive discourse in the social sciences has been more radical and experimental (Saltzman 2002). Its integration in the course has increased awareness of and sensitivity to the social standing and identity of all participants. The use of diverse anthropological tools enabled students to understand the community, its place, and its residents' ongoing lived experiences through for example casual conversations and in-depth interviews, participatory observations, the taking of field notes and visual documentation.

Some of these tools are not foreign to architecture and planning, but with an anthropologist onboard their implications have been discussed and examined. Students have used their professional skills to enhance knowledge acquired through anthropological methods, finding creative ways to map studied areas and their ethnographic observations. Apart from documenting their experiences and issues that arise during their fieldwork, they searched for ways to represent their findings in communicative ways to their 'clients'.[7]

The reflexive approach has allowed students to comprehend their multi-dimensioned identities and rethink their professional profiles. It enabled inward and outward considerations relating to social contexts and continuous learning from situations that are studied and analysed. An important assignment requires students to write three reflective journals during the semester. In the first journal, they explain why they joined the course, and reflect on their previous background and experience in working with communities. In the second journal, they describe their project development, providing personal perceptions, reactions and feelings when approaching the place and the local community. The third journal reflects on the course; they document and analyse the process they went through and its implications for their professional career and future personal decisions.

Projects developed during the course are identified and coordinated with local groups and NGOs. The idea for each project is loosely defined before the semester starts, and students are encouraged to choose their preferred project based on a description of the community, its location, the NGO involved, subject matter and suggested process, including readings and precedents. Local groups and NGOs work with the students throughout the semester, connect them to the community, help to structure the project, and often continue to develop and help implement the project with the local community after the semester ends. In selecting the projects three aspects are stressed: (1) direct contact with locals, not with a representative elite; (2) continuous and long-term relationship with the community and the NGO, mutual engagement, and commitment; and (3) the ability to complete the project within the timetable of the course.

The outcome of the collaboration with the community is often the basis for an actual project, to be further developed and elaborated through an advocacy process. Presentations of visual materials were found to be useful, not only during development stages of the final project, but also for the presentation of the product to all participants at semester end. Presentations are given to the community and allow residents and NGOs to approach decision-makers in order to explain their ideas. The presentations are useful for both internal processes, such as workshops, and external purposes, such as fundraising and other activities initiated by the community. This outcome matches the course's co-creation approach and its aim to work *with*, rather than *for*, local underserved and excluded communities, to assist them in understanding spatial processes, enrich them with professional knowledge, and build their capacity to be active in the urban arena. The fact that students often stay involved reflects the activism, civic engagement and political responsibility of community members and students alike.

LESSONS LEARNED

In what follows we provide insights into students' learning by adopting a critical view on fundamental dilemmas encountered during the course. The discussion focuses on issues that surfaced in in-class discussions, in students' journals, and in various presentations. Issues are interrelated and outline a dialectic tension inherent in the search for engaged professional practice. They express the reflexive processes put forward by the course and suggest fundamental contradictions between critical and projective pedagogy, i.e., a call for structural reform versus adjustments to existing systems, apparent amid personal and professional identities, the individual (me) and 'others', and particularly in the context of conflict zones, the political 'other' or 'othered'.

Professional versus Personal Identity

The dialogue with diverse communities aims for shared encounters and co-creation, as it generates for the students a space to reflect upon their own social-political positions. It encourages students to become aware of their complex identity vis-à-vis their professional training and, often for the first time, to consider the possibility of a professional career with NGOs and community activist groups. The students' multiple identities surface in relation to their professional identity, but also in relation to ethno-national, gender, and generational characteristics, in ways they had never encountered before. As planning and architecture students, their education is centred on skills and capacity building (Salama and Wilkinson 2007; Spiller and Clear 2014), ignoring and often dismissing other aspects of their identity in relation to professional positions, such as gender, or ethno-national affiliation.

Early in the semester, students are introduced to different NGOs, community groups, sites, and the proposed shared process for the semester. They are encouraged to select a site and community to work with, preferably one with which they do not share similar social characteristics. This is an attempt to move the students away from their 'comfort zone' and to create opportunities to overcome socio-cultural differences and stigmas. Mixed teams are encouraged, as well as, if possible, working with mixed communities, highlighting challenges of ethno-national boundaries.

Notwithstanding the effort to create opportunities for inter-ethnic and international dialogue, in a project with the Mossawa Center, the advocacy centre for Arab citizens in Israel, a team of three Arab women insisted on working as a team with a group of older Arab women. The students insisted that it would be easier for the women to communicate with them, since they shared the same culture and language.

The project outlined the urban experiences of older Arab women and aimed for urban infrastructure improvement.[8] Out of about 40 women who regularly attend meetings at Mossawa, the students ended up working with six women. These women were born before 1948 and came to Haifa as young children with their families, who had escaped or were expelled from their homes in the Galilee. For these women, the Mossawa weekly meetings are a meaningful social activity in which they exchange ideas and discuss various issues concerning their lives. They call themselves the "optimistic women", emphasizing their hopes for and confidence in the future.

The students were young Christian women, descendants of families who left their homes in the Galilee villages and came to Haifa or other towns in northern Israel. As young Arab women living in Israel, their professional identity has often conflicted with their other identities. Academic teaching is in Hebrew, and does not acknowledge the Arab students as a minority group. As Arab citizens of Israel, they live in the shadow of the Israel–Palestine conflict (Lustick 1980). They are citizens, but are discriminated against (Al-Haj 2004) and, as Arab women, they are further disadvantaged (Hertzog 2004; Sa'ar 2007). These cultural and socio-political differences are not germane to the students' professional identity. Their approach to the "optimistic women" was based on common language and culture, even though they were very different in other respects.

The weekly meetings took place at the Mossawa Center, at the women's homes, or during organized walks in the city. As the students strolled with the women through the streets of Lower Haifa, the women freely discussed their national, ethnic and gender characteristics. Their memories of life in the Arab neighbourhoods of Haifa were vivid and nostalgic. They pointed out places that had been important to them, in which their daily routines intermingled with larger social and political narratives. Through their personal accounts, they constructed a meaning that interwove the past with the present.

These experiences made the students face the gap between their personal and professional identity. During a class discussion, the students admitted that they were not used to talking about architecture in Arabic and did not know the necessary terms for explaining their professional life to the women. Trained as architects, the students were more interested in the future, expressing a professional desire for change. The women, on the other hand, expressed interest in the past and its political connotations. As one of the students explained in her journal:

> We came to the meetings interested in developing a proposal for the future ... I felt we had lived long enough with the past, all these remembrance days, plays, litera- ture ... everybody talks about the past ... The future meant nothing to the women, who kept going back to their stories of what was.

The encounter challenged the students' professional identity and its artificial separation from other elements of their identity. It made them realize the meaning of the past for the women, and their difficulties in facing the future. The past was seen not only as nostalgia, but as a way to cope with present-day hardships, as one of the students explained in her journal: "They are strong women who are trying to improve their habitat as much as they can ... most of them became widows years ago and raised their children on their own, facing many difficulties."

Being representatives of the academia and future professionals, students have the potential to mobilize change in less privileged communities. However, the students are also being changed. During the course, they undergo a process of identity formation that often confronts their professional and their personal identities and forces them to rethink their place in society.

The Other and Me

Confronting otherness has a transformative effect on students, making them rethink their place in the world (Astin 1999). As Banks (2004) explains, you cannot become the other; social, cultural and institutional worlds respond differently to people of colour, gender, ethnicity and nationality. However, you can make yourself an ally by deferring judgement, learning from the others' accounts, and supporting their struggles. Understanding contextualized structural positions of citizenship often occurs through direct contact with disadvantaged people (Beaumont et al. 2006).

While our students come from diverse ethno-national backgrounds, they are mostly privileged, and unaware of the connection between low-income and being part of a minority. The exposure to distressed environments is never easy, and although urban poverty is common, its reality is often new to the students. As a student noted in her journal:

> The first time we were asked to tour our [study] area was frightening, maybe because it was almost dark, maybe because of prejudice, or maybe because this was the first time I had encountered poverty exclusion. There is a difference between talking about it in class or seeing it in movies and talking directly with affected people.

Later, in the project which looked at the urban experience of Arab adolescents working on identity building at the Mossawa Center, the same student noted in her journal her perspective of the site as a Jewish architecture student:

> We pass by a building [an old traditional stone structure] and I say: "What a wonderful house!" The two young men answer: "This is nice? These buildings are all falling apart and nobody wants to live in them!" And suddenly I feel the distance between me and them, and I try to understand from where this stems. It is not only because I am looking at the place as an outsider. Our worlds are so fundamentally different.

The initial aim of the project developed with the Mossawa Center was to study the urban experience of young Israeli–Palestinian residents of Lower Haifa and to use their everyday lived experiences to explore problems and potentials. From the twenty regular members of Mossawa's youth group, three boys and two girls joined a team of three Jewish female architecture and landscape architecture students. The project began by walking together in Lower Haifa and discussing their shared perceptions of the area. These walks allowed an open exchange between the students and the youth, which gave the students a new perception of differences, but also an understanding of where they fit in, as one of them recalled: "In fact the tours, which I feared the most, opened for me a new understanding of something new and different … suddenly the pieces fell in place, and I could see my place in the shared process."

The realization of otherness was also experienced by the three Arab students who worked with the "optimistic women". Although they were part of the community, their age and professional training created a sense of separation. In spite of being respectfully aware of their Palestinian heritage, the students were more interested in action than in symbolic remembrance. The sites jointly explored by the women and the students tell the Palestinian story in Israel, and in Haifa in particular. But a closer examination revealed a more nuanced history, reflected in the women's personal memories. As one of the students wrote: "They [the women] have a deep desire to preserve 'the old' and to share their knowledge about space and history … keeping their memories alive through stories and descriptions." The difference between the women and the students is not merely in how they view their place, but essentially in how they interpret it. The generation gap is evident in the students' indifference to political meaning as compared with the women's ethno-national belonging.

Meeting the Political Other

The students' educational process, shared with local communities, made them realize the benefit of working effectively *with* target populations and not merely *for* them. However, within the context of the Israeli/Palestinian conflict, the course experience has also affirmed the value of engaged practice that brings to light political issues not usually discussed in the classroom. In the context of present-day Israeli society, discussing political issues is not easy. But, shared professional work in contested environment cannot avoid confronting the political 'other'.

For the three Arab students working with the "optimistic women", the project connected them professionally to their social and political milieu and forced them to reconsider their positions and identities. As one of them explained:

> I wonder if the project would have evolved differently if I had been a total stranger to the women. Living in their vicinity and being part of their society made them open up to me more easily. They assumed that I knew their background and the people they talked about.

The experience throughout the course has reinforced the students' and the women's shared ethno-political characteristics and made their national history more immediate to them. It evoked personal and collective memories embedded in the urban space, which made the students aware of their ethno-national identity. It aroused the students' political sensibility, often suppressed in professional setting, and made them feel the need to be more involved in their community. One of the students reflected in her journal on her renewed political interest: "I am going through a process, accelerated by this project; of renewed political interest … the encounter with the women has made me want to do something useful for my people." So, although the shared process revealed differences in the women and the students' worldviews, based on professional standpoints and on the generational gap, it disclosed their shared social status as a minority and brought political issues to the surface.

As opposed to the students working with their own community, the students working with the Arab youth of Mossawa were Jewish. One of them was from Kibbutz Baram, built after 1948 on the ruins of the Palestinian Biram village. The student brought this issue into class, contemplating what to tell the Arab youth and the group leaders at Mossawa. She ended up explaining her position openly, a decision that stirred a nuanced discussion of personal versus national identity and its affinity to political positions. This discussion was important not only for our students, but also for the Arab youth of Mossawa. It helped them gain greater tolerance for the other, and provided the opportunity to see people as individuals, rather than simply as part of a collective.

For Jewish students working on a project in the mixed neighbourhood of Haifa's Lower Hadar, organized through Shatil (Hebrew acronym for Support and Counselling Services for Social Change in Israel), meeting a mixed community was a transforming experience. The meetings revealed that residents of different ethnic and national groups, mainly Arabs who immigrated to Haifa from nearby villages and Jewish immigrants from the former USSR and Ethiopia, had no previous contact with one another. Assisted by Arab and Amharic translators provided by Shatil, the students developed a project with the residents, who, when confronted with the construction of an inner-city road and threatening their open spaces through their neighbourhood, connecting the Carmel Mountain and Lower Hadar, were compelled to work together.

Personal and group meetings made the students face the social and political complexities of the area. Meetings with Arab activists in the neighbourhood changed their worldviews, as one of the students noted in her journal after she visited an Arab house for the first time:

> Here I am sitting with a woman my age, which most likely I would not meet in other circumstances; apparently our worlds are so different, but also so close. The same hesitations about university and personal life, the same things that make us laugh or listen carefully.

The student later told us that when she left the Arab activist's house late at night, there was a radio announcement of a bomb explosion in Jerusalem. She turned off the radio unable to bear the news. Her experience mirrors others in community-engaged courses that provided transformative learning experiences, allowing Jewish and Arab students to re-examine social issues in a micro-climate of openness and intellectual rigor, thereby developing their commitment to encounter the 'other' and the 'othered'. As Golan and Shalhoub-Kevorkian (2014) report, by providing opportunities for reflection, these courses allowed students to build new networks of relationships within a deeply divided society.

However, although political issues surfaced throughout the course, the students seemed to be cautious about dealing with the political context of their activity. They often preferred to take a broad view that completely disregarded issues related to war and peace, the Israeli/Palestinian conflict, and the ongoing occupation of territories. The Palestinian Nakba was in the background, but never referred to directly. For example, in working with the "optimistic women", one student wrote in her journal of a woman in the group that had been uprooted from the village of Ikrit.[9] But her explanation was nuanced, with no reference to the meaning of Ikrit in the Palestinian national heritage. She either assumed that everyone knows about it, moving the burden of knowing to others, or perhaps did not want to bring up the issue and cause an argument.

Other researchers have shown how Palestinian students are concerned about expressing political opinions that are considered illegitimate in the hegemonic discourse in Israel (Golan and Rosenfeld 2015). When asked about it in an interview, they said they preferred to focus on their personal struggles, since the personal price for challenging the political system might be heavy. The fear of getting involved in political action raises questions about academic freedom and the reluctance of young people to study or discuss the political context of Israeli reality. Golan and Shalhoub-Kevorkian (2014) show how students and teachers in socially engaged courses draw a clear boundary between what they call 'society' and what they understand as 'political'. Issues raised in the classroom are not often discussed openly on campus, such as discriminatory laws and policies, social inequality, difference between Jewish and Arab students, between men and women, violation of human rights and obstruction of democracy. These findings suggest despair and distrust in the ability to change the situation. However, they could also suggest an attempt to build good and stable interpersonal relationships between course participants (Golan and Rosenfeld 2015).

In the context of an ethno-nationally contested city, issues of spatial justice, land rights and citizenship often come up. However, they are overshadowed by broader political issues that the students are not willing or able to approach. These limitations point to a basic dilemma inherent in the course between engagement and activism; between critique and dissidence. We often ask ourselves whether we should educate realistic professionals aware of their capacities, but also of their limitations, or should we encourage the students and their community partners to resist and oppose inequalities and injustices? Do we push students towards structural (political) change, or should we settle for reform that enhances everyday lives of marginalized communities? Yet, it is unclear to what degree the course pushes students towards dissidence, especially since it seems that the ones who take the course are the more politically aware and socially committed students. They might be ready to engage in activism, but can we take the risk of being considered starry-eyed political advocates?

CONCLUSION

Architecture and planning students, although concerned about place making, are often disconnected from people and places. Meeting with 'others' and learning about their everyday lives can be an enriching experience, though sometimes threatening and disturbing. It challenges students' previous perception about themselves, about others, about the profession and about the society in which they live. We found the reflexive approach useful for coping with these encounters, allowing open exchange of thoughts and impressions, sharing difficulties, and better understanding what students face. Personal attention and guidance created a safe space in the class and ensured a learning process that focused on problems arising from the field. Emotional processing of experiences was based on identification of difficulties and the ability to express them, in class, in personal discussions, and in journals. The journals we encouraged students to write turned out to be a place for reflection on the course and on professional and personal processes undertaken by each student. We found the journals an important tool for sharing internal struggles, doubts, dilemmas and conflicts, although often after we read them we had no answers, but rather more questions, and at best suggestions for further readings and for exploration of precedents.

Reflexive pedagogy demanded integration between different parts of knowledge building: the personal/intimate and the academic/intellectual. Knowledge based on own and on other students' experience was valuable. Students learned by themselves, for themselves, and about themselves, in a process that involved experiencing and inquisitiveness. As students grappled with the meaning of conflictual situations, not in an abstract way, but through lived, often-difficult experiences on the ground, they confronted the agency of professional practice in a volatile democracy. Through personal connection to places and people, social justice and human rights became reality, raising serious questions whether professional practice can overcome oppressive power systems and be useful in a complex socio-political world. In a growing de-politicized academic environment (Shenhav 2008) this is an ongoing challenge, demanding that political context be present in order to take community-engaged learning beyond its experiential dimensions.

Aiming to change political attitudes of students, we are often warned of the danger of higher education losing its basis of legitimacy if the distinction between political orientation and political commitment is blurred. Despite the need of community-engaged courses to develop sensitivity and capacity to contain opposing political positions, bringing political issues into the classroom could affect academic validity and endanger fieldwork credibility (Beaumont et al. 2006). However, can engaged education take a neutral stand towards political issues if it aims to affect students and motivate them to become active citizens and socially involved professionals? Can we avoid political discussions in which we and the students express our worldviews? (See Box 5.1.)

BOX 5.1 TIPS

- Establish continuous and long-term relationships with the community and the NGO through mutual engagement and commitment, to facilitate planning *with* (*not for*) the community.
- Use planning as a mean to promote relations between residents, the environment and its production, to mediate between critical and optimistic projective approach.

- Develop projects that are meaningful for the community and ensure they can be completed in the timetable allotted to the students.
- Use reflexive pedagogical methods to enable students to comprehend social situations by making them aware of their self in society (journals, discussions in class in a 'safe' space to reflect on experiences in the field); these should support emotional processing of experiences based on identification of difficulties.
- Include – if possible – staff skilled in anthropological/ethnographic methods to augmented fieldwork skills with diverse anthropological tools, such as casual conversations and in-depth interviews, participatory observations, the taking of field notes and visual documentation, to enable students to understand the community, its place, and its residents' ongoing lived experiences. Some of these tools are not foreign to architecture and planning, but it is useful to discuss, further examine, develop and refine their implications.
- Allow students to learn by themselves, for themselves, and about themselves, in a process that involves experiencing and inquisitiveness which is supported by personal attention and guidance.
- Enable direct meetings with locals (not representative elite) as this is an important factor in impacting and changing students' perception.
- Find ways to represent findings in communicative ways to communities, e.g. use visualization and on-site methods to explore participatory imagination and imaging of urban shared spaces, conceiving new ideas and conveying them to others through images and different forms of representation.

NOTES

1. The term 'Arabs', as used in Israeli discourse, refers to the Palestinian citizens of the state of Israel, but includes also Druze, Bedouins, and other groups living in Palestine prior to 1948, some of them that do not necessarily consider themselves Palestinians. This paper uses 'Arabs' and 'Palestinians' interchangeably, in order not to reify any specific title and to draw attention to the shifting and contextual character of identity.
2. Cities officially considered 'mixed' towns are: Haifa, Tel-Aviv-Jaffa, Lydda, Ramla, Acre, Upper Nazareth and Jerusalem, despite a growing Arab population in other cities, such as Karmiel, Afula and Beer Sheva, in which Arabs are not accounted for and thus their needs for services and amenities are not addressed.
3. Although the official estimate of the Arab population of Haifa is 11.3% (Haifa Statistical Abstract 2019), the unofficial estimate is over 20%, due to residents who live in Haifa but retain their official addresses in their Arab hometowns.

4. Planning is a graduate programme. Architecture and landscape architecture are graduate and undergraduate programmes.
5. This composition does not represent Haifa's demographic, as no Druze or Bahai attended the course.
6. Religious affiliation is often signified by head covers of Muslim and Jewish (married) women, and of Jewish men.
7. To learn more of these techniques see Kallus (2016, 2017).
8. The projects are not fully presented. To learn of this particular project, see Kallus and Shamur (2015).
9. Ikrit (إقرت or إقرث) was a Palestinian Christian village located 25 kilometres northeast of Acre on the Lebanese border. It was seized, forcibly depopulated and razed by the Israel Defence Force during the 1948 war. Its inhabitants, who fled to Lebanon and neighbouring towns, fought for the right of return to Ikrit in Israeli courts and in well-publicized cultural and artistic activities.

REFERENCES

Al-Haj, M. (2004) The status of the Palestinians in Israel: A double periphery in an ethno-national state. In A. Dowty (ed.), *Critical Issues in Israeli Society* (pp. 109–126). Westport, CT: Praeger.

Angotti, T., Doble, C. S. and Horrigan, P. (eds.) (2011) *Service-Learning in Design and Planning: Educating at the Boundaries*. New York: New Village Press.

Astin, A. W. (1999) Student involvement: A developmental theory for higher education. *Journal of College Student Development* 40(5): 518–529.

Astin, A. W and Astin, H. S. (eds.) (2000) *Leadership Reconsidered: Engaging Higher Education in Social Change*. Battle Creek, MI: W. K. Kellogg Foundation.

Astin, A. W. and Sax, L. J. (1998) How undergraduates are affected by service participation. *The Journal of College Student Development* 39(3): 251–263.

Bandyopadhyay, S., Lomholt, J., Temple, N. and Tobe, R. (eds.) (2010) *The Humanities in Architectural Design: A Contemporary and Historical Perspective*. London: Routledge.

Banks, J. (2004) Teaching for social justice, diversity and citizenship in a global world. *The Educational Forum* 68(4): 296–305.

Beaumont, E., Colby, A., Ehrlich, T. and Torney-Purta, J. (2006) Promoting political competence and engagement in college students: An empirical study. *Journal of Political Science Education* 2(3): 249–270.

Bell, B. and Wakeford, K. (eds.) (2008) *Expanding Architecture: Design as Activism*. New York: Metropolis Books.

Ben-Arie, R. (2016) The Haifa urban destruction machine. In H. Frichot, C. Gabrielsson and J. Metzger (eds.), *Deleuze and the City* (pp. 179–192). Edinburgh: Edinburgh University Press.

Boal, F. W. (1996) Integration and division: Sharing and segregating in Belfast. *Planning Practice and Research* 11(2): 151–158.

Bollens, S. A. (1998) Urban planning amidst ethnic conflict: Jerusalem and Johannesburg. *Urban Studies* 35(4): 729–750.

Bollens, S. (2000) *On Narrow Ground: Urban Policy and Ethnic Conflict in Jerusalem and Belfast*. Albany, NY: SUNY Press.

Bolton, G. (2010) *Reflective Practice, Writing and Professional Development*. London: Sage.

Bose, M., Horrigan, P., Doble, C. and Shipp, S. C. (eds.) (2014) *Community Matters: Service-Learning in Engaged Design and Planning*. London: Routledge.

Boyer, C. M. (1996) *The City of Collective Memory: Its Historical Imagery and Architectural Entertainments*. Cambridge, MA: MIT Press.

Butin, D. W. (2010) *Service Learning in Theory and Practice: The Future of Community Engagement in Higher Education*. New York: Palgrave Macmillan.

Calame, J. and Charlesworth, E. R. (2009) *Divided Cities: Belfast, Beirut, Jerusalem, Mostar, and Nicosia*. Philadelphia: University of Pennsylvania Press.

Campus Compact (2000) *Presidents' Declaration on the Civic Responsibility of Higher Education*. http://www.compact.org/wp-content/uploads/2009/02/Presidents -Declaration.pdf.

Corburn, J. (2003) Bringing local knowledge into environmental decision making. *Journal of Planning Education and Research* 22: 420–433.

Cupers, K. (2005) Towards a nomadic geography: Rethinking space and identity for the potentials of progressive politics in the contemporary city. *International Journal of Urban and Regional Research* 29(4): 729–739.

Dovey, K. (2001) Memory, democracy and urban space: Bangkok's 'path to democracy'. *Journal of Urban Design* 6(3): 265–282.

Dutton, T. A. and Mann, L. H. (eds.) (1996) *Restructuring Architecture: Critical Discourses and Social Practices*. Minneapolis: University of Minnesota Press.

Faier, E. (2005) *Organizations, Gender and the Culture of Palestinian Activism in Haifa, Israel*. London: Routledge.

Falah, G., Hoy, M. and Sarker, R. (2000) Co-existence in selected mixed Arab-Jewish cities in Israel: By choice or by default? *Urban Studies* 37(4): 775–796.

Fenster, T. and Yacobi, H. (2005) Whose city is it? On urban planning and local knowledge in globalizing Tel Aviv-Jaffa. *Planning Theory and Practice* 6(2): 191–211.

Fincher, R. and Iveson, K. (2008) *Planning and Diversity in the City: Redistribution, Recognition and Encounter*. London: Red Globe Press.

Golan, D. and Rosenfeld, Y. (2015) Learning from the successes of academy-community courses in Israel. Giluy Daat (Opinion) 7: 13–36.

Golan, D. and Shalhoub-Kevorkian, N. (2014) Community-engaged courses in a conflict zone: A case study of the Israeli academic corpus. *Journal of Peace Education* 11(2): 181–207.

Goren, T. (2008) *Cooperation in the Shadow of Confrontation*. Ramat-Gan: University of Bar Ilan Press (Hebrew).

Greeley, A. (2017) *Remaking Urban Citizenship: Organizations, Institutions, and the Right to the City*. London: Routledge.

Gregory, A. and Heiselt, A. (2014) Reflecting on service-learning in architecture: Increasing the academic relevance of public interest design projects. *Globalizing Architecture: Flows and Disruptions*. 102nd ACSA annual meeting proceedings.

Haifa Statistical Abstract (2019) *Strategic Planning and Research Division*, Chapter 2: Demographics, p. 67 (Hebrew).

Hardin, M. C., Eribes, R. A. and Poster, C. (eds.) (2006) *From the Studio to the Streets: Service Learning in Planning and Architecture*. Sterling, VA: Stylus Publishing.

Hayden, D. (1995) The Power of Place: Urban Landscapes as Public History. Cambridge, MA: MIT Press.

Hefetz, S. and Kallus, R. (2018) Educating planners as social entrepreneurs: The potential of community-based professional training. *PlaNext* 7: 27–40.

Hertzog, H. (2004) 'Both an Arab and a woman': Gendered, racialised experiences of female Palestinian citizens of Israel. *Social Identities* 10(1): 53–81.

Holston, J. (2008) *Insurgent Citizenship: Disjunctions of Democracy and Modernity in Brazil.* Princeton, NJ: Princeton University Press.

Holston, J. and Appadurai, A. (1996) Cities and citizenship. *Public Culture* 8(2): 187–204.

Kallus, R. (2013) Reconstructed urbanity: The rebirth of Palestinian urban life in Haifa. *City, Culture & Society* 4(2): 99–109.

Kallus, R. (2016) Citizenship in action: Participatory urban visualization in contested urban space. *Journal of Urban Design* 21(5): 616–637.

Kallus, R. (2017) *Planning in a Mixed City: Professional Responsibility, Social Change and Spatial Justice*. Haifa: Social Hub, Technion (Hebrew).

Kallus, R., Ben Arie, R. and Zaatry, H. (2020) Palestinian Urbanity in Haifa: Utopia or Heterotopi?, Chapter 11 in: Julia Urabayen and Jorge Leon Casero (eds), *Difference in the City. Postmetropolitan Heterotopias as Liberal Utopian Dreams* (pp. 143–162). NYC: Nova.

Kallus, R. and Shamur, T. (2015) Professional education in an ethno-nationally contested city: Architectural students engage with their professional and national identities. *Journal of Architectural and Planning Research* 32(1): 40–54.

Karkabi, N. (2018) How and why Haifa has become the 'Palestinian Cultural Capital' in Israel. *City & Community* 17(4): 1168–1188.

Kimmerling, B. and Migdal, J. S. (2003) *The Palestinian People: A History*. Cambridge, MA: Harvard University Press.

Kolodney, Z. and Kallus, R. (2008) From colonial to national landscape: Producing Haifa's cityscape. *Planning Perspectives* 23(3): 323–324.

Landry, C. and Wood, P. (2012) *The Intercultural City: Planning for Diversity Advantage*. London: Routledge.

Larsen, L., Sherman, L. S., Cole, L. B., Karwat, K., Badiane, K. and Coseo, P. (2014) Social justice and sustainability in poor neighborhoods: Learning and living in southwest Detroit. *Journal of Planning Education and Research* 34(1): 5–18.

Lustick, I. (1980) *Arabs in the Jewish State: Israel's Control of a National Minority*. Austin: University of Texas Press.

Marcos, R. and Weiland, U. (eds.) (2013) *Handmade Urbanism: Mumbai, São Paulo, Istanbul, Mexico City, Cape Town: From Community Initiatives to Participatory Models*. Berlin: Jovis.

Moely, B. E., McFarland, M., Miron, D., Mercer, S. and Ilustre, V. (2002) Changes in college students' attitudes and intentions for civic involvement as a function of service-learning experiences. *Michigan Journal of Community Service Learning* 9(1): 18–26.

Moore, D. T. (2010) Forms and issues in experiential learning. *New Directions for Teaching and Learning* 124: 3–13.

Nishishiba, M., Nelson, H. T. and Shinn, C. W. (2005) Explicating factors that foster civic engagement among students. *Journal of Public Affairs Education* 11(4): 269–285.

Rabinowitz, D. and Monterescu, D. (2008) Reconfiguring the 'mixed town': Urban transformations of ethnonational relations in Palestine and Israel. *International Journal of Middle East Studies* 40: 195–226.

Reardon, K. and Forester, J. (eds.) (2015) *Rebuilding Community after Katrina: Transformative Education in the New Orleans Planning Initiative*. Philadelphia: Temple University Press.

Roakes, S. L. and Norris-Tirrell, D. (2000) Community service learning in planning education: A framework for course development. *Journal of Planning Education and Research* 20: 100–110.

Roberts, B. (2015) Looking for the outside: How is architecture political? *The Avery Review* 5 (February): 1–5. http://averyreview.com/issues/5/looking-for-the-outside.

Robertson, J. (2002) Reflexivity redux: A pithy polemic on 'positionality'. *Anthropological Quarterly* 75(4): 755–762.

Sa'ar, A. (2007) Contradictory location: Assessing the position of Palestinian women citizens of Israel. *Journal of Middle East Women's Studies* 3(3): 45–74.

Salama, A. and Wilkinson, N. (eds.) (2007) *Design Studio Pedagogy: Horizons for the Future*. Gateshead: The Urban International Press.

Saltzman, C. (2002) On reflexivity. *American Anthropologist* 104(3): 805–813.

Schön, D. (1987) Educating the Reflective Practitioner. San Francisco, CA: Jossey-Bass.

Schön, D. (1983) *The Reflective Practitioner: How Professionals Think in Action*. New York: Basic Books.

Segev, T. (1984) *1949: The First Israelis*. Jerusalem: Domino Press (Hebrew).

Shenhav, Y. (2008) Sociologists and the Israeli occupation of Palestinian territories. *Israeli Sociology* 9(2): 263–270 (Hebrew).

Shepherd, A. and Cosgriff, B. (1998) Problem-based learning: A bridge between planning education and planning practice. *Journal of Planning Education and Research* 17(4): 348–357.

Sletto, B. (2010) Educating reflective practitioners: Learning to embrace the unexpected through service learning. *Journal of Planning Education and Research* 29(4): 403–415.

Somol, R. and Whiting, S. (2002) Notes around the Doppler effect and other moods of modernism. *Perspecta* 33 (Mining Autonomy): 72–77.

Soria, K. M. and Mitchell, T. D. (eds.) (2016) *Civic Engagement and Community Service at Research Universities: Engaging Undergraduates for Social Justice, Social Change and Responsible Citizenship*. New York: Palgrave Macmillan.

Spiller, N. and Clear, N. (eds.) (2014) *Educating Architects: How Tomorrow's Practitioners Will Learn Today*. London: Thames & Hudson.

Stohr, K. and Sinclair, C. (2006) *Design Like You Give a Damn: Architectural Responses to Humanitarian Crises*. Melbourne: Metropolis Books.

Stohr, K. and Sinclair, C. (2012) *Design Like You Give a Damn: Building Change from the Ground Up*. New York: Harry N. Abrams.

Watson, D., Hollister, R. M., Stroud, S. E. and Babcock, E. (2011) *The Engaged University: International Perspectives on Civic Engagement*. London and New York: Routledge.

Wight, I., Kellett, J. and Pieters, J. (2016) Practice – reflection – learning: Work experience in planner education. *Planning Practice & Research* 31(5): 500–512.

Winkler, T. (2013) At the coalface: Community–university engagements and planning education. *Journal of Planning Education and Research* 33(2): 215–227.

6. Challenges in education of participatory planning: collaborating with patients and physicians to plan mental health facilities

Elsa Vivant

INTRODUCTION

This chapter presents a project workshop with Master's students in urban planning. The originality of this workshop pertains to its audience and to the subject: how to relocate a mental health facility, working with patients and staff (nurses, medical doctors, psychologists, managers). The students had to consider the urban conditions of the location of a new mental health care facility in Paris, based on a prospective survey and an understanding of the urban context. They reflected on how to destigmatize people with mental health disorders, and how to empower them in a context of changing therapeutic practices and hospital management. The first particularity of the exercise was the fact of working from the perspective of a care institution on urban changes, rather than from that of a planning institution. In order to understand the needs, expectations and uniqueness of the potential users of the future hospital, the students designed and implemented work sessions with patients, which is the second particularity of this project workshop.

After presenting the workshop's different stages, this chapter focuses on an analysis of the conditions and difficulties of such an innovative and inclusive approach. It considers the content of the project workshop, the role of the sponsor (the hospital), the societal issues addressed in urban planning, the relations to the users, what and how the students learnt, the construction of a professional identity, and the role of the supervisor. Behind the particularities of this project workshop on a subject seldom studied in urban planning (mental health), in which an experimental methodology was applied (working sessions with users of a mental health institution), this experience informs more general reflection on the ethics of planning practices and the education of future practitioners. The chapter shows how working in collaboration with professionals from health care institutions helps students to build their professional identity as urban planners. The activities carried out with the patients supported a more comprehensive and participatory approach to planning for the users' sake. This project also revealed that urban planning is constantly challenging its own practices by paying new attention to marginalized segments of the population.

AN UNUSUAL PROJECT WORKSHOP

Within the curriculum of the Master's in Urban Planning at the *École d'Urbanisme de Paris* (Paris School of Urban Planning),[1] students run a project workshop in partnership with a public or private urban planning institution.[2] The subjects studied are diverse (e.g., urban renewal, transit-oriented development, inner-city revitalization, etc.), and are established and negotiated with a sponsor, who may have particular expectations (prospective-type thinking, development of proposals for site management, programming study on a specific project, etc.). The results of the work are documented in a written report and presented orally to the sponsor. The format for the workshop is intense, consisting of one to two full days per week for ten to twelve weeks for which attendees earn ten ECTS credits for their participation. Students are allocated a dedicated place, a classroom, where they can store material and display it on the walls, and where they meet to work outside of the sessions that usually last the entire day. The teacher plays a major role in the workshop. He/she accompanies students in a novel approach where the accent is on reformulating the problem and not necessarily solving it. The teacher is also in charge of the identification of a subject and the formalization of relations with the partners, who must be convinced to "play the game" in this educational exercise. The project workshop creates relationships (between students and the teacher) of a particular nature, established in close proximity and fostered over time by regular contact.

Usually, the sponsor works in the field of urban planning. In the case presented here, however, the subject of the project workshop derived from the educator's notion that mental health is an understudied issue that might raise challenging ethical questions for future professionals. I support the idea that the university has to offer an environment for students to experience projects that expand their horizons. This requires, however, that all the parties are convinced of that, and above all the university. In a context where professionalization is often understood as ready-to-work training, I (like many colleagues) argue that planning is firstly a reflexive practice (Schön 1983), and therefore that the purpose of planning education is to offer space for reflexivity that transcends the implementation of good practices. The project workshop is a unique opportunity to place students in a situation of dialogue with the social world, to connect to contemporary and emerging issues, and to open up to other ways of thinking and doing. Working on issues that appear to be far removed from urban planning makes students aware of socio-political and ethical implications of planning practice.

To enrol the mental health institution to work with an urban planning school (without a clear understanding of what urban planning is and how it can enlighten their practices and problems), the partnership was based on a largely open agreement and no financial commitment. Due to the particularity of the public concerned by the project workshop, a convention covered the students' insurance and confidentiality. This contractual vagueness seemed to be a necessary condition for the enrolment of partners unfamiliar with the project workshop and its outcomes.[3] The project workshop presented here was part of a compulsory curriculum but, because of the sensitive nature of the subject, a choice of three proposals was offered.[4] Eight students[5] chose to participate, motivated by the social dimension of the topic (considering a marginalized population), its originality (mental health), the novelty of working with users, the fact of working with a partner outside the world of urban planning (the hospital), and the transversal dimension (cutting across urban and social issues).

WORK IN PARTNERSHIP WITH MENTAL HEALTH INSTITUTION

The issue of mental health is quite new or even unprecedented in urban planning. Yet, the changes of mental health institutional practices (at least in France) have urban impacts. For a long time, mental health facilities were relegated to peri-urban or rural settings, and patients hidden and excluded from society. Today, with new therapies, an ideological turn, and financial austerity, psychiatric hospitals are shrinking, and a new paradigm of care is emerging that implies new duties, practices and needs for institutions to cure mental health diseases. How can this stigmatized population's right to the city and to human dignity be considered? Can planning contribute to their destigmatization? These are some of the questions raised by this experiment.

Understanding Mental Health Issues

A first pedagogical challenge was to help students to understand and problematize issues related to mental health and its complex and ambiguous relationship to urban space. To grasp this complexity, the students investigated the city (analysis of statistical data) and local care services supply (from professional directories), the governance of mental health in Paris (interviews with professionals), and the evolution and practices of the world of mental health (through bibliographic research). They also worked towards a better understanding of mental health disorders, the difficulties that they entail in daily life, and users' expectations of care institutions (interviews with professionals and community leaders, documentaries, exhibitions, films and comics). In order to share the students' results and understanding of these issues, I present the main elements here.

The post-war period was strongly characterized by challenging alienism in psychiatry. Therapeutic approaches changed under the influence of psychoanalytical approaches, and advances in medication helped significantly to reduce the hospitalization of patients. Additionally, in France a new principle of territorial organization of mental health care (called *sectorization*) resulted in the creation of outpatient care facilities in the communities and the removal of hundreds of beds. As a large asylum in the suburbs of Paris was underused, the health authorities decided to move its last remaining services from its historic site (and to sell this valuable land) to a more central site – despite protests by the staff and especially by the residents in the neighbourhood of the new hospital. Typically, the location of a mental health institution within a community raises questions in terms not only of neighbours' acceptance (an expected NIMBY effect), but also of patients' privacy (they can been seen entering the facility) and the accessibility of care (Coldefy 2010; Coupechoux 2014; Coutant and Wang 2018; Dollé 2001; Foucault 1972; Hochmann 2015, Lévy 2012; Michel 2009; Pinon 2001).

The general trend was accompanied by the broadening of perspectives, from psychiatry (a medical specialty that treats psychological disorders) to the concept of mental health that involves everything related to health, the environment, well-being, and social inclusion (Ehrenberg 2004; Rhenter 2010). People with mental health disorders are no longer locked up (for life) in hospitals outside the city; they work and live in the city, like any other citizens. Hospitalization is now only a last resort, for a short period of time. However, mental health problems can hinder patients' ability to access work and housing.

Based on this understanding of mental health issues, the students identified a set of paradoxes that the concept of proximity allows us to articulate and examine critically. The geographical proximity of patient care and living spaces is becoming more of a sensitive issue with respect to privacy and confidentiality, as patients visiting the institution can be recognized by people who know them. The presence of the hospital in the city can also cause neighbourhood disturbances. The working sessions with the patients revealed that, contrary to what we had imagined, they had various practices within the city and were quite mobile, finding their way and moving around (sometimes on long and complex journeys) like any other urbanite. These understandings changed the framework of thinking in planning. The students' work turned towards a more conceptual reflection on the concept of proximity, by analogy with other facilities where the question of proximity arises according to various logics (geographical, temporal, organizational, etc.). They sought to understand the extent to which the location of an outpatient facility should be thought of in terms of geographical proximity or accessibility.

Working with the users (both patients and medical staff) and being attentive to the diversity of points of view, led the students to question the question. Instead of proposing solutions, they reframed and rephrased the sponsor's problem in order to accompany his reflection. Their work evolved from urban planning to a prospective approach in the service of critical examination of organizational issues. While keeping in mind the challenges of maintaining the quality of care underpinned by a logic of public service, patient empowerment and destigmatization, the students devised two contrasting programmatic concepts:[6] the *city of mental health* (a grouping together of care and support structures) and the *hospital outside the walls* (acting as a gradual disappearance of treatment centres). More than proposals to implement, these programmatic concepts are in fact two sides of the same reformulation of the sponsor's request: *to create a new model of care* (to be exemplary and to learn to heal, to live with the mental health disorder and to live together), and *to put mental health in the public space* (as a political and material space) (Bonal et al. 2016).

Build a Professional Identity as an Urban Planner

Usually, project workshop partners (developer, community organizer, local municipality, etc.) are familiar with urban planning issues. Here, however, the students were faced with people who had no knowledge of urban planning, whose logic in action and governance they had to understand. They also had to demonstrate teaching skills by translating the usual methods and thinking of urban planners into comprehensible terms. The abstruseness of medical jargon mirrored that of urban planning, which had to be discarded to adapt its level of discourse to different audiences. Surprisingly, the students felt more comfortable expressing themselves as urban planners than they had experienced in previous internships or workshops. They did not feel like students in urban planning but rather as urban planners, talking to mental health professionals, peer-to-peer, each learning from the professionalism of the other. At minimum, they expressed a sense of greater legitimacy to assert themselves as professionals.

The hospital professionals were at once the sponsors of the project workshop, the experts on the subject, and the future users of the facility. Within the hospital team, there were differences in the understanding of mental health issues and the reorganization of the care services. At each steering meeting, various points of view were expressed, which had to be understood in light of the position of each one in relation to the others, e.g., between nurse and administrative director, or psychiatrist and psychologist. This plurality required the students to adopt a balanced position so as not to take sides in debates specifically pertaining to the institution. They became aware that an intervention in project management assistance did not necessarily require the formulation of well-argued proposals in response to the problem raised by the sponsor, but rather the creation of a space of debate, where the challenge lay more in the clarification of contradictory issues. They then assumed a new role of mediator between the stakeholders, to create the space and the debate around a public problem: How to accommodate mental health disorder in the city? As one student put it: "the most significant aspect of the work is not the result but the audience it creates [...] if there are many different people at the final discussion, it will be something different to discussing a proposal on mental health in the city". As a result, the students' work evolved from urban planning to a prospective approach. As noted above, they developed strategic concepts instead of feasible proposals. To build the framework of a debate between the actors, based on their investigation and their prospective problematization, the final discussions took the form of a half-day of collective reflection, bringing together different professionals and actors of mental health services. Following the presentation of the work, the participants (staff from various departments of the hospital and other professionals concerned by the topic) were divided into four groups to discuss the issues raised by the students (*to put mental health in the public space* and *to create a new model of care*).

The reflexivity of the urban planners played out in their offer of assistance to project management where the mission (through the meetings and the learning it generated) transformed the planners themselves and led them to reconsider their own expertise in a reflective way. To move, to reformulate, even to reverse the question was possible only on the basis of argumentation, education and explanation of the approach, in order to "empower the sponsor" (as one student put it). Urban planning could then become a practice which supports change. The problem raised by the hospital highlighted the fact that the relocation of an activity had to be understood in terms of its internal logic: the management constraints (reduction of resources, rationalization of real estate), the professional and therapeutic doctrines, society's perception of it, the human resources management issues, users' practices and perceptions, urban constraints and opportunities. It was, however, also a question of staying in one's place (as a planner) without taking sides in debates peculiar to the world of mental health, while being aware of the stakes of these debates. Working along with various professionals and above all with patients led the students to give greater importance to the needs of the target population of a project and to "think for people instead of for the project itself" [sic]. This was the very meaning of the civic commitment of urban planning that this project workshop reaffirmed.

WORKING WITH PATIENTS IN A PSYCHIATRIC HOSPITAL

As briefly mentioned above, the main focus of this project workshop was to work with patients of mental health institutions in order to gain a better understanding of their experiences in and of the city. Even though it had become standard practice in urban planning to take users into consideration, the meaning and the terms that this implies are not stable. Beyond principles, this experience with patients with mental health disorder raised many questions for participatory planning: Which users were to be taken into account? For what purposes? What was the value of the knowledge produced? What was really going on in the meeting with users?

How to Work with Users

Working sessions with patients helped to further the understanding of the perceptions of people with mental health disorders and of their uses of the city. The information and knowledge produced was intended to inform the relocation of the new facility. Following the advice of psychologists, the sessions were conducted with young people with early psychosis who had an interest in the city and transportation (some spent their free time in the subway, others know the timetables by heart). Four working sessions designed by the students were scheduled. Without any experience of participative practices, the students were inspired by survey methods studied in class, and by animation techniques learnt in an animation centre or theatre workshop. Each one lasted two hours. They were planned according to the requirements of the health care facility and were added to the usual schedule of the university.

The first session was thought of as an opportunity for everyone to meet. Above all, it was about getting to know "the other" and to feel accepted, so that the patients would participate in other sessions and trust the students. It was also a moment when the students themselves confronted their own fears and prejudices. The exercises involved an inter-individual encounter such as the mirror game and the blind guide. Students and patients, in pairs, looked at each other face to face, holding each other's elbows, with physical contact. These playful exercises were a way to remove the barriers and to accept the presence of others. In the following session, the students asked the patients to guide them around the neighbourhood in small groups. The goal was to make them talk about the choice of the path, their preferences, their habits, and their knowledge of the neighbourhood. Contrary to the students' expectations, the activity was very different, depending on the group. One patient started to run, another refused to go out, others did not speak, and so on. This served as a reminder that whatever the exercise (and the audience), we could not foresee how the participants would react to a proposal, nor what knowledge would be produced. From a pragmatic perspective, this walk, like other activities carried out with patients, was an experience of inquiry shared by all, that shifted perceptions and, as such, produced knowledge (of the other, of oneself, of situations). The third session was held in the cafeteria of the health care facility. Patients were asked to describe or to draw their daily commute, so that their movement around the city, the obstacles they encountered and the tactics they used to overcome them could be understood. Mental maps were thought of as a medium of speech, elaboration and enunciation of facts and representations. Students noted and drew what they were told by the patients, who drew busses and their dangerous mirrors, the basement of the subway station, a scooter, etc. All the sessions were the subject of a formalization (new photo of the guided walks, description of the stories of journeys, etc.) recorded in a booklet of which the patients received copies during the final session hosted at the university, in a spirit of reciprocity. On that occasion, the students were in turn the patients' guides on campus. As at the end of any collective adventure, this morning ended with a group photo, some sadness, and hugs.

"Give a Voice to Those Who Never Speak"

The description of the working session should not hide the many questions that were raised. The first type of question was linked to the nature of the facility to be relocated (a mental health facility) and to the diversity and particularities of the users concerned: doctors, nurses, families and, above all, patients. Despite the importance given today to consideration for the residents in urban planning, some users, such as people suffering from mental health disorders, are not taken into consideration. How can planners work along with them and their vulnerability in a participatory planning process? What credit can be given to patients' words? How can patients be persuaded to participate? To what extent can their voice be heard and considered in the planning process? These issues were discussed at length during the workshop. Although they arise within the framework of any participative approach, here they took on a particular meaning with regard to the users concerned: people suffering from mental health disorders, whose access to autonomy is limited. There was also a question of method: What do we observe? How to observe without "giving the impression of doing the same thing as the psychologists" (as one student commented)? For one, taking notes in this situation is tricky. On several occasions, this student felt uncomfortable about being in an explicit position of observer: "I found it weird to note. I began to notice. I felt that it was not easy. I felt like I was studying birds, watching patients like guinea pigs". Others, on the contrary, experienced this observation as a moment of sharing, with the patients checking the notes, asking for modifications, and so on.

  These concerns relate more broadly to the fear of hurting others that many students reported, as well as to an ethical consideration on the very meaning of the process. At the end of each working session with patients, speaking times were planned between students and professionals from the hospital to analyse the situations experienced, understand the daily realities of the patients, be attentive to gestures or words not to use, and so forth. The question of physical contact appeared as a point of vigilance. Looking at each other, being looked at, touching and being touched by the other are sometimes difficult experiences for patients, especially when they are adolescents facing the upheavals of puberty. For the psychologists, the sessions were new situations in which the patients' reactions revealed a new aspect of their personality. They saw it as part of their own therapeutic work. In the relationship a form of reciprocity also played out, in the attentiveness and the listening. Over the course of the working sessions, the object of knowledge changes. Through the relationship that was formed with these users, it was not so much the practices and perceptions of the patients themselves that fed the reflection, but the understanding of their plurality and the reflexive gaze that it induced. The students understood that there were no specific practices or needs of a supposed "mental health disorder" population. They had as many practices and needs as did any other urbanites. It was undoubtedly on this point that this experience was the most unique and instructive. It raised the students' awareness of the ways in which planners understood social complexity. Getting students to work with people suffering from mental health disorders is by no means trivial and induces a great deal of reflexivity amongst them about their investment in the process, the meaning of their work, and the ethical dimensions of urban planning.

Fighting Prejudice

Awareness of prejudice resulted from a reflexive process to challenge prejudice, which lasted throughout the project workshop. The first session was essential in initiating the participants' relationship to one another. Gradually, fears were allayed over the course of the meetings, and prejudices disappeared, making way for an equally destabilizing observation. Behind a category (people suffering from mental disorders), each patient had perceptions and practices concerning space that were specific and unique to him or her. These were not devoid of rationality, even though it was not evident. For instance, like anyone else, the young patients were able to come to the mental health outpatient facility alone every day, and had their own tips to find their way in the city and the complex Parisian subway system; they even had tactics and alternative routes in case of incidents. As the work progressed, representations changed. The differences in practices and perceptions of space were more inter-individual than specific to any one category of people suffering from mental health disorders. Beyond otherness, this diversity related to the awareness of the plurality of uses of the city. "Living with the disease is about looking at those who live differently, and at how we live together. There is a mirror effect: it makes me wonder about myself", commented a student. As trite as this statement may seem, it refers to the limits of categorizations and questions urban planning practices. Not to give in to generalization is also a way of thinking about the destigmatization of mental health disorder, because by this experience, the students "were confronted with [their] own barriers", having realized that the patients, in fact, are "like us", as one of them put it.

While the whole process was rich in learning from others and from ourselves, certain situations reminded us that organizing such a meeting is not easy and that the experience could have been short-lived. Impatient to return to the psychiatric hospital after an initial, touching encounter, the first moments of the second visit gave rise to doubt, when a patient greeted us in a very vulgar way. It seemed normal for the psychologists, as this was the patient's usual way of expressing himself, but we all felt uncomfortable. Moreover, while these meetings created a relationship between patients and students, what exactly was the nature and place of this relationship? An incident was to lead us to discuss it at length with the psychologists of the institution. At the end of the third session, at the patients' request, the students gave them their cell phone number. A few minutes after the end, several female students received a lot of love messages from one of them. They worried about it and so did I, because the institutional framework in which the workshops took place engaged my responsibility. They were aware that these phone number exchanges were problematic, but did not know how to react and did not dare to say no. Their discomfort reflected their feelings of guilt for creating a relationship with no tomorrow, with patients they knew were fragile and isolated. To resolve the situation, the psychologists organized a meeting during which a discussion was launched on the notion of relationship, what it triggered in each person, its asymmetry, and the feeling of guilt that followed. Faced with this feeling ("I feel almost guilty: we create the relationship and we don't know how to manage it" said a student), the psychologists reassured the students by drawing a parallel with the relationships that are formed in a summer camp, between instructors and children. They also mediated by reframing, with the patients, the meaning of our intervention. This unprecedented situation provided professionals with a new framework for analysing their patients' behaviour. Through this situation, students learned to set the framework of a professional relationship; as one of them said, "You have to have professionalism in the relationship". This called into question the limits of benevolence, regarding how to listen, what to do about particular words, and how to listen and consider while being aware that the other person is suffering from a mental disorder. In urban planning discourse and practice, it is generally said that we cope with users. The experience here was different: it was about learning to be in a relationship with the user and learning about them.

CONCLUSION: LEARNING THE CIVIC DIMENSION OF PLANNING

The project workshop and the intensive group work process involved emotional burdens and tensions that the subject of mental health exacerbated. This workshop was all the more demanding and intensive as the sessions with the patients were added to the usual programme and disrupted the workflow. They contributed to the students' personal commitment to the process. Due to the sensitivity of the subject, special attention was paid to the students' well-being, leaving ample room for debate and moments of collective and individual debriefing to discuss with them their own learning as urban planners. Although the outcomes for the students (and the teacher as well) were unquestionably positive, initiating a participatory project workshop with a vulnerable population requires the teacher to be attentive to the side-effects. In this respect, I had benefited from the support of the health care professionals and psychologists, who were aware of the difficulties and challenges of these interactions. All of this required time and a room for long discussion with the students, where they could express their feelings and their doubts, as much as their learning and questions. They expressed not only their concerns but also their enthusiasm, in a workshop that differed (by the subject, the sponsor and the collaborative approach) to their expectations when they chose urban planning: "This is great. This was not expected in urban planning. We talk about it around us. People are amazed". Working sessions with patients led the students to give greater importance to the needs of the users of a project. Four two-hour working sessions were enough to become aware of the diversity of users and to change their perceptions of the problem. As one of the students explained, working with patients leads one to "think for people instead of for the project itself". This is the very meaning of the civic commitment of the urban planner that this workshop reaffirmed. During the first few weeks of the work, the students became familiar with mental health issues, and worried about moving away from urban planning. In the end, the workshop opened up new perspectives for reflection. Other new topics are consequently likely to emerge, as for mental health, opening new fields of possibility for these young planners. "By questioning mental health, we are putting ourselves in a different position as urban planners who are 'making the city'. It clarifies that urban planning is also a civic engagement" (a student).

This teaching experience underscores the importance of practice in the teaching of urban planning (Vivant 2018). It reinforces the idea of a reflexive practice of urban planning that is constructed and questioned by the encounter with new situations and issues. Like other project-based disciplines, such as architecture and design, urban planners build their professionalism through practice and reflexivity, through the different projects and subjects on which they work (Schön 1983). This implies the teacher's strong involvement in the process, along with an awareness of and attentiveness to the disturbing effects of such encounters. While a project workshop is an ideal exercise for students to familiarize themselves with the realities of the professional world, it is also the space where they can invent and experiment with new practices. (See Box 6.1.)

BOX 6.1 KEY CHALLENGES AND IMPLEMENTATION TIPS

Working with a mental health institution raises particular challenges but also creates opportunities beyond those that emerge when working with more traditional in community organizations and NGOs.

Working and collaborating with patients with mental health disorders requires deep engagement, sensitivity and students becoming familiar with an entire new set of concepts, jargon and issues. Having sufficient time/credits allocated and good access to health care professionals is helpful for students and staff to immerse themselves with the topics. A full day of teaching per week for a whole semester plus additional study time is considered appropriate for the module. It has also been useful to make enrolment voluntary to ensure stronger commitment by the students.

Dealing with anxieties by students in regard to the challenging topic is helped by having regular feedback, a low teacher to student ratio (e.g. 1:8–10) and regular discussion sessions and dedicated time to reflect.

While university–community collaborations benefit from some kind of pre-set contractual relationships – it is advisable to keep such arrangements vague without financial commitment to avoid lock-ins and pre-programming failure due to the impossibility to ensure pre-set deliverables in such novel engagement situations.

In turn, the experimental and interdisciplinary nature of the project lends itself to unusual explorations, building professional identity (as the essence of planning needs to be explained to a very different profession) and students' reflexivity and civic engagement.

NOTES

1. In September 2015, the IUP (Institut d'Urbanisme de Paris – Paris Institute of Urban Planning, part of Université Paris-Est Créteil) and the IFU (Institut Français d'Urbanisme – French Institute of Urban Planning, part of Université Paris-Est Marne-la-Vallée) joined forces to form the EUP – *École d'Urbanisme de Paris*, or Paris School of Urban Planning – and offer a new curriculum in urban planning and development within the University Paris Est.
2. This kind of teaching by practice is mandatory in French urban planning curricula.
3. The assessment of the students' work – that resulted in the production of two reports (one on the diagnostic phase, and one explaining the two conceptual proposals), two public presentations (one at university and one for the hospital managers) and a half-day working session with thirty professionals – was based on the output and the working process itself. All of the students were awarded the highest grade.
4. The other proposals concerned: the transformation of an industrial area into a residential one; and the planning of new business developments near a future transportation hub.
5. Geoffrey Bonal, Laura Esteve, Floriane Lavigne, David Pinto, Pauline Roquet Montégon, Alexandra Spyridopoulou, Yousra Toujgani, Uta Von Stebut.
6. They organized themselves in two groups of four, worked for a full week, and challenged their different proposals every day.

REFERENCES

Bonal, G., Esteve, L., Lavigne, F., Pinto, D., Roquet Montégon, P., Spyridopoulou, A., Toujgani, Y. and Von Stebut, U. (2016) *L'établissement public de santé Maison Blanche dans le 19ème arrondissement de Paris: diagnostic et proposition.* Rapport d'étude, École d'urbanisme de Paris; Université Paris Est Marne la Vallée.
Coldefy, M. (2010) *De l'asile à la ville: une géographie de prise en charge de la maladie mentale en France.* Thèse de Géographie.
Coupechoux, P. (2014) *Un monde de fous. Comment notre société maltraite ses malades mentaux.* Paris: Seuil.
Coutant, I. and Wang, S. (eds.) (2018) *Santé mentale et souffrance psychique. Un objet pour les sciences sociales.* Paris: CNRS Éditions.
Dollé, J.-P. (2001) L'architecture de l'hôpital psychiatrique comme symptôme de l'évolution récente de la ville. In La Ferme du Vinatier (ed.), *Architecture et psychiatrie. L'hopital: espace de soin, espace urbain* (pp. 25–31). Lyon: Éditions la Ferme du Vinatier.
Ehrenberg, A. (2004) Remarques pour éclaircir le concept de santé mentale. *Revue française des affaires sociales* 1: 77–88.
Foucault, M. (1972) *Histoire de la folie à l'age classique.* Paris: Gallimard.
Hochmann, J. (2015) *Histoire de la psychiatrie.* Paris: Presses Universitaires de France, Que sais-je?
Lévy, A. (dir.) (2012) *Ville, urbanisme, et santé, les trois révolutions.* Paris: Éditions Pascal.
Michel, A. (dir.) (2009) *Ville et santé mentale: projections, politiques, ressources, symptôme.* Paris: Éditions Le Manuscrit.

Pinon, P. (2001) Architecture et thérapie. L'hospice de Charenton comme "instrument de guérison". In La Ferme du Vinatier (ed.), *Architecture et psychiatrie. L'hopital: espace de soin, espace urbain* (pp. 15–23). Lyon: Éditions la Ferme du Vinatier.

Rhenter, P. (2010) Les conseils locaux de santé mentale, un nouveau modèle pour les partenariats? *Vie sociale* 1(1): 151–163.

Schön, D. (1983) *The Reflective Practitioner: How Professionals Think in Action.* New York: Basic Books.

Vivant, E. (2018) Accompagner l'implantation d'un établissement de soins psychiatriques. Les enseignements d'un atelier de programmation urbaine avec les usagers. *Cahier Ramau* 9: 86–101.

7. Beyond the classroom: new skills through community–university outreach

Camila D'Ottaviano and João Farias Rovati

INTRODUCTION

The subject addressed in this chapter is based on community outreach[1] experiences promoted in two Brazilian Architecture and Urbanism courses, one in Porto Alegre, at the Faculty of Architecture of the Federal University of Rio Grande do Sul (UFRGS), and one in the city of São Paulo, at the School of Architecture and Urbanism of the University of São Paulo (USP). In the national context of Brazil, both are highly ranked public institutions offering free undergraduate and graduate (Master and Doctoral) education. This status is, in itself, important as in Brazil there are significant differences between public and private universities. For example, public institutions are responsible for almost all the scientific research conducted in the country. According to the evaluations of the Ministry of Education, the best Brazilian universities are public. However, 75% of Brazilian undergraduate students (about 8 million) are enrolled in private institutions.

According to the Federal Constitution, a fundamental characteristic of Brazilian universities, whether public or private, is the accomplishment of teaching, research and community outreach activities. The successful establishment of community outreach in the institutional framework, however, is relatively recent. An important milestone in this process was the creation, in 1987, of the Forum of Brazilian Public Universities Community Outreach Divisions[2] (FORPROEX). But only in 2012 was a National Community Outreach Policy in fact agreed on. This policy resulted from long-standing discussions and consolidated the understanding of community outreach as an instrument to provide the closer links between universities and society in order to address the deep social inequalities existent in Brazil.

During the last decade, community outreach has advanced in different areas, including the fields of urban planning and urban studies. Experiences have multiplied and community outreach has been successfully established as a unique training tool and space for young urban planners as evidenced by its growing presence in seminars and meetings promoted by the National Association of Graduate Programs and Research in Urban and Regional Planning (ANPUR) and ANPUR's publications (D'Ottaviano and Rovati 2017, 2019). In 2016, however, this progression was severely interrupted when President Dilma Roussef was deposed by a government coalition committed to ultra-liberal policies. Since then, the country has experienced a political, economic and, above all, an institutional crisis. The freezing of public investments[3] in areas such as health, social security and education, determined by the coup government,[4] now threatens the very continuity of community outreach as a possibility to articulate education and research and, especially, as a training space that goes beyond the classroom limits. In this context, urban planning public policies have also been strongly questioned.

The critical analysis in this chapter addresses these issues; it is organized in four parts. In the first part we describe the institutional framework of community outreach activities in Brazil: its historical evolution and establishment in higher education, advances and potentialities, and its specificities. Second, we will present characteristics of the universities and programmes at the undergraduate level at two Brazilian institutions and elaborate on the pedagogical tools the authors used in outreach practices associating them to Paulo Freire[5] (1973, 1996) and his notions of *transformative action*, *dialogical action* and *praxis*. In the third part, two specific accounts are provided of exemplary outreach experiences. From the critical analysis of these experiences, we uncover possible ways for the continuity and deepening of community outreach as a training experience in urban planning via innovative and flexible teaching arrangements. Fourth, we will conclude by highlighting the current challenges in the training of young urban planners in the context of the Brazilian public university structure and to community outreach.

INSTITUTIONAL FRAMEWORK OF COMMUNITY OUTREACH IN BRAZIL

In Brazil, academic education and university structure are generally based on the "principle of inseparability between teaching, research and community outreach".[6] However, traditionally the implementation of this 'principle' has been quite diverse. Brazil is home to more than 2,500 institutions formally recognized as 'higher education' ones. Out of these, about 200 are formally classed as 'universities' – a very diverse world of public, private, confessional and community institutions with local, regional and national remits. And in whatever format, community outreach is considered an established activity in all these institutions.

According to FORPROEX (2012), the earliest Brazilian experiences related to outreach date back to the beginning of the 20th century, when some São Paulo colleges, which later gave rise to USP, made references to "community outreach activities". In the early 1930s, while establishing "the bases of the Brazilian university system", the federal government included community outreach among its main purposes. In the early 1960s, community outreach appears prominently in the guidelines of the University Reform National Seminars promoted by the National Students Union (UNE). In 1962, the first Community Outreach Service was created at the University of Recife. Directed by Paulo Freire, the service played an important role in establishing community outreach as a "form of commitment of universities with popular sectors" (Britto 2017, p. 28). But this conception was opposed after the military coup of 1964. The dictatorship imposed limits for the practice of 'intellectual freedom' and 'university autonomy'; however, it continued the process of incorporating community outreach into the university system, now oriented mainly by geopolitical conceptions related to national 'security', 'development' and 'integration' – as it was the case of the Rondon Project,[7] focused on the Amazon.

Only from the mid-1980s, after the end of the dictatorship, an open and pluralistic debate restarted to advance an institutional consolidation of community outreach within the Brazilian university system. In 1987, the Forum of Brazilian Public Universities Outreach Divisions Executive Vice-Presidents was created and in 1988, the new Federal Constitution established the "principle of inseparability between Teaching, Research and Community Outreach". This definition supported the creation, in 1993, of the Program for the Promotion of Community Outreach (PROEXTE) and, within the scope of the National Law of Guidelines and Bases for Education (LDB), approved in 1996, the formalization of community outreach as one of the three main purposes of the Brazilian University, alongside teaching and research.

Another important initiative to institutionalize community outreach was the creation of the National Community Outreach Plan, developed and approved in 1998 by FORPROEX (2001 FORUM). More recently, the national education plans for the periods 2001–2010 (PNE 2001–2010, Federal Law 10,172/2001) and 2014–2024 (Federal Law 13,005/2014) defined universities' responsibilities within their institutional functions of Teaching, Research and Community Outreach. It was decided that a minimum of 10% of the total credits required for graduation should be fulfilled "in programs and projects of Community Outreach, directing their action, primarily, to areas of great social relevance" (Federal Law 13,005/2014, Strategy 12.7). Since then, organizations such as FORPROEX, the National Outreach Network and the Association of Universities of the Montevideo Group have been working on the establishment of community outreach policies that are no longer limited to local actions. In 2012, based on the discussions and deliberations of FORPROEX, the

Community Outreach National Policy was established (FORPROEX 2012). A recent definition of Community Outreach highlights a broad focus:

> Community Outreach is the educational, cultural and scientific process that articulates Teaching and Research in an inseparable way and enables the *transformative relationship* between University and Society. The Community Outreach is a two-way path, with assured transit to the academic community, which will find in society the opportunity to elaborate the *praxis* of the academic knowledge. Upon returning to the University, teachers and students will bring a learning that, subject to theoretical reflection, will be added to that knowledge. This movement, which establishes an *exchange* of systematized, academic and popular *knowledge*, will have as consequences the production of knowledge resulting from the confrontation with the Brazilian and regional realities, the democratization of academic knowledge and the effective participation of the community in the University's practice. In addition of collaborating to this dialectical process of theory/practice, Community Outreach is an interdisciplinary activity that supports an integrated view of the social. (FORPROEX 2012, pp. 21–22, emphasis added)

In short, it can be said that in present-day Brazil, community outreach is broadly understood as *an instrument to bring the University closer to society, necessarily involving a two-way interaction.* According to FORPROEX, for example, this "approach" and "two-way interaction" aims above all to "educate in a sensitive manner" participants to the "social problems" and to enable them to formulate public policies:

> Community Outreach has the potential not only to sensitize students, teachers and technical-administrative personnel to social problems. As an activity that also produces knowledge, it also improves the technical and theoretical capacity of these actors, thus making them more capable of offering subsidies to governments in the elaboration of public policies; better equipped to design, if they hold any public office, these policies, as well as to implement and evaluate them. (FORPROEX 2012, pp. 35–36)

However, the outreach definition has been subject to different interpretations. In fact, activities associated with community outreach in Brazil are extraordinarily diverse and do not always embrace a 'double-way interaction' or empower their participants. Sometimes community outreach is simply seen as 'everything' which is not teaching or research including the mere possibility of providing services – as in, for example, providing courses very similar to those ordinarily given at universities to other audiences. A recent study revealed that, at times, even technical assistance and consultancy activities for companies and public authorities involving remuneration and even contracts of high financial value are classed as community outreach (Rovati and D'Ottaviano 2017).

COMMUNITY OUTREACH IN PORTO ALEGRE AND SÃO PAULO

Institutional Context and Characteristics

Before further discussing the community outreach experiences of the Faculty of Architecture at the Federal University of Rio Grande del Sul (UFRGS) and the School of Architecture and Urbanism at the University São Paulo (USP), it is valuable to provide some institutional context for these two host institutions. The UFRGS was founded in 1934 as University of Porto Alegre. It is the main university education centre in the Southern region and is considered today one of the top five Brazilian federal universities. Currently the university has over 50,000 undergraduate and graduate students. USP, also founded in 1934, is part of São Paulo's state universities system. Like UFRGS, USP was created from the assembly of autonomous undergraduate programmes in the city of São Paulo. USP is currently the largest public university in the country with almost 100,000 students enrolled in undergraduate and graduate programmes.

Furthermore, it is important to highlight the specificities of training and education for professional urban and territorial planners in Brazil, where, in contrast to most European or North American countries, there are practically no undergraduate programmes for education in planning. Instead planning education is enabled via Architecture and Urbanism programmes. Only at the graduate level (Master, Doctorate) are there programmes exclusively dedicated to urban or territorial planning.

UFRGS and USP's Architecture and Urbanism programmes were created in the second half of the 1940s. Both are results of student-led movements that questioned the historical link between Architecture, Engineering and Fine Arts. During the late 1940s, the first Brazilian 'autonomous schools' of Architecture were created in São Paulo, Porto Alegre, Belo Horizonte and Rio de Janeiro. The establishment of each one of these courses also led to the creation of new autonomous schools within the structures of the two universities. The course and the School of Architecture and Urbanism of the University of São Paulo (FAUUSP) were created in 1948 as an outcome of the mobilization of the then students of the Architect-Engineering programme at the Polytechnic School. In the case of UFRGS, the Architecture programmes created in 1945 were originally hosted in the schools of Engineering and Fine Arts. Subsequently, following the students' mobilization both programmes merged and the School of Architecture was created in 1952.

UFRGS's Architecture and Urbanism undergraduate programme consists of 10 semesters of full-time teaching, with classes in the morning and at night, totalling 4,470 class hours.[8] The programme enrols 55 new students every semester. According to its pedagogical programme it facilitates

> the training of professionals able to organize the physical environment, in accordance to social needs and natural or built environment constraints. This activity, which involves the production of isolated or complex buildings, as well as urban space organization, in any scale or dimension, implies the preparation of studies, projects and plans, with the corresponding details and execution. (Comgrad-Arq 2018)

In order to complete the degree, a student must attend 56 theoretical and practical compulsory subjects and at least five theoretical and practical elective subjects, offered by different departments, especially the departments of Architecture and Urbanism. Within the structure of UFRGS, community outreach is organized and supported by the Division of Community Outreach; and, in the School of Architecture, by the Community Outreach Commission.

FAUUSP's undergraduate programme in Architecture and Urbanism at USP also lasts 10 semesters full-time and requires a total of 5,880 class hours.[9] A hundred and fifty students are selected each year through local and national selection. According to its programme statement the degree

> aims to train generalist professionals capable of understanding the needs of individuals, social groups and communities in relation to the design, organization and construction of interior and exterior spaces, encompassing urban planning, building, landscaping, conservation and the valorisation of the built heritage, the protection of natural environment balance and the rational use of resources. (FAUUSP 2019)

The FAUUSP pedagogical project values the complexity of a profile always in transformation, prescribing the formation of a professional

> open to critical and historical analysis, design and technological experimentation, theoretical refinement, confrontation of diverse social and urban situations, exceeding the current official professional system basic subjects and assimilating wider academic purposes of the Public University as a whole. (FAUUSP 2014, p. 5)

To obtain the degree, a student must attend 61 theoretical and practical compulsory subjects and 12 theoretical and practical elective disciplines, offered by different departments, notably by the departments of Architecture History, Design and Technology. Within the structure of USP, the community outreach is organized and supported by the Division of Culture and Community Outreach; and, at FAUUSP, by the Committee on Culture and Community Outreach.

Until 2018,[10] in both universities community outreach activities were not compulsory and were formally considered as complementary activities. The projects usually offered one-year scholarships for the students. For USP the scholarships were provided by the University. At UFRGS scholarships were provided by the University and by the Federal Government. In addition to the possibility to have a scholarship, some of the students engaged themselves in the community outreach projects based on their desire to contribute to social movements and special subjects such as social housing, *favelas* improvement or community work.

Community Outreach: Dialogical Action, Praxis and Close Bond with Society

As already noted, the institutional structure of Brazilian University is based on the Teaching–Research–Outreach tripod. However, despite its long tradition, and being an integral part of the institutional structure of our universities, community outreach usually does not receive the same attention and support dedicated to teaching and research from the university administration. Moreover, at the conceptual level, community outreach is marked by strong ambiguities; in this sense, as it has been observed in the previous section, part of the actions so named are in fact limited to service activities or to the mere transmission of knowledge to selected audiences.

From the authors' perspective, however, community outreach, when used as a tool to break with daily academic and traditional teaching practices, can hugely influence the training of future urban planners. It is not just about innovating or experimenting new teaching and learning practices. It is a matter of adopting as guiding principle of these practices and experiments the *close bond* with the local setting and society, and the *commitment* to reduce the stark social and territorial inequalities that characterize Brazilian society. Because it is mainly through community outreach "that the university has the chance to be flooded by social and popular movements, non-academic knowledge and the cultural dynamics of the city, being itself a public space and public sphere par excellence" (Britto 2017, p. 31).

As such the authors' notion of community outreach builds epistemologically and conceptually on three ideas elaborated by Paulo Freire (1973, 1996):

- the importance of knowledge for a *transformative action*;
- the need of *dialogic action* for knowledge; and
- *praxis* as a way of acting within and for the society.

From this point of view all such activities are therefore developed from a close interplay between teacher and student, researcher and researched. All activities include long periods of direct observation, the use of all the senses (listening, seeing, dialogue) and the ability to deal with uncertainties and errors, always present in these sorts of processes. In fact, the experience and recognition of "errors" humanize the extensionist logic and provide a more complex and complete formation process.

Methodologies are developed on a case-by-case basis, that is, they are designed for each project or situation. They always include as a fundamental principle fieldwork, interdisciplinary collaboration and the development of activities in a collective and cooperative way with the population that is the object of the action or study, aiming to establish a knowledge exchange dynamic. As Paulo Freire points out, outreach necessarily involves a willingness for *delivering*

> [...] something brought by a Subject who is "within the wall" to those who are "beyond the wall" or "outside the wall" [...] [And where] Educating, and educating oneself for the purpose of liberation, is the task of those who know that they know little (for this very reason they know that they know something and can thus succeed in knowing more) in dialogue with those who almost always think they know nothing. (Freire 1973, pp. 7, 10–11)

In each of our projects and activities we reaffirm a certain understanding of outreach, broadly defined as a

> field of experimentation of dialogic approaches of interaction between University and Society, with an aim to confront social, technical or aesthetic issues relevant to the daily routine of their urban or rural life, by engendering academic and ordinary, popular knowledge consolidated by oral and gestural tradition, [which] is presented as a fair counterbalance to the exclusionary principle contained in the logic of confinement. (Britto 2017, p. 32)

The experience of interaction with the concrete demands of populations implies the involvement of the students with a reality that they are often unaware of. This experience, together with collective work, decisively contributes to the education of a qualified professional not only as a 'technician', but also and mostly as a humanized and socially committed individual:

> One of the first knowledges, indispensable to those who, arriving at favelas or at realities marked by tradition of our right to be, intends that their presence will become coexistence, that their being in the context will become being with it, it is the knowledge of the future as a problem and not as inexorability. It is the knowledge of History as a possibility and not as determination. *The world is not. The world is being.* [...] My role in the world is not only that of who verifies what happens, but also that of who intervenes as subject of occurrences. I am not only the object of History, but also its subject. In the world of History, culture, politics, I realize not to adapt myself but to change it. (Freire 1996, p. 76, emphasis added)

As emphasized, community outreach still occupies a relatively marginal position in Brazilian universities, which value especially research and development of 'pure knowledge'. University professors are 'academics'; and when they engage in 'practical' activities they usually do so to respond to 'market' demands. From this point of view the 'social' stands aside. In the case of Architecture and Urbanism programmes, this is very evident. For example, project teaching is almost always focused on the demands of a small part of society, precisely the one that has the resources to hire architects. This situation is criticized by Agamben referring to Ludwig Tieck's story *Des Lebens Überfluß* (Life's Superfluity), which

> [...] depicts two penniless lovers who gradually renounce all possessions and all outside life to the point where they live dosed up in their room. Finally, when they can no longer find wood for fuel, they burn the wooden ladder connecting their room with the rest of the house, and are left in isolation from the outside world, owning nothing and alive to nothing but their love. This ladder – Tieck gives us to understand – is experience, sacrificed by them to the flames of 'pure knowledge'. (Agamben 1993, p. 15)

Agamben's comment seems to be particularly appropriate to the context addressed here. We understand that community outreach activities directed to the 'social', such as the ladder can offer students the experience of another kind of knowledge, different from 'pure knowledge' pursued by the research world. But the question is how to incorporate this 'ladder' to the routine of our universities? The following cases are intended to answer this question.

CASE EXAMPLES

The experiences and analyses briefly presented hereafter refer exclusively to community outreach activities carried out in Porto Alegre (UFRGS) and São Paulo (USP). They focus on the potential of teaching–learning processes practised "beyond the walls" of our universities (Freire 1973). Designed in the context of Architecture and Urbanism modules, such experiments are closely linked to the notion of *habitat social production*, that is

> [...] to all those processes that generate inhabitable spaces, urban components and dwellings, which are carried out under the control of self-producers and other non-profit social agents. They may result of individual families acting separately, of informal organized groups, social enterprises such as cooperatives and residents' associations, or nongovernmental organizations, professional unions and even philanthropic institutions that serve emergencies and vulnerable social groups. The self-management modalities range from spontaneous individual to collective self-production, which implies a high organizational level of participants and, in

many cases, complex processes of production and management of habitat components. (Ortiz Flores 2006, pp. 3–4)

All cases include active and continued contact between students and the population. Some projects are the result of students' autonomous initiatives – projects that we supervise and, in some cases, only monitor.

Orquídea Libertária [Libertarian Orchid], Porto Alegre, 2014–2015

With the technical assistance of the City-in-Project, Teaching, Research and Outreach Laboratory (CPLAB) of the UFRGS Faculty of Architecture, the *Orquídea Libertária* residential complex was developed by the Cooperativa de Trabalho Mista Solidária Utopia e Luta (COOPSUL).

The university's participation began following an invitation from COOPSUL to Professor João Rovati to lead on the design for a housing complex. The idea was to develop a complex with 50 housing units. A community outreach project was then prepared and approved by UFRGS and as part of this, four scholarships were offered to undergraduate students.[11] These students, under the supervision of Professor Rovati, supported all activities with COOPSUL for two years (2014–2015). According to one of the students the activities were

[…] ongoing work that began few months earlier by the social technical group and by COOPSUL – a work that sought to guide the members of the cooperative on the operation of the [housing] programme, with the project and the documents needed to participate; motivate and organize everyone […] (Baumbach 2015, in Rovati 2015, p. 7)

Based on methodology developed by Usina,[12] the CPLAB team developed a participatory process with future residents to design the project. Five workshops were held with a group of members of the cooperative, where they discussed the social and political objectives of the process and the architectural design itself. Using interactive and creative ways, the future residents of the *Orquídea Libertária* were invited to reflect about themes such as the urban design, the housing units, future furniture, materials, communal spaces and the neighbourhood (see Figures 7.1 and 7.2). After ten months of work, a more complete version of the architectural design of the *Orquídea Libertária* complex was presented to its future residents. Again, according to one of the students:

the Project was a very good experience as it was made for real people, with real problems and demands that are very common in Brazil. (Baumbach 2015 in Rovati 2015, p. 11)

This experience made it possible for teachers and students to learn about the specificities of the architectural project for a population of great social vulnerability. The action was marked by instances of deep interaction between teachers, technicians, students, residents and popular leaderships, but also by conflicts between the different actors involved in the action that finally led to its interruption.

Source: Ong Cidade.

Figure 7.1   First workshop with families – participatory tools

Square in Jardim Jaqueline, São Paulo, 2016–2017

Developed by the FAU Social and supervised by Professor Karina Leitão, the second example's aim was to improve a public square located in Jardim Jaqueline *favela* (west of São Paulo). The students' involvement with the community began during an academic undergraduate activity. At the end of the regular semester, a group of students decided to continue the activities with the community of Jardim Jaqueline. They were joined by graduate students (Master and PhD students) from LabLaje collective. All work was unpaid and voluntary.

Source: Ong Cidade.

Figure 7.2   Second workshop with families – thinking about the project

Under the supervision of Professor Leitão, the students learned that one of the main problems was the lack of leisure space for children and the elderly. In response, they looked for areas in the surroundings where a small square could be created. Following negotiations involving residents and municipality technicians, they managed to develop an agreement with a shopping centre located next to the *favela* by which the shopping centre ceded a small plot just beside their parking lot and donated the necessary funds for the creation of a leisure area (materials and equipment).

The project and its implementation were accomplished with the participation of the residents, especially the children. Upon completion, the project has become a key example for the students of the interaction success between university, community, public power and private sector that helped to make the project feasible.

REFLECTION

All projects had/have as a central pedagogical proposal the development of teaching-learning experiments based on the experience of innovative pedagogical practices, always based on the direct observation of the study sites, dialogue, close interaction, active and solidary participation between all the participants – students, residents, technicians, teachers and population in general. We can affirm that, undoubtedly, in the two metropolises, the projects have greatly contributed to the sensitive recognition of the 'world' and the real and daily needs of different social segments. Additionally, the students had to face the difficulties of designing and implementing an urban project, including the negotiation with the varied participants and difficulties to access funding.

It is important to highlight that the students that join community outreach projects are usually willing to experience the real city, with its real people. Nevertheless, while rewarding on one hand, quite often the outreach experiences and realities caused anguish and frustration amongst the participants. The frustrations derived from mainly two reasons: (i) the mismatch and divergence between 'university times' with institutionally imposed deadlines and mandatory periodic evaluations, and the 'times within the city', sometimes more urgent and at other times exceeding the duration of academic semesters; and (ii) the difficulty to implement the designed projects, given the almost permanent lack of resources or funding. As such, instructors have made a deliberate effort to discuss these frustrations with the students; this helps to illustrate the important role all the activities play in the communities as well as highlight that such mobilization and self-awareness plays a role in the development of their professional identities as young architects and urbanists.

CONCLUSIONS

Today in Brazil, advocacy in favour of community outreach as a training tool in urban planning is rooted in two core aspects: (i) that a *close bond with society* can only be developed through a daily experience with the social fabric of society; and (ii) that these daily experiences must have a *public dimension*.

The modest community outreach actions described, have as *modus operandi* the bond between Architecture and Urbanism students with the urban and social environment to which they belong and are part of, and the involvement with concrete social demands of great complexity. In order to face each of them, we have proposed alternative paths, new co-creation pedagogies and new project practices based on the contact with and recognition of the other, the knowledge exchange and dialogical action. The opportunity of this *experience* has proved important to our students, even in the cases of interrupted and unfinished projects, when students have the challenge of learning from 'failures' (Rovati 2015).

According to Agamben, "[modern man's] incapacity to have and communicate experiences is perhaps one of the few self-certainties to which he can lay claim" (1993, p. 13). It may be an exaggeration to invite Agamben to comment on our unpretentious teaching practices for urban planning, but we believe that through projects such as the ones described here, it is possible to use *experience* as a fundamental pedagogical tool that by means of a close bond with society converts trivial teaching moments into real learning.

It is indeed this *experience* that strengthens community outreach as a *political action* and as a *public space*, a privileged *locus* of interaction between university and society. Political action supposes a *civic choice* of life in the city and within society. Community outreach as political space must inevitably be guided by the exercise of democracy, by the struggle against social inequalities and prejudices, by social justice improvement and by the fraternal dialogue and partnership between the 'different stakeholders'. As such, community outreach represents a *space-time* of experimentation that seeks and creates knowledge that transforms.

Paulo Freire's statement of "understanding we became able to intervene in reality, an incomparably more complex task that generates new knowledge than simply adapting to it" (Freire 1996, p. 76) is a good summary that captures learning from community outreach. As planners, in order to intervene in reality, we need socially, ethically and politically *committed* theoretical and conceptual basis that encompass the *complexity* of the society in which we are placed. Community outreach as transformative action is made possible through the experimentation that (a) embraces diversity, (b) surpasses pre-existing disciplinary boundaries, (c) confronts the false dichotomy between theoretical and practical activities, and (d) from effectively articulating professional practice with teaching and research.

Through community outreach, we also have the opportunity to reaffirm the important *public dimension* of our universities, precisely

> for being a field of action that engenders teaching and research processes through the constant experimentation of dialogical interaction dynamics, the purpose of which is to place its production of knowledge at the service of society (as generated products or developed processes) aiming to expand participatory conditions for the populations outside the university, especially those living in a state of vulnerability, exclusion and discrimination of any kind. (Britto 2017, p. 30)

We face today an enormous challenge: to enhance the experiences and practices of our students' education beyond the classroom, guaranteeing the *close bond with society* and, at the same time, defending the role of public universities in the 21st century as a major player in the promotion of just cities

(Fainstein 2010). Therefore, to think and practise community outreach means to reflect about the public dimension of the university and the meaning of knowledge itself, asserting its critical *role to provide transformative experiences*. The authors strongly believe that community outreach has an enormous value as an engaged training tool. Above all, because, without giving up the rationality implied in scientific knowledge, it sustains *praxis* guided by sensitivity. (See Box 7.1.)

BOX 7.1   IMPLEMENTATION TIPS

- As community outreach activities have uncertain outcomes in terms of delivery etc., learning outcomes need to be carefully phrased.
- Students will need to be supported to overcome frustration if projects fail.
- Having a coordination office and support within the institution to help liaise with community organizations is likely helpful and removes burden from the professoriate.
- Outreach activities cannot follow a fixed design and need to be developed and shaped on a case-by-case basis.

ACKNOWLEDGEMENTS

We would like to thank colleagues from ANPUR's executive board 2015–2017 for their support. This chapter is in part the result of reflections about university outreach and teaching of urban planning since 2015 as members of ANPUR's executive board. We would like to thank also our colleagues from FA-UFRGS and FAUUSP – Jorge Bassani, Caio Santo Amore, Karina Leitão, Bruno Mello and Martina Lersch – our long-standing interlocutors in this debate.

NOTES

1. For the purpose of this chapter we will use the expression 'community outreach' to designate our university outreach activities and institutional structure as defined by UFGRS English website.
2. Community outreach is part of the regular curricula of all undergraduate courses in Brazil.
3. Public funding is important for community outreach activities and projects as a way to guarantee human and material resources (for example: free care in public university hospitals is done by students as a community outreach service).
4. Constitutional Amendment No. 95 (2016) that froze the maximum public expenditure for the next 20 years and heavily jeopardizes investment in education and other public services.

5. Paulo Freire (1921–1997), a prominent Brazilian Educationalist is best known for his book "Pedagogy of the Oppressed" (1968), which is considered one of the foundational texts of the critical pedagogy movement.
6. Federal Constitution, Article 207: "Universities enjoy didactic-scientific, administrative and financial, and patrimonial autonomy, and *will obey the principle of inseparability between Teaching, Research, and Outreach*" (emphasis added).
7. UFRGS Rondon Project: http://www.inf.ufrgs.br/rondon/?page_id=13.
8. In Brazil undergraduate courses carry a significantly higher number of class hours than customary in Europe or the USA.
9. Beside architecture and urban planning FAUUSP's degree includes landscape design, graphic design and industrial design.
10. In December 2018, the Federal Resolution no. 7 established that 10% of the undergraduate class hours must be engaged with community outreach activities. Higher education institutions have until December 2021 to implement the new directives (D'Ottaviano 2019). This new law did not influence the experiences presented in this chapter.
11. All the students that participate in community outreach projects, with scholarships or not, have activities hours assigned to their scholar credits.
12. Usina is a housing movement technical support group based in São Paulo.

REFERENCES

Agamben, G. (1993) *Infancy & History: Essays on the Destruction of Experience.* New York: Verso Books.

Britto, F. D. (2017) A extensão universitária em tempos de crise [Community outreach in times of crisis]. In C. D'Ottaviano and J. Rovati (eds.), *Para Além da Sala de Aula. Extensão Universitária e Planejamento Urbano e Regional* [Beyond the Classroom: University Outreach and Urban and Regional Planning]. São Paulo: ANPUR/FAUUSP. Retrieved from http://anpur.org.br/public/publicacoes/livros/para_alem_da_sala_de_aula.pdf.

Comgrad-Arq (2018) Apresentação [Presentation]. Porto Alegre: UFRGS/FA, 2018. Retrieved from https://www.ufrgs.br/comgrad-arq/apresentacao/.

D'Ottaviano, C. (2019) Extensão em movimento [Community outreach in movement]. In C. D'Ottaviano and J. Rovati (eds.), *Além dos Muros da Universidade: Planejamento Urbano e Regional e Extensão Universitária* [Beyond the University Walls: Urban and Regional Planning, and Community Outreach]. São Paulo: ANPUR. Retrieved from http://anpur.org.br/wp-content/uploads/2020/01/livro-II_al%C3%A9m-dos-muros-da-universidade_final.pdf.

D'Ottaviano, C. and Rovati, J. (eds.) (2017) *Para Além da Sala de Aula. Extensão Universitária e Planejamento Urbano e Regional* [Beyond the Classroom: University Outreach and Urban and Regional Planning]. São Paulo: ANPUR/FAUUSP. Retrieved from http://anpur.org.br/public/publicacoes/livros/para_alem_da_sala_de_aula.pdf.

D'Ottaviano, C. and Rovati, J. (eds.) (2019) *Além dos Muros da Universidade: Planejamento Urbano e Regional e Extensão Universitária* [Beyond the University Walls: Urban and Regional Planning, and Community Outreach]. São Paulo: ANPUR. Retrieved from http://anpur.org.br/wp-content/uploads/2020/01/livro-II_al%C3%A9m-dos-muros-da-universidade_final.pdf.

Fainstein, S. S. (2010) *The Just City*. Ithaca, NY: Cornell University Press.

FAUUSP (2014) Projeto Político Pedagógico [Political Pedagogical Project]. São Paulo: FAUUSP. Retrieved from http://www.cg.fau.usp.br/Documentos/02_-_projeto_politico_pedagogico-ppp__out_revisado_fev_2014_.pdf.

FAUUSP (2019) Arquitetura e Urbanismo [Architecture and Urbanism]. São Paulo: FAUUSP. Retrieved from http://www.cg.fau.usp.br/Cursos_arq.asp.

FORPROEX – Fórum de Pró-Reitores de Extensão das Instituições Públicas de Educação Superior Brasileiras (2012) *Política Nacional de Extensão Universitária* [University Outreach National Policy]. Porto Alegre: UFRGS.

Freire, P. (1973) Extension or communication. In P. Freire, *Education for Critical Consciousness*. New York: Seabury Press.

Freire, P. (1996) *Pedagogia da Autonomia. Saberes necessários à prática educativa* [Pedagogy of Autonomy: Necessary Knowledge to Educational Practice]. São Paulo: Paz e Terra.

Ortiz Flores, E. (2006, October) Producción social del hábitat. Componente estratégico de las políticas de estado [Social production of the habitat: Strategic component of state policies]. Paper presented at the XV Asamblea de Ministros de Urbanismo y Vivienda [XV Assembly of Ministers of Urbanism and Housing], Montevideo, Uruguay.

Rovati, J. F. (2015, September) Cidade e moradia: os erros deles e os nossos [City and housing: Their mistakes and ours]. Paper presented at the 3º Congresso Internacional da Habitação no Espaço Lusófono – CIHEL [3º International Housing in the Lusophone Space Congress], São Paulo, Brazil.

Rovati, J. and D'Ottaviano, C. (2017) Os territórios da extensão universitária [The territories of university outreach]. In C. D'Ottaviano and J. Rovati (eds.), *Para Além da Sala de Aula. Extensão Universitária e Planejamento Urbano e Regional* [Beyond the Classroom: University Outreach and Urban and Regional Planning]. São Paulo, ANPUR/FAUUSP. Retrieved from http://anpur.org.br/public/publicacoes/livros/para_alem_da_sala_de_aula.pdf.

8. Collaborative and innovative participatory planning pedagogies: reflections from the Community Participation in Planning project

Gavan Rafferty, Grazia Concilio, José Carlos Mota, Fernando Nogueira, Emma Puerari and Louise O'Kane

INTRODUCTION

This chapter presents an innovative pedagogy to teach participatory planning, developed during a two-year collaborative project, *Community Participation in Planning* (CPiP), involving Ulster University (UK), Community Places (UK), the University of Aveiro (Portugal) and the Politecnico di Milano (Italy). Funded by the European Union's (EU) Erasmus+ programme, CPiP aimed to enrich student learning on different models of civic engagement and offer the space to rethink interactions between spatial planning practitioners and local communities. In embedding real-world learning with spatial planning curricula to facilitate innovative ways for conceptualizing and operationalizing how citizen participation in planning can be taught in higher education, CPiP demonstrates how context-based experiential learning in higher education aligns with the emerging rise – and challenge – of the 'third mission' activities of contemporary universities.

This chapter discusses the pedagogical innovations developed to engage students in what can be considered 'risky' learning environments (Barnett 2004; Rooij and Frank 2016). For planning students across the three partnering academic institutions, these learning environments consisted of working with different communities of 'geography' (e.g., residential neighbourhoods) and of 'interest' (local authorities and/or community development organizations) on short longitudinal live or 'real' participatory planning projects. This project-based learning pedagogy, supported by the shared international learning platform created through CPiP, exposed students to complex situations across different European locations. In effect, this broadened the contextual and conceptual backdrop for knowledge co-production and critical reflection across geographical and cultural boundaries.

The chapter proceeds as follows. Firstly, it outlines the contextualization and conceptualization of the CPiP project, positioning the work of CPiP within the wider theoretical and pedagogical terrains. In particular, it frames how CPiP embraced a co-learning and co-design pedagogy for teaching participatory planning skills that was experiential, iterative and developmental within the wider context of preparing students to become transformational agents. Secondly, the chapter discusses the operationalization and reflections of the participatory planning pedagogy. Thirdly, the chapter draws together conclusions from the pedagogy for both planning education and contributing to universities' civic engagement.

CO-DESIGNING PEDAGOGIES FOR PARTICIPATORY PLANNING

In recent decades, planning education has witnessed a much richer theoretical, research-informed base and advocacy-orientated approach, with greater pedagogical experimentation that tries to enhance student learning and experience (Cognetti and Castelnuovo 2014; Ritchie et al. 2017). Such experimentation is now necessary for addressing the aims of the New Urban Agenda and achieving the United Nations' Sustainable Development Goals, which calls for innovative pedagogies that demonstrate the transformational potential of planning. In designing the CPiP project, the overarching aim was to create a learning platform that augmented student experiential learning by enlarging the geographical, cultural and political arenas beyond those that students were already exposed to in the immediate environs of their home academic institutions. Accompanying this was the ambition to challenge customary participation methodologies, which traditionally tend to be short-lived and interactive in quite limited ways (Kitchen 2007).

CPiP chiefly focused on creating an innovative co-design pedagogy across Aveiro, Belfast and Milan to educate future planners on new and different models of civic engagement and to rethink interactions between practitioners and communities. A key pedagogical consideration was to create cross-sectoral, -cultural and -national learning, across three geographically, culturally and politically different contexts, that embedded the temporal socio-spatial uncertainties and challenges associated with participatory planning. The project facilitated novel ways of connecting student cohorts with real-world communities to co-learn about participation, to co-design engagement strategies and to co-create inclusive practices. This included academics redesigning module content and incorporating 'live' projects to help students understand what constitutes 'community' and how multiple communities (of interest, place, practice and learning) can become more meaningfully involved in shaping spatial planning (physical development) outcomes and co-designing the delivery of public services.[1]

CPiP partners wanted to strengthen their respective teaching practice for building the capacity of students, and selected practitioners involved to: (1) better engage with and negotiate present realities and unknown futures, and (2) recognize the range of actors and 'voices' in contemporary society. These themes also shaped the academics' pedagogical perspective, in representing ways for students to integrate substantive and practical knowledge, specifically in relation to deliberative and advocacy practices of spatial planning (Lang 1983). Collectively, the CPiP team assert that there can be three different approaches to embedding real-life practice in spatial planning education, particularly in relation to teaching participatory approaches:

1. 'Real-world' as a *case study* (typically related to physical and built environments) to observe: mainly oriented to skill students in conducting spatial analysis, identifying problems through physical evidence, and returning to the classroom to develop spatial solutions.
2. 'Real-world' as a process to '*plug-in*' to and work with risk and uncertainty: oriented to expose students to complex socio-physical contexts of urban transformation; identifying urban planning and design scenarios to interact with real-life urban transformation processes.
3. 'Real-world' as a '*living laboratory*' for immersion and experimentation: oriented towards community activation and co-actor activism, which through meaningful collaboration, framed in a 'co-productive' mode, explores ways of co-designing interventions and making small tactical actions for collective benefit.

CPiP academics placed particular emphasis on exposing students to the third perspective. This pedagogical framing produced a *blended learning* approach, underpinned by the notion of facilitating dialogic inquiry (Escobar 2011; Wells 1999), between individual and collective learning through engagement with professionals and civic actors across different cultural contexts. For CPiP, the classroom, or 'planning/design studio', was considered a complementary reflective learning space blended with specific 'urban living labs' (ULLs) (Concilio and Rizzo 2016; also see Marsh 2008 on territorial living labs) occurring between actors in real-world processes. The combination between learning processes developed both on campus and in 'real-world environments' strengthened the link between *thinking* (about participation) and (delivering) *action* in participatory planning situations. This process builds on the work of Mäntysalo et al. (2011) and Galison (1999, 2010) that recognize value in 'trading zones' for framing the process of learning-to-action.

This supportive co-learning approach offered opportunities to link *thinking* and *action* via multi-contextual environments that enhanced the collaboration between different stakeholders, moving towards Arnkil et al.'s (2010) Quadruple Helix concept, which presents significant opportunities and benefits for enhancing student learning by offering greater social inclusivity and robustness. Students were challenged through their learning process to consider comparisons between different national, regional and local practices. This encouraged students to digest and internalize theoretical knowledge and reflections, as well as to develop improved case-based reasoning across different local planning practices. Crucially, students recognized the significance of context-dependency, allowing them to critically reflect on comparative approaches and consider the challenges, barriers and opportunities for the transferability of knowledge and practices. Central to framing this reflexive approach, nurtured in the project by linking classroom learning with 'plug-in' and 'living lab' experimentation, was Schön's notion of the 'reflective practitioner' (Schön 1983, 1987). Like Schön, CPiP colleagues tried to nurture a pedagogy that generated 'learning *in* action' during those modules connected with real-world experimentation. Due to the real-world nature of the experimentation, CPiP partners acknowledged that (often-unforeseen) complexities can occur in working with communities of geography, interest or practice (Boelens and De Roo 2014). Acknowledging such complexity in urban contexts highlights the growing need to prepare future planners to value, and work in, transdisciplinary environments to share challenges, co-create knowledge and co-design solutions and actions. Consequently, CPiP's pedagogy, in linking Aveiro, Belfast and Milan, allowed planning students to be "supported to cope with uncertainty and planning for an unknowable future in a pluralist society" (Rooij and Frank 2016, p. 478). While acknowledging that complexities can occur in working with communities of geography, interest or practice, planning students were encouraged to view themselves, not as neutral observers, but as active participants who engaged with unstructured problems in a process of social interaction and mutual learning.

OPERATIONALIZING PARTICIPATORY PLANNING EDUCATION: LEARNING *IN* ACTION

The conceptualization above enabled academics to co- and re-design teaching modules across their respective institutions to provide students with the opportunity to 'live' with uncertainty, complexity and dilemmas in participatory planning learning and practices. This involved two core CPiP activities – teaching modules and local projects in Aveiro, Belfast and Milan – working in synergy.

In each city, the pedagogical design was to either 'plug-in' to or create local participatory ('living laboratory') projects to capture civic engagement practices and facilitate knowledge co-production that provided the context-based learning in modules. Students' assessment integrated problem-solving and design thinking that tried to add a social impact lens to their coursework, in producing a 'product' that not only demonstrated student learning, but which would be of use to practitioners or communities (e.g., stakeholder analysis information, community engagement strategies, or urban design initiatives to activate community participation). While local projects in each participating city were distinctive, given their different geographical and cultural contexts, there were common threads that connected the local projects and modules, particularly, the focus on stimulating genuine, inclusive multi-actor participation in practical spatial planning exercises. These core interlinked pedagogical activities were complemented by two community workshops in each location, occurring up-front to inform the wider CPiP project and modules, followed by three blended mobility study exchanges, running parallel to modules, consisting of a minimum of four students, three local practitioners and three civic actors from each location (Figure 8.1).

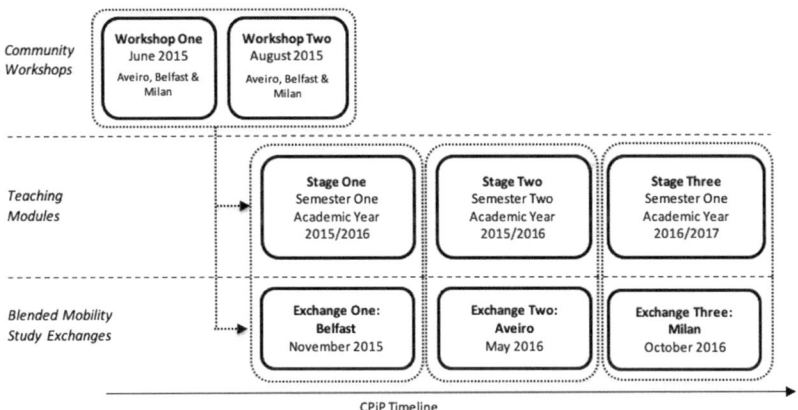

Figure 8.1   *CPiP delivery illustrating three-stage semester model*

Teaching Modules and Local Projects

In Aveiro, the teaching modules and local CPiP project were initially exploratory to create a participatory initiative. *Vivó Bairro* (old neighbourhood of Aveiro) was developed as a city centre urban regeneration project in collaboration with relevant stakeholders (mainly CORDA, a commercial and tenant association, and the municipality of Aveiro). During the first semester (September to December 2015) in the Master's of Urban and Regional Planning, at the University of Aveiro, first year cohorts were involved via two modules (*Strategic Spatial Planning* and *Urban Public Space*), followed by the *Policies for Urban Revitalization* module, scheduled for the second academic year of the Master's course. Each of three modules involved approximately 20–30 students. During the second semester (commencing February 2016), a set of digital platforms were created to share the knowledge produced and to increase collaboration and learning between students, local authority staff and community members, under the umbrella of *Vivó Bairro*. The initiative was envisaged as an ephemeral event to be collectively crafted, which could simultaneously demonstrate possibilities of, and be a catalyst for, change. That is, on the one hand, to be able to reveal the richness of material, immaterial and social resources that can be mobilized when a community becomes motivated to act upon a shared goal. On the other hand, attracting the attention of citizens, private agents and public authorities to the unsuitability of an urban condition can trigger collective efforts to alter that situation, and reveal the seeds of new relations amongst agents with a renewed willingness for further collaborative action. *Vivó Bairro* was implemented as an 'action-research project' (Cognetti and Castelnuovo 2014) focused on knowledge co-production between the university and the local community and applying this (newly) combined knowledge to bring about change and nurture collective action.

In Belfast, the local CPiP project was a collaboration between academics and postgraduate students at Ulster University, representatives from Connswater Community Greenway (including local residents and interest groups), and planning professionals in Community Places. The project focused on mapping stakeholder analysis, co-designing strategies that promoted inclusive engagement and co-productive working, and co-proposing spatial interventions with an emphasis on inter- and intra-community interaction around the shared space asset of an emerging greenway in East Belfast. The teaching modules at Ulster University incorporated into CPiP were selected from the PgDip/MSc Community Planning and Governance and MSc Planning, Regeneration and Development courses. Adopting the three stage/semester approach, as noted above, the specific postgraduate modules aligned with CPiP were: *Collaboration and Boundary Spanning* (academic year 2015–2016, Semester 1), *Sustainable Place Making* (academic year 2015–2016, Semester 2), and *Inclusive Engagement Methods* (academic year 2016–2017, Semester 1), with the latter a re-designed module, based on the emerging learning from the CPiP Project. There were approximately 15–20 students in each module.

In Milan, the teaching modules and local CPiP project were organized within the framework of the broader *ReLambro* intervention plan,[2] focusing on the planning and urban design of public green areas (parks) that intersected with the Lambro River, which is situated on the eastern side of the Milan municipality. Approximately 50–60 students were involved in each module, from the MSc in Architecture and from the BSc in Science of Architecture and Urbanism of the School of Architecture, Urbanism, Engineering and Construction (former School of Architecture and Society). Academics and students were considered relevant actors in contributing to and developing the local planning processes. They were active in raising awareness, both at community and institutional levels, and in creating dialogue between existing communities and several municipalities involved. The three teaching modules were not conceived to produce expert-driven design proposals, rather they had been considered real-time supports to embed participation needs that would enable the co-creation of design interventions. Each of the three modules and associated studio-based working adopted a different focus. The first module was designed to initiate or activate spatial awareness and discover (new) communities. The second module developed urban design projects as so-called 'community traps' to attract the attention and action of (existing and new) communities and institutions. The third module worked collaboratively with communities to co-design spatial solutions.

Blended Mobility Study Exchanges

Blended mobility study visits supported the learning and transfer of participatory practices across organizational, local and national levels in the three participating countries. In addition to CPiP partners, the three blended mobilities brought together 10 participants from each location, consisting of members of local communities, local authority staff and higher education students, to share good practice and discuss the complexities of contemporary civic engagement. These exchanges occurred during academic semesters to enable the participation of selected students and for wider dissemination of learning back into linked modules across each academic institution as participating students returned (see Figure 8.1). During these visits, study exchange participants engaged in local institutional events, site visits and meetings with local communities. This was supported by virtual communication to extend the blended approach for exchanging ideas and good practice. At the end of each exchange, participating students reported back to their peers to enrich module context and wider student learning experience, connecting the mobility exchange learning to their 'live' projects aligned with their module. While each module had different assessments, aligned to their wider programme level learning outcomes, students were to reflect on how the learning captured and disseminated through the study exchanges informed their module coursework that linked with their local 'live' project in either Aveiro, Belfast or Milan.

PEDAGOGICAL REFLECTIONS

The multi-context-based pedagogy and longitudinal nature of CPiP, operating for nearly two academic years, was fruitful in revealing the complexities and commonalities in contemporary understandings of 'community', 'planning' and 'participation'. Student feedback confirmed how exposure to different 'real-world' participatory initiatives enriched the learning experience on modules across the three planning courses, which through the innovative co-designed pedagogy, offered a synthesis of knowledge co-production and practical skills development that benefited students in each location.[3] For example, the range of context specific issues, (established and emerging) engagement mechanisms and conflictual perspectives amongst different civic actors provided students with a much deeper empirical understanding of contemporary participatory planning practice. One Aveiro student stated how "knowing different European perspectives is good for the enrichment of our knowledge … and will [help] me to improve how I can act in my own city".

Many local practitioners and civic actors welcome these types of 'engaged university' pedagogies, as they view these as 'safe spaces' within which to grapple with often contested issues. The input from academics and students can challenge the 'status quo', offer fresh thinking and push others to go beyond conventional participatory approaches. Such engaged work can produce 'win-wins' for both practitioners/communities and students. For example, one Belfast student acknowledged "how models of participation could support engagement to bring different communities together … and foster relationships", allowing students to appreciate the value and application of participation models to real-world scenarios and offering insights for practitioners to better inform their future practice and actions.

The blended mobility study visits component of the pedagogy enabled participants to debate the role of *knowledge* and *action* in facilitating participation. Unlike traditional module learning, the longitudinal connection between academics, students and practitioners through CPiP created a familiar and conducive environment to continue critical conversations in the separate local CPiP projects and participatory planning pedagogies on campus. A key learning outcome for students – and other participants too – was exposure to place-based knowledge exchange among actors. Through cross-sectoral and cultural interaction, there was deeper learning and reflection on the dynamic interplay between knowledge and action. The critical exchange between students and practitioners drew out a much richer appreciation of the interdependencies between *those involved* in participation (i.e., the 'actors'), the *sources and assets* available from which participation can be mobilized and benefit from (i.e., the 'resources'), and the role of the *physical and cultural characteristics* of a locality (i.e., the 'place').

The 'lived experience' pedagogical dimension, in the study visits and connected modules, enabled CPiP partners (academics, students and professionals) and wider participants (local government officers and civic actors) to reflect on how the flow from knowledge exchange into action is not necessarily a linear process, and that the concept of knowledge is often complex and undervalued in the context of participation. For example, creating inclusive spaces to share knowledge, such as traditional consultation events, or public meetings, does not automatically align ideas, create shared knowledge or co-produce joint action. Another learning reflection from CPiP's adopted pedagogy emerging during the study exchange conversations, and supported in classroom reflections, was around the *construction of knowledge*, typically co-created through participatory mechanisms, and the *application of knowledge*, which subsequently gets applied into practice through shared actions. The cross-sectoral and cross-cultural discussions with 'actors', about 'resources' in different 'places' enabled students to engage in participatory 'trading zones', where knowledge was exchanged and aligned so that it offered prospects for creating joint actions.

The pedagogy offered innovative ways for academics and students to question assumed knowledge and participatory practices by broadening the empirical base for observation by, as one CPiP partner notes, "discovering the relevance of different participation cultures in different countries, and specifically in different contexts". As every neighbourhood, city or region is different, students could better appreciate the need to adopt place-based thinking that reflects on local context and assets to produce a distinctive participatory approach. To help with teaching participation to planning students, the learning from CPiP demonstrated the importance of framing knowledge co-production within a place-based approach when trying to conceptualize and operationalize participatory planning activities. A challenge for many students, whether in the planning discipline or across other disciplines, is arguably not the acquisition of knowledge, but the synthesis of knowledge emerging from different sources. Therefore, during CPiP, academic staff and students grappled with ways in which to work with such complexity, given the range of diverse knowledge and views across different actors that typically emerge in participatory exercises. To support students in this endeavour, CPiP academics generated a knowledge co-production schema that would allow students to better appreciate the segments of knowledge co-production and to provide them with an analytical tool for organizing ideas/information (Figure 8.2).

This conceptual framework helped students to organize and visualize various stages associated with knowledge co-production that would guide them in navigating through complex participatory exercises dealing with

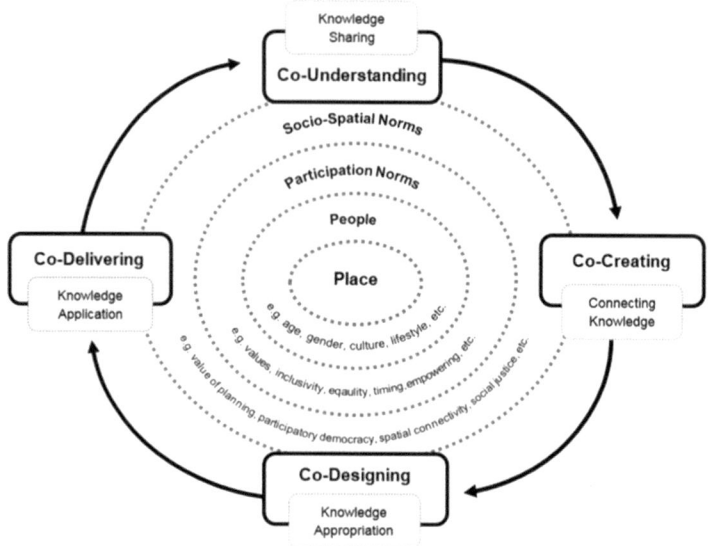

Figure 8.2   *Conceptualizing knowledge co-production in participatory
               planning exercises*

multiple 'voices' and knowledge. In addition, this model allowed students
to consider various factors, or norms, influencing participatory practices that
may differ from place to place. CPiP's multi-context pedagogy, and the complexities revealed in real time, provided a unique backdrop and opportunity for
producing this conceptual framework that supported students in their learning
– and hopefully their future practice – to proactively engage, and grapple,
with knowledge co-production in participatory planning exercises. Based on
CPiP's cross-sectoral and transnational learning, participatory practices for
knowledge co-production follow four stages:

1. *Co-Understanding (using Knowledge Sharing)*: better appreciation of
    place dynamics, characteristics, assets and perceptions by participants
    sharing knowledge and nurturing reciprocity.
2. *Co-Creating (by Connecting Knowledge)*: the opportunity to connect
    pre-existing tacit knowledge through participation, with actors working
    together, spanning professional and sectoral boundaries, to generate
    shared explicit knowledge.

3. *Co-Designing (from Knowledge Appropriation)*: using external knowledge to produce mutually beneficial interventions and outcomes, perhaps in the form of a vision, plan, strategy, etc., that are co-designed, and which embed a sense of shared ownership.
4. *Co-Delivering (through Knowledge Application)*: utilizing the newly generated explicit knowledge to implement a co-designed vision/approach and actively work towards achieving outcomes to transform place, capitalizing on trust, respect and commitment engendered through co-productive participation. Delivering co-produced places also produces new (internalized and externalized) knowledge through a complex and collaborative learning experience.

Framing knowledge co-production this way offered a pedagogy that moved beyond didactic teaching styles of describing participatory approaches to planning students towards experimental ways of exposing students to the potential opportunities and complexities of real-world co-production in participatory planning through action learning.

CONCLUSION

The pedagogical approach established through CPiP demonstrates, and reaffirms, the important civic dimension to planning education, which supports universities in achieving their expanding 'third mission' contributions. Given the disciplinary expansion and the contextual conceptions of planning, students are frequently exposed to problem-based teaching, learning and assessment on real-world dilemmas and complexities, which tend to be geographically near to their university. This pedagogical approach has been, and continues to be, central to many planning academics. However, the significant advantage offered through CPiP was expanding the teaching and learning environments beyond the immediate local geographies of the university campus, responding to the argument that graduates need to appreciate how planning is context-dependent and socially constructed (Rooij and Frank 2016). In doing so, it provided academics and students with a broader contextualization and conceptualization of real-world participatory planning challenges, offering staff the opportunity to design transformative pedagogies that exposed students to dilemmas and uncertainties (Barnett 2004, cited in Rooij and Frank 2016) and the multiplicity of activities and interests across different European planning contexts.

Like the planning academy, universities are now re-engaging with wider society to contemplate their social impact. There is an increasing emphasis now placed on the third mission of contemporary universities – civic engagement – complementing and enriching teaching and research functions

(Pinheiro et al. 2015). Planning, with its applied nature, can combine teaching and research with civic engagement/impact. For CPiP academics, teaching students about how stakeholders can participate in planning processes should not be considered at a purely theoretical level. Specifically referring to urban/ spatial planning disciplines, the CPiP experience demonstrates that scientific research, teaching and social engagement should no longer be considered as three independent arenas. Rather, teaching and research should be embedded within the social engagement dimension (Figure 8.3). Therefore, planning education, with appropriate pedagogical design, can provide universities with ways to make genuine connections between teaching, research and social engagement for civic impact. The knowledge institutions involved in CPiP all played a strategic role in steering urban visions, engagement strategies, community creation, interaction and empowerment, which enriched the collaboration between academia and communities. In this respect, CPiP represented expressions of the 'engaged university', which is an important aspect of contemporary higher education. For example, Ulster University has recently articulated 'civic contribution' to be at the heart of its new strategic vision (Ulster University 2016), encouraging academics to consider their capacity to enhance social and economic development. In Milan, not only the CPiP experience followed this direction, but, like Ulster University, Politecnico di Milano has initiated civic-orientated instruments and programmes, e.g., *PoliSocial*,[4] a programme for applying and building university knowledge and excellence through engagement and social responsibility, and *Mapping San Siro*,[5] a research-action project of Politecnico di Milano's Department of Architecture and Urban Studies exploring forms of production of scientific knowledge as a tool for dialogue.

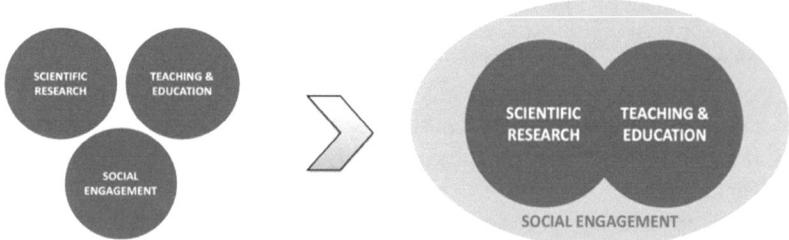

Figure 8.3   Embedding teaching and research in social environment

Similarly, in Aveiro, the University has been engaging with new ways of collaborating with regional and local entities and communities, that go far beyond traditional assistance or consultancy work. The pioneering work of developing a joint policy design process to frame a regional development programme, involving eleven municipalities in the region, illustrates the ways in which multidisciplinary academic knowledge and competencies can be mobilized to create a shared understanding of regional development dynamics and challenges amongst stakeholders. This is ultimately a knowledge empowering and capacity building process that enables re-interpretation of communities' own situation, needs and prospects.

Working as university teams in real-world situations can be challenging, especially given the time-bound nature of university semesters and scarce resources available, as well as the balance that should be pursued between the engagement of local communities and the expectations/results of such work. The limited time available during a university semester is also a clear restriction to create a successful 'learning *in* action' experience for actors involved that truly embeds 'co-design' and 'co-production'. Potential barriers could arise when 'plugging-in' real-world processes that are not mature enough, or when they are already institutionalized. In the first case, the interaction of the students and knowledge institutions with real-world processes might be relatively difficult to create and sustain. Such interaction needs to be triggered, and space for innovation needs to be nurtured, which might not be an easy task during a university semester. In the second case, the space available for action may also be restricted, with existing (institutional/conventional) structures possibly becoming barriers for stimulating fresh thinking or innovative actions. As demonstrated in CPiP, when a hybrid situation was created, the teaching and learning pedagogy tended to be more successful in strengthening the collaborations and relationships between the students, knowledge institutions and local communities.

It may be possible to co-design multi-contextual learning opportunities across modules in multiple academic institutions. The added value of CPiP – in financing study exchanges – was to sustain longitudinal context-based action learning environments equipping future planners with the knowledge and skills necessary for broaching uncertainty and complexity when undertaking citizenry participation in planning. Even without financed study exchanges, the collaborative exchanges between academics, via conferences and online professional networks, offer opportunities for them to co-create learning curricula that simultaneously embed real-world exchanges across different contexts into modules at multiple institutions. Perhaps not sustainable for long periods, as curricula or collaborations change, but a concerted effort over a shorter time frame can significantly enrich the student learning experience and provide academics with valuable insights for innovating their pedagogy.

Preparing planning students with the skills to add value to, and stimulate transformative action in, real-world environments is core to contemporary planning education. Didactic teaching methods for preparing students to work in the complex, and often 'messy', world of participation is not sufficient anymore. CPiP's pedagogical approach of nurturing exchange and critical reflection across different socio-planning cultures engendered deep discussion and learning around what constitutes (local) knowledge and action, particularly when planners and civic actors engage in participatory exercises. In a world of ever-increasing voices and competing interests, planning students need to benefit from engaging with a diverse range of stakeholders to better consider ways of co-learning new participatory practices, co-producing knowledge through equal and reciprocal relationships and co-designing community engagement and place-making strategies that act as catalysts for improving action and outcomes. (See Box 8.1.)

BOX 8.1   IMPLEMENTATION TIPS

- Early engagement between academic staff to re-design – and co-create – modules and to align similar learning outcomes across different planning degree courses.
- Meaningful and honest discussion with local actors (communities of geography and practice) to agree mutual interests and build a common purpose, particularly in relation to what the module learning (and pedagogy) is trying to achieve and to manage expectations (e.g., what will be produced/the outputs).
- Careful explanation of 'co-creation' and 'co-production', both to students and civic actors, so that a shared understanding is established.
- While financial barriers exist to support actual study exchanges, a substitute would be to integrate virtual exchanges using digital technologies, which would expose students to different contexts and enrich their learning experience.

ACKNOWLEDGEMENTS

The CPiP partners would like to acknowledge the support of European Union funding through the Erasmus+ programme. The insightful and valuable contributions made to teaching and learning through CPiP were only possible by the active involvement of local civic actors, local government staff, university students and supporting academic colleagues in Aveiro, Belfast and Milan.

NOTES

1. In Northern Ireland, the delivery of public services is now coordinated through a process known as 'community planning', introduced through the Local Government Act (NI) 2014, placing a duty on local authorities to initiate, facilitate and maintain community planning in their area, working with statutory partners and local communities to enhance social, economic and environmental well-being.
2. Further information on the *ReLambro* intervention plan is available (in Italian) at http://82.149.33.231/relambro/.
3. Further feedback and reflections from CPiP participants (students, practitioners and academics) are available in an online video, available at https://www.youtube.com/watch?v=1O1a0BZgvpI&feature=youtu.be.
4. http://www.polisocial.polimi.it/it/home/.
5. http://www.mappingsansiro.polimi.it.

REFERENCES

Arnkil, R., Koski, A., Järvensivu, P. and Piirainen, T. (2010) *Exploring Quadruple Helix: Outlining User-Oriented Innovation Models*. Finland: University of Tampere.

Barnett, R. (2004) Learning for an unknown future. *Higher Education Research & Development* 23(3): 247–260.

Boelens, L. and de Roo, G. (2014) Planning of undefined becoming: First encounters of planners beyond the plan. *Planning Theory* 15(1): 42–67.

Cognetti, F. and Castelnuovo, I. (2014) Learning in action. Mapping San Siro: An exploration into city/university collaboration. Paper presented at 2nd Annual AAE Conference 2014 Living and Learning, UK: University of Sheffield. Accessed 18 February 2015 at https://re.public.polimi.it/handle/11311/941359#.WH1LTvmLQ1I.

Concilio, G. and Rizzo, F. (2016) *Human Smart Cities: Rethinking the Interplay between Design and Planning*. Cham: Springer International Publishing.

Escobar, O. (2011) *Public Dialogue and Deliberation: A Communication Perspective for Public Engagement Practitioners*. Edinburgh: UK Beacons for Public Engagement.

Galison, P. (1999) Trading zone: Coordinating action and belief. In M. Biagioli (ed.), *The Science Studies Reader* (pp. 137–160). London: Routledge.

Galison, P. (2010) Trading with the Enemy. In M. E. Gorman (ed.), *Trading Zones and Interactional Expertise: Creating New Kinds of Collaboration* (pp. 25–52). Cambridge, MA: MIT Press.

Kitchen, T. (2007) *Skills for Planning Practice*. Basingstoke: Palgrave Macmillan.

Lang, J. (1983) Teaching planning to city planning students: An argument for the studio/workshop approach. *Journal of Planning Education and Research* 2(2): 122–129.

Mäntysalo, R., Balducci, A. and Kangasoja, J. (2011) Planning as agonistic communication in a trading zone: Re-examining Lindblom's partisan mutual adjustment. *Planning Theory* 10(3): 257–272.

Marsh, J. (2008) Living labs and territorial innovation. In P. Cunningham and M. Cunningham (eds.), *Collaboration and the Knowledge Economy: Issues, Applications, Case Studies*. Amsterdam: IOS Press.

Pinheiro, R., Langa, P. V. and Pausits, A. (2015) The institutionalization of universities' third mission: Introduction to the special issue. *European Journal of Higher Education* 5(3), 227–232.

Ritchie, H., Sheppard, A., Croft, N. and Peel, D. (2017) Planning education: Exchanging approaches to teaching practice-based skills. *Innovations in Education and Teaching International* 54(1): 3–11.

Rooij, R. and Frank, A. (2016) Educating spatial planners for the age of co-creation: The need to risk community, science and practice involvement in planning programmes and curricula. *Planning Practice & Research* 31(5): 473–485.

Schön, D. A. (1983) *The Reflective Practitioner: How Professionals Think in Action*. New York: Basic Books.

Schön, D. A. (1987) *Educating the Reflective Practitioner: Toward a New Design for Teaching and Learning in the Professions*. San Francisco, CA: Jossey-Bass.

Ulster University (2016) *Five & Fifty: Five Year Strategic Plan; Fiftieth Year Strategic Vision 2016 –2034*. Accessed 7 March 2018 at https://www.ulster.ac.uk/fiveandfifty/strategicplan.pdf.

Wells, G. (1999) *Dialogic Inquiry: Towards a Sociocultural Practice and Theory of Education*. New York: Cambridge University Press.

Additional Resources

CPiP materials from the Erasmus+ Project Results Platform are available at https://ec.europa.eu/programmes/erasmus-plus/projects/eplus-project-details/#project/2014-1-UK01-KA200-001803.

CPiP – Learning Report is available at https://ec.europa.eu/programmes/erasmus-plus/project-result-content/40ad1202-862c-4ce2-830a-b89a8e0beebc/CPiP%20Learning%20Report.pdf.

CPiP – Participatory Skills Framework is available at https://ec.europa.eu/programmes/erasmus-plus/project-result-content/8cca1880-da5f-4067-91f0-b53c350c2780/CPiP%20Participatory%20Skills%20Framework.pdf.

A video produced to capture the learning and reflections from the CPiP project is available at https://www.youtube.com/watch?v=1O1a0BZgvpI&feature=youtu.be.

PART III

Developing new classroom-based competencies

9. Urban design studio as a critical learning space within the architecture curriculum: the evolving pedagogical approach to "PROJECTO 5"

Teresa Calix

INTRODUCTION

The course *Projecto 5* is the last of five design studios for students of the University of Porto's Integrated Master's in Architecture[1] (IMArc) though the first really focusing on urban issues. Although the city and urban spaces always frame architectural design exercises throughout the IMArc, multi-scale practice that reflects on urban issues and on the collective space system is only worked on as a critical dimension of design in the final year. The *Projecto 5* studio represents a learning space which is particularly concerned with the interaction between urban actors, forms of citizenship and common life. Hence, the theoretical knowledge acquired previously in different courses of the IMArc, essential for a more comprehensive understanding of the present-day urban condition, is only effectively applied within a practical framework and instantiated in this studio.

The practical urban experience presented as an academic exercise to the students becomes a platform for experiencing and building awareness of the critical issues and future challenges related to contemporary urban environments. Topics like planning uncertainty, urban management complexity, the crucial importance of the economic conditions in setting priorities for intervention (measuring effects in order to select and reject intervention options) and the social and political instability that determine the difficulties in establishing consensus, are addressed within the scope of Portuguese urban culture, where it has always been easier to seize opportunities to make projects than to implement plans for the future.

Projecto 5 differs significantly from the traditional studio at the Faculty of Architecture at the University of Porto (FAUP) which focuses on architectural design – giving particular attention to spatial relationships and correctness of form, shape, shade and light, architectural language, materials and local context as promoted by Álvaro Siza and Eduardo Souto de Moura's oeuvre. Instead, it represents an alternative learning space, challenging students with a different view in their final steps to complete the Master's course and enter the professional world. The exercise proposed to the students requires a new mind-set and an approach that they have not experienced before. Starting with a previously selected area of relevant complexity, they are expected to learn how to discuss the diversity of urban topics, to interrelate, integrate and experiment with them, considering different urban actors and their specific agendas, without a previously suggested functional programme, directions or instructions of any kind.

The exercise recognizes that to complete their knowledge on architecture and urbanism, within the main issues related to urban areas, it is essential to consider a different methodological framework of learning by doing, which also implies reflecting on the site and transformation expectations before starting to carry out 'design tasks' from a pre-set intervention programme. In a sense, the overall ambition of this course is that "students would grasp that the most elevated purpose of design is to be mankind's way of participating in evolution, using the vast knowledge we have acquired to be guided more by choice than by chance" (Buchanan 2012). This process of design think-ing also recognizes that the scope of architectural intervention is becoming increasingly complex. Present-day reality is highly challenging and requires new kinds of approaches, more comprehensive skills and far-reaching modes of thinking, teaching and communication.

As a critical, although limited, learning space, where ideas raise a very broad range of issues for discussion and design exploration, *Projecto 5* will be explained in the present chapter by considering four topics: (1) *the foun-dational learning concept and the evolving historical context* will address the origins of the design studio; (2) *the current syllabus and its didactics* refer to the current practice; (3) *the new pedagogical practices* highlight pedagogical innovations related to the studio; and (4) *future challenges* which summarizes difficulties and suggestions for implementation.

THE FOUNDATIONAL CONCEPT AND THE EVOLVING HISTORICAL CONTEXT

Projecto 5 was established in the late 1990s by Professor Manuel Fernandes de Sá,[3] seeking to "provide conditions for the development of an in-depth reflection on the issues of city and territory, discussing methods of approach and planning instruments; disseminating a strategic reasoning for intervention; proposing ways of managing the uncertainty underlying intervention in the city; introducing the question of pluri-disciplinarity and practising city design and control of the urban scale" (Sá 2003, pp. 10–11). "From strategy to the project" (Portas 1998) is an essential text for the conception of *Projecto 5*. Portas,[3] recognizing that the expression "Urban Project" is not new since it had "already been used to connote unitary architectural projects of appreciable dimension and complexity" (1998, p. 114), claimed that:

> what distinguishes the present stage is, on the one hand, the importance of strategic programming with the consequent autonomisation of the work programme. On the other hand, it is distinguished by the untimely seizure of opportunities on offer or that the cities themselves provoke and on yet another hand, by the organisational processes or mechanisms set up to involve the different partners upon whom the implementation depends, in the shortest time, of a complex project. And finally, by the bi-unequivocal and not merely hierarchically dependent relationship, that the project tends to establish with the plan, or in other words, what we call a new style of planning or … a new style of project. (1998, p. 115)

Conceived as an interactive process, linking theoretical knowledge and practice, *Projecto 5* creates an ambivalent learning experience: on one hand, the exercise to be developed must go beyond a formalist view of the urban question enabling in-depth understanding of the territory and providing a professional approach that supports intervention in the city; on the other hand, it must complete the training of future architects in terms of planning,[4] allowing and enhancing their capacity to intervene – both by defining the overall strategy or programme to implement in different stages and by designing the shape of particular actions – and, therefore, to bring architecture into the field of planning (Sá 2003, p. 4). This education for planning within an architecture programme hopes, indeed, to contribute to the training of urbanists with a more comprehensive and broader view.

Situated in the overlapping space of plan, process and project areas of influence, *Projecto 5* also hopes to contradict a recurring practice in architectural education in which:

> Problems in the design studio generally start with the abandonment of carefully formulated briefs which are replaced by fancifully elaborated scenarios – a tactic that severs contact with any reality which is dismissed as too mundane and demeaning to stimulate students' creativity and teachers' attention (some of whom seem unable to master and keep up with that reality). Yet if undertaken with sensitivity and skill, and with imagination fuelled by insight into reality rather than flight from it, the formulation of a convincingly apt narrative or conceptual image can be a potent design aid. Indeed, something of this sort has always underpinned the best architecture. (Buchanan 1989, para. 10)

So, although taking place after a four-year curriculum that heavily emphasizes morphological aspects of architecture, *Projecto 5* expects to broaden the range of issues raised and discussed within the proposed assignment. Students will need to synthesize issues within a fully developed urban design that considers multiple scale proposals, various stages of development and ultimately seeks to deepen students' understanding on urban reality. For the above reasons, within the scope of *Projecto 5* the 'Urban Project' is considered the learning and design framework par excellence. It provides the link between urban planning and architectural design, both from the point of view of public space design as well as the complex design–process–plan interaction. This must consider the dynamics of the society – taking into account, but not limited to, the demands of the urban actors formulated in a given moment – and the complexity of contemporary reality – short-term actions and long-term effects. These conditions reflect, therefore, that certainties and uncertainties are indispensable conditions to be addressed in each proposal envisaged or materialized.

In the time between the conception of *Projecto 5* (about 20 years ago) and the present, the world and didactics have evolved. For example, curricula and syllabus were transformed as a result of the changes in the surrounding educational environment. In the case of FAUP the architecture degree consisted previously of a six-year Bachelor's degree and is now a five-year Master's degree. These changes resulted from adaptations to implement the Bologna Agreement and the three-cycle system of Higher Education in Europe. The loss of one year led to a significant reduction of compulsory subjects in the area of Urbanism and related social sciences which in turn inadvertently reduced students' awareness of urban and social issues such as the successive transmutations of dynamic territorial realities arising from contemporary fluidity and instability (Bauman 2000; Innerarity 2004) of matters which, in particular, concern the *res publica*.

The risk for architectural education is like before, although in a different global context, that "Instead of the difficult and self-effacing task of establishing real needs and appropriate programme, students tend to be encouraged to elaborate the most fanciful even farcical scenarios as impetus to design." Furthermore, and emphasizing this tightening of educational complexity, on the contrary to current reality, "it is surprising how few schools teach urban design – and of those that do, how narrow and particular is their approach and how much very relevant twentieth-century [and twenty first century, could one add] thinking on the subject they tend to ignore" (Buchanan 1989, para. 7).

So, in addition to addressing the absences of subjects in the IMArc curriculum, *Projecto 5* didactics were also modified in order to consider the changes brought about by the increasing number of new territorial processes and societal changes related to economic globalization and all its different forms of physical materialization in Portugal at the turn of the millennium.

At the time when *Projecto 5* was defined, the urban growth cycle that started in the 1970s had increased considerably, related to two important yet linked political circumstances: the implementation of democracy[5] followed by integration within the European Economic Community[6] and the resulting funding available. Together they made it possible to implement the Portuguese demo-cratic welfare state, compelling the state to invest in public infrastructures and facilities, while the production of new housing was mainly in the hands of the private real estate sector. The circumstances demanded state responsibility for drawing up plans and regulations, for supervising private initiatives and guar-anteeing the availability and the adequate performance of public services. In the 1990s, the prevailing logics were those related to a seemingly unstoppable growth, mainly private but accompanied by strong public investment in public structures and facilities (buildings and networks) that were to be at the disposal of the majority of the population, ensuring the development of the country, responding to local needs and seeking to reduce existing inequalities.

During this time Portuguese Architecture and Urbanism as academic dis-ciplines and professional fields experienced a positive change in their impor-tance, visibility, demands and complexity of assignments (architectural and urban projects), in the plurality of clients and in the diversity and sophistication of programmes. While the period was characterized by state investment, both in planning and in providing infrastructures and public services, the decision to build and the choice of housing and business locations were mainly driven by market requirements and individual preferences. However, this era of cumulative improvements came to an end in the mid-2000s, changing the means available, expectations, and, of course, calling into question known intervention paradigms. The established, and well-known, planning tools and logic of investment which sought to address scenarios of urban intensity, density and expansion, ceased to make sense and continue to fail to the present day. What seems certain is that the logic of intervention based on growth and almost exclusively depending on the leverage of areas positively influenced by the dynamics of intensification as it was in the past can no longer suffice.

Therefore, *Projecto 5* is expected to present a pedagogical process and a space for critical reflection on the newer and greater uncertainties that concern spatial development and change and its actors. The course must reflect on various scales and behaviour and their convergence on certain subjects or conflicting values; discussing new methods and tools for approaching this, underlying a strategic reasoning of intervention, which, in many circum-stances, may require highly selective tactics concerning the investments to be made on the basis of their potential future effects.

This learning experience is to enhance students' capacities to understand the different facets and multiple layers that constitute the complexity of contem-porary reality as well as to intervene in a continuously changing environment, filling the absences of previous learning spaces and the limited discussion on relevant urban subjects, understood in a comprehensive, integrated and eminently practical perspective. It also ensures that the IMArc students will be able to develop new skills of observation and interpretation of a broader reality and to operationalize a complex territorial entity, recognizing the scales, processes, times and also the (not so well known) values of the present and the future options that lie within this.

THE CURRENT SYLLABUS AND ITS DIDACTICS

Projecto 5 is understood as a laboratory and represents a platform for experimenting with the problems associated with practice and the recognition of urban issues and interventions in contemporary urbanization. The long-term exercise proposed in *Projecto 5*, situated between the plan and the project, presupposes questioning and recognizing the themes and the materials underlying an approach that takes place within the scope of the Urban Project.

In practical terms, a cohort consisting of approximately 80 to 100 students is divided into groups (of three to five students each) and presented with a complex urban territory without well-defined boundaries (just pointing out an area to start the debate) or a previously defined programme. Students are challenged to study it, understand it and define the best possible programme, considering the political and social agenda and a short- or medium-term time frame. The syllabus considers four phases linking the development of the exercise with complementary practical and theoretical initiatives (see Figure 9.1).

The **first phase**, running for six weeks (see Figure 9.1), is the 'prospective characterization'. Based on careful observation and a thorough selection of issues encountered in the territory, the 'prospective characterization' establishes the basis for an intervention strategy: the operationalization of a prospective vision, capable of establishing ways to improving urban identity and image, of anticipating upcoming changes and anticipating potential destinations. The label 'prospective characterization' contains its meaning within itself. It means project but also analysis, since 'prospective' allows us to see ahead or to anticipate the future while 'characterization' distinguishes features but also highlights the character or the characteristics of what is being observed. So, one could say that prospective characterization is intentional, grounded in arguments and must be substantiated. However, it is not holistic, does not reproduce reality but interprets. For this reason, it is important that the students are aware that the prospective characterization, although useful and necessary to move forward, is poorer, reductive and less diverse when seen in comparison to the complexity of reality.

In order to operationalize this phase, students are urged to recognize the methods and instruments available to survey, examine, identify, decipher, dissect, or dissociate evidence empirically collected or found in maps, charts, photos, plans, statistical data, studies and so on. While this process of data collecting takes place, the keys to apprehend reality and the observation matrix arise along with the definition of measures and appropriate scales, and the selection of indicators and values considered important to register. Additionally, while classifying, typifying, categorizing issues and urban materials, students also learn to establish different forms of association. These serve to represent particular interpretations of the territory, to register or describe a perspective, highlighting the value of particular links, networks or systems.

The interpretations must integrate some properties from reality, such as the diversity of values, complexity, dynamic qualities, multiple layers, multiple scales, and trends in order to avoid misunderstandings. They also have to consider a systemic perspective that reinforces and qualifies the internal and external connections, the material and immaterial dimensions, guaranteeing the interrelationship and cohesion of the different actions, considering the social and institutional context and considering the structuring role of certain physical elements as well as the determining value of their relative position. In short, it is expected that the students understand the different issues at stake; that they recognize what is important to characterize. Through asking questions – such as What to choose? How to justify the choice? or On what does the choice depend? – they start to set up possible areas of reasoning and grounding decisions. This process of thinking deals with diverse and sometimes conflicting interests, ranging from knowledge, experience, ethics, to ideology, principles, models, values, or even time, among others. They are also affected by the requirement of proposing an urban strategy grounded on a vision for the city and, furthermore, the need to seek and produce a collective consensus. The underlying principles of urban qualification – and for that reason the exercise proposed to students – demand the definition of a consistent, reasonable and well-informed point of view on the territorial reality.

In the **second phase**, running for six to seven weeks (see Figure 9.1), the growing awareness of the students will lead to the definition of a systemic vision and the proposal of an intervention strategy – that will define the main goals and will support several related proposals, which together contribute to determining the programmatic options recommended for implementation. The conceptual arguments and design solutions resulting from these two interacting phases – the prospective characterization and the elaboration of the strategy – debated and built within groups of students, ensure that the overall proposal of each group represents a collectively discussed vision or hypothesis (to test) of a transformation for a particular territorial context, which results from the synthesis of the cross-disciplinary research carried out and considers heuristic validation initiatives. The programmatic options to implement and the definition of intervention limits are based on the aforementioned strategic reasoning and on the designation, within the group, of more restricted areas of intervention, which are recognized as priority areas for the implementation of the previously drawn up urban concept.

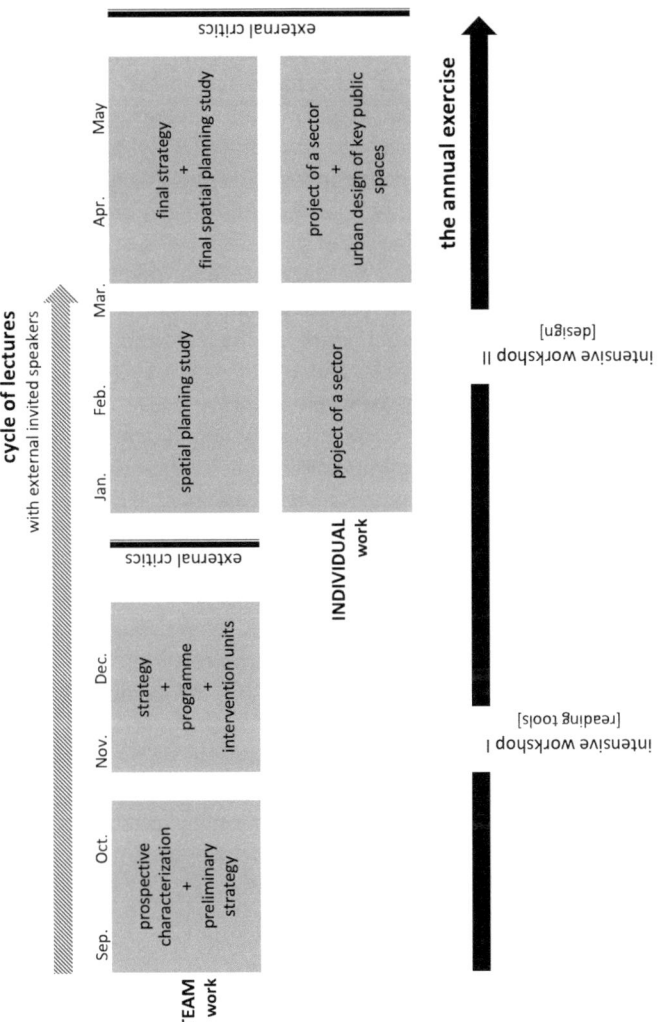

Figure 9.1   Syllabus schedule

Following the completion of these two phases each student will individually develop a particular urban sector with key public spaces – as part of the **third, and fourth phase** (each again six to seven weeks long, see Figure 9.1) – approaching scales of morphological concretization and the technical language of their materialization. Ultimately, all the proposals have to be formulated in the conceptual frame previously explained, ensuring the further development of the intervention programme; however, if, throughout this process, grounds for amendments arise, they should be negotiated within the group, and if needed lead to requisite adjustments in the overall strategy. The strategic approach – by establishing the ideal and the principles of urban transformation and by considering a systemic perspective that strengthens and qualifies internal and external links – will ensure the interrelationship and cohesion of the different initiatives and transformative actions.

Throughout the four different phases, the Urban Project, understood as the framework for experimentation and also as a research process, presents a set of specific curricular requirements that guarantee, on the one hand, the construction of a holistic and operative standpoint and, on the other hand, the acknowledgement of the complex interplay between different issues and technical contents. It is up to the teacher to encourage careful and in-depth observation and interpretation of the explicit and implicit dimensions that are involved in the different processes that materialize in the area and above all contribute to increasing the students' critical capacity to observe, interpret and formulate proposals. In this process, it is essential to raise awareness of the three degrees of abstraction and simplification that are decisive to move forward: (1) empirical observation, (2) recognition of types and rules, and (3) singularities and dissonances, and the integration of strategies and project solutions – without completely forgetting the complexity of the multi-layered territory that is the focus of the studio.

Student work is assessed at the end of each phase; assessment considers the performance of each student individually as well as their contribution to teamwork. The final mark will result from the weighting of the various evaluations and of the progress that the student made on their development path.

NEW PEDAGOGICAL PRACTICES

Supporting Multi- and Trans-disciplinarity

Complexity implies the need to bring together complementary subjects such as Geography, Sociology, Engineering, Economics, Law, and Landscape Architecture, among others. It highlights, above all, the importance of these different subjects – and, in particular, their common intersecting and overlapping issues – to the reasoning of future architects. Consequently, it is essential that various specialists are involved in the design studio to speak to different topics and presenting different perspectives on the same issues. Likewise, it is also considered important to invite local politicians or stakeholders to share their views, to explain the challenges they face and the ways they envisage how to respond to them. The theoretical knowledge and the expertise in technical issues, of the former, and the political or business ideals, of the latter, help students to understand multiple aspects of reality and take positions through design.

By including 'specialists' and stakeholders in the learning process, two complementary pedagogical objectives are addressed. First, it allows students to be sensitized to a diversity of topics that interfere with contemporary reality, even if they do not manage to master them as a whole. Second, it enables different positions, opposing arguments, to be presented, forcing the students to make decisions and sometimes take sides through an informed and reasoned process which will guide them towards the elaboration of their proposal(s) and which they have to substantiate. Evidence of complexity will approach real-world conditions, broadening the recognition of challenging issues that have to be considered in the near future, as they face the reality of their profession.

The individuals to invite are an outcome of the selection of particular subjects or methods and are based on the requests made by students to deepen research in the territory under study. This pedagogical approach has given rise to a set of classes that complement the design studio by bringing in various external professionals. Moreover, these classes are opened to the entire academic community to maximize debate and benefit.

Supporting Communication Skills

It is also essential to promote student competencies regarding the graphical representation of a dynamically synthesized process in its different scales, objectives and scopes. The language of the project fosters the use of different types of drawing and communication materials – such as diagrams, perspectives, or sketches. These, in addition to the more common (and better known) technical architectural drawings, made by hand or computer-aided design systems – that are fundamental to the narrative of the project, instantiate a kind of storytelling as both a research, design and communication tool.

General storytelling techniques are presented as a means of reasoning and for sharing results. By offering a more persuasive and effective way of delivering information than that of using only technical 'dry' images, this 'tool' is an important way of presenting arguments and persuading others, enforcing essential competencies for the future role of the architect as mediator or facilitator. In order to stress this approach and the importance of communication, students have to present their project at the end of each phase to their colleagues and teachers. At the end of the second and the fourth (last) phase, these presentations – of 10 to 15 minutes – include in addition the presence of technical or political members of the municipality concerned and other specialists. The interactions with external critics emphasize the importance of communication skills since the guests have no knowledge of either the proposals or their evolution and react according to what is presented to them. The choice of design materials, schemes or maps to be shown and rhetoric are fundamental to guarantee that the essential content is presented well and offers a clear understanding of the project.

Supporting the Development of Community Engagement Skills

Beyond the long-term exercise, but still within the scope of the curricular unit, complementary activities involving intensive workshops are organized. These workshops are available to all students enrolled in the course, and, although participation is not mandatory, it is strongly advised. For those who participate, the workshop evaluation adds an extra contribution to the final assessment. These workshops, which temporarily suspend the *Projecto 5*'s exercise, are organized in partnership with a municipality different from the one in which the annual exercise is being developed. Workshops are timed strategically and consider what can be gained in methodological terms for the long-term exercise. Typically, workshops that take place in the first semester, are to focus on characterization tools and workshops in the second semester focus on concrete design solutions. At least the intensive workshop in the second semester always takes place, because it is easier to find a partner institution interested in the exercise that allows students to achieve the pedagogical objectives of this activity.

Within the workshop framework, students are challenged to carry out in just one week of intensive work the design of a set of concrete public spaces and solving related challenges selected by the municipality. Ensuring the collaboration of local government and local institutions, and being noticed by citizens and collective entities, these initiatives have sought to facilitate a specific practical experience which is close to the actors who are transforming the territory and their demands and needs. The experience is therefore relevant and stimulating for the future architects who feel closer to real problems. Feedback on these workshop activities is quite good since students feel that the work they produce effectively matters and the debate it provides is really important for locals and local institutions. These more socially sensitive initiatives also contribute to questioning students' disciplinary stances resulting from the 'architecturally shaped' education making some of the issues related to the architect's social responsibility even clearer.

Pedagogically speaking, these short workshop activities in an area different from the territory of the main exercise allow students to experiment with approaches and ideas (for data collection, public participation or design) that respond to a more acute challenge, testing them for later integration in the development of the main exercise and task. They can return with more skills, different tools and perspectives to the long-term exercise. What is more, within the scope of design skills, students can discuss innovative solutions for different urban spaces, materializing concrete actions by addressing smaller areas and different scales of resolution. The knowledge obtained through experimentation during a very short period of time requiring a clear, tangible and immediate answer is then applied to the scope of the exercise of longer duration. In addition, these initiatives help students to keep mobilized and interested in the one year-long project.

FUTURE CHALLENGES

Although the foundation of this course was developed some 20 years ago, it has only quite recently emerged that both the opportunities and the visibility of the relationship between university, local institutions and society have been intensified and extended.

The resilience and dynamic syllabus of the course allows for the continuous adaptation to emerging challenges. The course is sufficiently flexible to incorporate controversial urban issues as well as embrace the unceasing renewal of ideological principles and criteria that inform strategic and design options and determine the students' response.

The ability to relate to transformation and disruption, in a world that is undoubtedly changing at a breath-taking pace, is the main reason that it can be asserted that *Projecto 5* promotes an innovative learning environment. Moreover, the interactions it establishes with the actors in the territory and the reflection that students produce regarding this, have given rise to two distinct and important outcomes: students' greater familiarity with the complexity underlying actual urban contexts and with the arguments and challenges commonly recognized and accepted by the decision-makers; and the increased interest of public actors in the students' perspective, even if (or maybe because) it is less constrained than a more realistic professional approach. Indeed, the feedback of partner municipalities has been very positive and others who have become familiar with the experiences previously developed are increasingly interested in collaborating both in the long-term exercise as well as in the intensive workshops.

These results are to some extent small steps towards a broader strategy that seeks to reshape the role of universities, and especially the mission of the school of architecture, enhancing its relationship with society, by disseminating and applying knowledge which is not only theoretical but also obtained through practical experimentation. By aspiring to this proximity to the territory and its community, the university also guarantees the ability and willingness of future professionals to identify and work with values (intellectual, cultural, environmental, and so on) that can further determine the future development of global society.

The pedagogical framework and its various levels of reflection are based on a long-time learning experience, embodied in the current annual duration of *Projecto 5*. This condition has been maintained until present and it is contrary to the preponderant tendency of higher education programmes exclusively organized into semesters.

Indeed, the development of a multi-scaled Urban Project over the period of an entire academic year allows group work and individual work to alternate and especially enables the interconnection of both spaces of reflection in an interdependent and dialectical process that mimics negotiation procedures in order to achieve the consensus required for a collective vision and decision making while promoting individual design progress.

The long-term also enables the recognition and the taking advantage of the specificities of drawing (as a tool to research or represent) and design (as a concept to be drawn) while understanding the communication process as a synthetical process that should be able to differentiate levels of uncertainty that are embodied in the proposal through their various forms of representation and consider the different times of their realization. By evaluating the certainty and uncertainty of solutions and by relating the former to further development through urban design and the latter to a more diagrammatic representation, students set design priorities, deepening and detailing what is more feasible, according to circumstances, and overcoming the rigidity of morphological or programmatic solutions that can be changed over time or better defined in the future. What students learn most is to explore not just form but the countless forces at work that need to be reorganized and resolved.

For future architects this learning laboratory creates the experience of the ambivalent condition of the architect's profession: on the one hand, the responsibility to participate in the public definition (the common good) of the conditions of action of private actors (individual interests); and on the other hand, the conscious action of designing in the public's service, considering principles and rules that are beneficial and shared by a given community and which in this way bind society. Thus, it is hoped that *Projecto 5* ensures a critical learning space that contributes to the ability of Architecture (and architects) to positively address the problems of contemporary urban territories. (See Box 9.1.)

BOX 9.1 POTENTIAL DIFFICULTIES AND IMPLEMENTATION TIPS

Setting up a long-term exercise

Due to the need of a significant time input by students, it is highly advisable to deliver the exercise over two semesters. This also allows students to experience the area in different seasons/conditions and enables relationship building with local institutions. To ensure long-term buy-in, domestic students receive credit only if they complete both semesters. Stimulating activities (such as the intensive workshops; expert lectures etc.) may be introduced to sustain the momentum of the project. While foreign exchange students can add value (see below) they may be able to attend only one semester and care needs to be taken that their partial involvement does not impact negatively on other learners.

Establishing relations with the institutions in the field

It is essential to work with local organizations that have a real interest in local territory and are interested in interacting with students. Although other institutions or organizations can take part in the process, municipalities are considered as main partners. It is important to meet with their representatives before the beginning of the academic year to agree on the intervention area, main challenges to address, deliverables, and schedules to engage with students.

Bringing experts to the classroom

It is important to connect students with real-world experts and complementary disciplines that might increase the levels of knowledge about the territorial reality they are dealing with. This was a successful approach used in our context to secure availability of professionals and practitioners with particular topic expertise already before the beginning of the academic year in anticipation of the needs that might arise as the exercise progresses.

Ensuring effective teamworking

Working in teams can be rewarding but also challenging. Thus, it is vital to clarify at the start that special emphasis will be placed on the contribution of each student to group work. Reinforcement of this message, enhancing collaborative working and decreasing potential tensions can be facilitated via weekly meetings with the whole group of students to discuss both team and individual work.

International students

It is essential to encourage discussions arising from different cultures and visions of the territory. For this reason, we suggest that international exchange students are integrated in teams – even if they only can participate for one of the two semesters. International students can provide valuable external viewpoints and share precedents from elsewhere, while they themselves can gain precious insights into local culture.

NOTES

1. The Integrated Master's in Architecture (IMArc) offered by the Faculty of Architecture of the University of Porto is a five-year Master's degree. It provides access to professional activity and/or the practice of research.
2. Manuel Fernandes de Sá (1943–) is an architect. He was a Full Professor at FAUP and the coordinator of the urban design studio.
3. Nuno Portas (1934–) is a widely known architect in Southern Europe and Latin America, with a pedigree in teaching, research and public administration. He was a Full Professor at FAUP responsible for the theoretical courses in urbanism.
4. In Portugal there is no urban planning degree at this moment, although it existed in the recent past for a short period of time. Thus, most Portuguese urbanists have a degree in Architecture or Civil Engineering.
5. After 48 years of dictatorship, democracy was restored in 1974; the Carnation Revolution started as a military coup but was soon linked to an unanticipated and popular campaign of civil resistance.
6. Portugal joined the European Economic Community in 1986.

REFERENCES

Bauman, Z. (2000) *Liquid Modernity*. Cambridge: Polity Press.
Buchanan, P. (1989) What's wrong with architectural education? Almost everything. [Electronic version]. *The Architectural Review* 19(5). https://www.architectural -review.com/today/1989-july-whats-wrong-with-architectural-education-almost -everything/8637977.article.
Buchanan, P. (2012) The big rethink part 9: Rethinking architectural education [Electronic version]. *The Architectural Review* 232(1388). https://www.architectural -review.com/essays/campaigns/the-big-rethink/the-big-rethink-part-9-rethinking -architectural-education/8636035.article.
Innerarity, D. (2004) *A Sociedade Invisível*. Lisbon: Editorial Teorema.
Portas, N. (1998) From the strategy to the project. In A. V. Milheiro and J. Afonso (eds.), *Nuno Portas, Prémio Sir Patrick Abercrombie UIA 2005*. Lisbon: Ordem dos Arquitectos.
Sá, M. F. (2003) Programas, conteúdos e métodos | relatório. In M. F. Sá, *Planos operativos de escala intermédia: caracterização técnica e arquitectónica*. Porto: FAUP.

10. Addressing the interplay of design-based disciplines and social sciences in urban development education

Lukas Gilliard, Nadia Alaily-Mattar and Alain Thierstein

INTRODUCTION

Cities continue to exist as administrative entities. However, the normative logic of city boundaries, indeed the very logic of the concept of the city as a definite bounded entity, is at odds with the logic of contemporary urbanism. With growing awareness that the urban extends beyond city limits, and that increasingly problems faced locally can neither be solved at the local city level nor at the national level, the regional scale gained importance towards the end of the last century. Today, polycentric urban regions are a hot research topic in the field of spatial sciences, signalling a shift from territorially embedded to relational conception of space (Harrison 2013). Yet the region is not an autonomous subject or container with neat boundaries.

The studio project presented below focuses on the creative tension between the urban as 'networks of multi-scalar connections' and 'cities as bounded territories'. The idea of the studio is to contemplate the emerging spatial patterns of the urban beyond the category of the city. Within this context of an increasingly relational world amidst the territorial pervasiveness of cities, how do we understand the spatial reality at the crossroads of urban transition, today? And what transformations in spatial organization do we envisage to guide the evolution of urban societies, whose quotidian habitats mess up our overtly neat conceptualizations of space?

Steering the development of relational urban networks requires new approaches that go beyond the established instruments of urban planning. Instruments that are bound to administrative responsibilities and boundaries, which are no longer effective in creating positive momentum for sustainable development. Under these conditions, spatial planners will rarely work alone on projects. The growing complexities demand cooperation with architects, landscape planners, transport engineers, economists or sociologists depending on the task and situation. Today's urban development is co-created (Rooij and Frank 2016). The competencies required to steer development of the urban realm in the 21st century are scattered among various disciplines.

In response, scholars observe that an increasing number of disciplines become concerned with the development of cities and regions. Study programmes that try to prepare graduates for planning and development practice have proliferated over the last decades resulting in a diverse offer of degrees beyond the established undergraduate and postgraduate degrees of spatial planning (Frank et al. 2014; Frank and Kurth 2010; Gilliard and Thierstein 2016). As more and more experts with different disciplinary backgrounds become involved in planning and development processes, new methodologies need to be developed that facilitate working across disciplinary boundaries.

Universities play a key role in equipping graduates with the required competencies, yet thus far, undergraduate and postgraduate programmes usually align with the traditional disciplinary structure of faculties and departments. Students adopt ways of thinking and doing that are specific to their discipline. The deeper students dive into their field of expertise, the more difficult it becomes to bridge between different terminology, methodology and work ethics.

In order for inter- or transdisciplinarity to become the academic paradigm for today's and tomorrow's transformative challenges, universities need to counteract the increasing specialization and compartmentalization in academia by placing greater emphasis on interdisciplinary research and teaching. In the field of urban development, inter- and transdisciplinary teaching requires bringing together students from various spatially relevant disciplines to work collaboratively on projects that are close to practice. Project-based learning environments, such as the design studio, need to become learning platforms that are not only open to design-based programmes but also to students from the social sciences and engineering, to name just two of the most relevant.

The chapter presents a pedagogical approach for an interdisciplinary design studio which tries to prepare students for the complex challenges of steering regional development. Two main ideas feed the planning concept that underlies this course.

First, as planners acknowledge the 'wicked' nature of urban planning problems (Rittel and Webber 1973) in which neither the problem in need of planning nor its solutions can be objectively or unequivocally defined, they are questioning the usefulness, appropriateness and impact power of their current repertoire of spatial planning instruments and tools. They are challenging their accepted wisdoms and are beginning to draw on a post-rational spatial planning discourse. This has left "planning in crisis" as the title of Schönwandt's (2008) book asserts. This pertains to both planning theory and practice. On the theory side, "planning theoreticians are in a state of turmoil. Nothing is accepted; everything is questioned" (Alexander quoted in Schönwandt 2008, p. 19). In terms of planning practice, the threat of insignificance and lack of political relevance looms (Friedmann 1998; Kegel 2006; Kunzmann 2000; Lendi 2008; Schönwandt and Jung 2006; Tschirk 2008), as planning practice continues to be based on an idealized perception of the state's social and technological competence to act tied into a relatively strict and inflexible straitjacket of rules and regulations.

Hence, today's planning 'trouble' (Butler 1990) can be understood as a moment of heightened self-consciousness; a creative crisis in which planners attempt to get organized in the wake of a paradigm shift. This means that the need to plan is not put into question, the need to plan is still acknowledged, rather, the question is how to plan in the context of systems that have fuzzy boundaries (Vester 2012) and "ambiguous causal webs" (Rittel and Webber 1973, p. 167). As planners acknowledge that causes and effects are separated in time and space, they are questioning the usefulness, appropriateness and impact power of their current repertoire of spatial planning instruments and tools.

Second, the practice of planning changes and transformations of spatial environments draws on scientific endeavours, while in itself not being a pure scientific exercise. Rather, spatial planning is a political process that continues to be embedded in existing normative ideals while being informed by spatial experts. Within the controlled laboratory setting of academia, then, the engagement of design disciplines with social and economic sciences and the humanities acquires accentuated importance for developing spatial planning approaches, which manage both the constraints of science and promise of design beyond normative and political restraints.

The chapter assesses the method of trend analysis as a discursive tool for experts from various disciplines. The trend analysis is based upon Vester's (2012) sensitivity model (SM) – a cross-impact analysis that can be conducted without the help of complex modelling. The SM works as a 'boundary object' (Wenger 2000) – a discursive procedure executed by experts from various fields. We hypothesize, that, firstly, the trend analysis helps a heterogeneous group of experts to prioritize different aspects of planning over others, and secondly, helps them to translate analytical findings into impact-oriented interventions.

The remainder of the text is structured into three parts: A general course description provides an overview about the institutional context, the learning objectives, the course structure, and the assessment form. We will then discuss in detail the trend analysis method as the core element of our pedagogy. And lastly, we will reflect upon the value of our approach.

COURSE DESCRIPTION

Institutional Context

The studio is the first semester project of the MSc 'Urbanism – Landscape and City' at the Technical University of Munich (TUM). The programme is open to students from a variety of backgrounds, such as architecture, landscape architecture and planning, town planning, civil engineering, environmental planning, geography and sociology. Applicants for the programme undergo a competitive selection process. Students are expected to have a strong disciplinary foundation in their fields, as well as the interest and open-mindedness to look beyond one's own nose. Students enrolled in the programme are early career individuals. Most students have at least one year of work experience in their associated fields. They have decided to return to the university in order to acquire more knowledge and skills based on their experience in practice, rather than to fulfil qualification requirements.

The Institute of Urban Development designs and supervises, among other tasks, the first year's studio project. The project is worth 12 ECTS points (based on the standardized European Credit Transfer System), which corresponds to 40% of students' weekly workload. In other words, students have two days every week to work exclusively on the design project. Since 2014, 15 to 30 students have joined the course each year to work in four to six groups of three to five students. Due to its placement within the first semester of the two-year curriculum, the project sets the stage for students from various disciplines enrolled in this programme to comprehend the complexity of urban spatial development, and to engage in dialogue and exchange of skills and insights with peers from different disciplines. The learning process is a search for appropriate approaches to address problems caused by such complexity.

Learning Objectives

The main learning objective is to train students to master appropriate skills and knowledge for a newly emerging interdisciplinary urban and regional development practice. Students are asked to adopt a critical stance in respect to the current state of planning while being expected to master the principles and instruments of planning, at the same time.

The development of the learners' capacity also depends on what 'bag' of skills these students bring with them. The challenge in this course is to enable (1) a multi-disciplinary exchange of skills, and (2) the development of interdisciplinary design proposals. Students who are trained in disciplines with a design focus (e.g., architects, and landscape architects) engage with students who come from disciplines with strong analytical focus (e.g., geographers, and sociologists). As a result, both the analytical and design capacities of students are developed.

Beyond the teaching of skills, our goal is to provide students with knowledge on the key principles of 21st century planning and development practice. For us, the following six key principles should guide practice in the future (Wiese et al. 2014): (1) relational definition of space, (2) an inter-scalar perspective, (3) futures thinking, (4) impact orientation, (5) strategic orientation and (6) producing debate-enabling end products. The application of these six principles are the main capacities that the learners develop.

By adopting the relational notion of space, students bridge gaps between the various disciplines concerned with spatial transformation. Doing so enables them to search for 'biological solutions' (Vester 2012), where they are effective rather than forcing solutions within the frontiers of individual fields of expertise or the territorial confines of defined mandates of activity. The inter-scalar perspective is key in this regard. Practically, students zoom into a city quarter when required or consider the nation state as the appropriate scale of analysis in other domains.

The course endorses the fact that "the future cannot be 'predicted' but alternative futures can be 'forecasted' and preferred futures 'envisioned' and 'invented' – continuously" (Sardar 2010, p. 178). Hence, a key capacity that the learners of this course develop is considering several alternative futures rather than one.

Impact orientation means considering the impact of interventions on future developments. Impact can be experienced in the short-, medium- or long-term. More importantly though, is the consideration of impact chains. Future visions should consider interrelated impact chains while simultaneously not becoming too vague. This will force students trained in design disciplines to carefully consider the underlying hypotheses of design proposals. Simultaneously, it encourages the analytically based disciplines to break away from the constraints of analysis and consider the possibilities of design!

Owing to the 'wicked nature' (Rittel and Webber 1973) of planning problems in the urban domain both the goals and the process for achieving them are open for debate. Unlike the military or corporate sector, adopting a strategic orientation in urban planning is not about 'increasing profit' or 'winning the battle', rather it is about selectivity of action and developing a coherent narrative that includes stakeholders and is process- and impact-oriented.

The end products of the application of these key principles provide a much-needed link between plan making and decision-making. The end products are proposals for change. They are debate-enabling end products that serve as consistent story boards, against which public authorities can check the effectiveness and consistency of their decisions.

Structure

For the purpose of the course, each year, we select a different area of transition within the metropolitan area of Munich (German: Europäische Metropolregion München (EMM)) as focus for the design studio project. Over the years, we have worked on various subareas of the EMM (more information: http://www .re.ar.tum.de/lehre/abgeschlossene-projekte/).

The objectives of our studio projects are (1) to identify the key opportunities and threats for sustainable development based on multi-scalar analyses, and (2) to propose possible and desirable functional and spatial futures using a time horizon of 30 years from the present. Towards this objective, it is vital to strategically manage the interplay between metropolitan functionalities and local particularities. This can be done by steering density, land use and mobility patterns of the urban–rural continuum while taking a regional perspective.

The course is organized into lectures, workshops, and studio work. Students work in assigned groups completing three consecutive assignments. Group work is a vital aspect for the success of this project. The exchange of background experience that each student brings, in addition to dialogue and negotiation, pushes the discussion forward and enriches the solutions that each group presents.

The first assignment is dedicated to analysing the focus area; it encompasses (a) physical spatial analyses which all groups carry out, and (b) thematic analyses which cover several interrelated themes, for which each student group is assigned one theme according to its 'expertise'. The findings of these analyses highlight the strengths and weaknesses of the focus area. The idea of the first assignment is not to be all encompassing. Rather the objective is to identify the key issues at stake, and sieve through the particular spatial components of these key issues. At the end of this first part of the course, students are able to organize and innovatively visualize their comprehension of thematic strengths and weaknesses of the area under study, categorize these at different scales, and understand the linkages of different scales of analyses.

In the second assignment, new student groups are formed in such a way that each group is a mix of 'experts' from the preceding assignment. These newly formed groups work together until the end of the semester. The second assignment brings the time dimension to the fore. Urban development is a dynamic process that projects into an unknown future. Users' requirements, tastes, values and lifestyles evolve over time. Population characteristics are dynamic. Demography today is certainly different than the one in the future. The objective of this assignment is to derive evidence-based, possible, and desirable alternative futures for the focus area under investigation. Each group proposes one alternative future set at +30 years. With alternative future, we mean a narrative of future functionalities alongside schematic visualizations of the spatial dimension of this identified future. For the purpose of providing evidence, students are asked to engage in a trend analysis – the core methodological feature of the course.

The third and final assignment is focused on the development and specialization of a selected alternative future concept. By now, the students have identified the key issues for the focus area and have developed a conceptual proposal of an alternative future that addresses these challenges in a desirable manner. The objective of this final assignment is to move from a concept to a spatial development strategy. The challenge in this assignment is to move from ideas conceived in numerical and narrative forms to images, and then from images to plans. This entails thinking of the urban in terms of connections, networks, relationships and mobility, rather than only static land uses.

Assessment

The assessment is based upon three presentations of the student groups, six submitted A1 posters, and eight-page text for a brochure. The students' presentations are key tools with which students are trained to convey their findings and proposals orally. Experts and local stakeholders are invited as guest critics. The presentations are between 15 and 18 minutes. A key learning objective that is being assessed is the ability to communicate complex ideas in a sharp and focused manner. This requires the combining of rhetoric and a diverse set of visuals that draw on classical urban planning graphics such as maps as well as analytical graphics from other disciplines to assist in the delivery of the message. Figures 10.1–10.3, while not readable in detail, provide an impression of the diversity of graphical tools and expressions that emphasise the co-creative interdisciplinarity of the studio.

TREND ANALYSIS

Urban development is a dynamic process that projects into an unknown future. The trend analysis and futures thinking approach is paramount for assignment two and assists students in identifying pertinent levers of control.

The objective of the second assignment is to derive evidence-based, possible and desirable alternative futures for the focus area under investigation. The trend analysis conducted by the students is to help (a) structure the discussion about the future, (b) capture the systemic relations between trends, and (c) uncover information that is implicit in the discussion but not yet visible. With

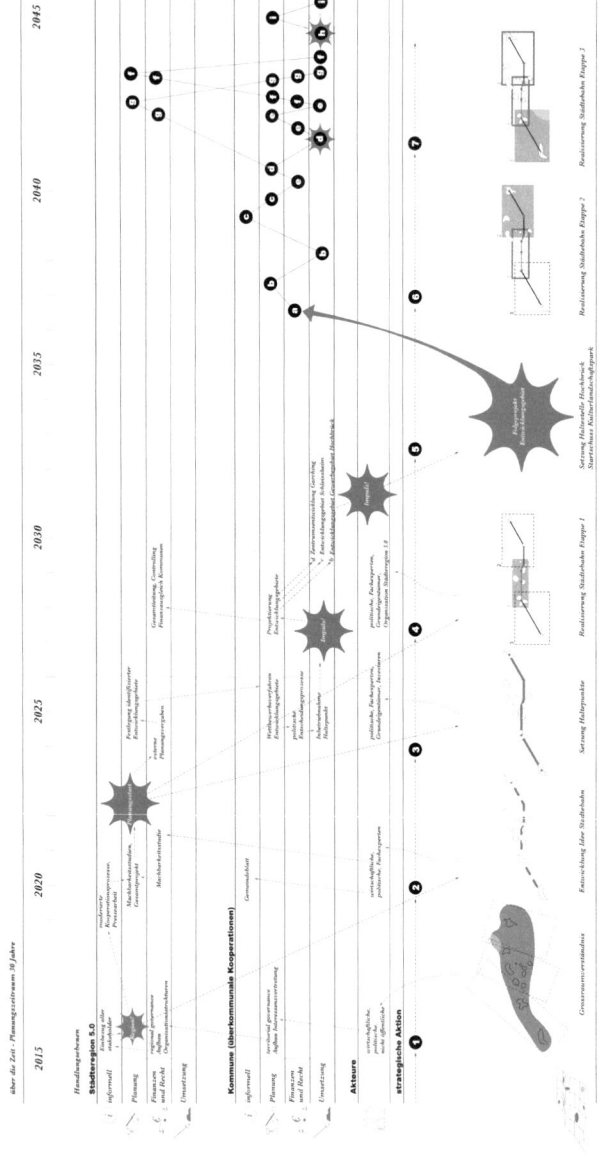

Source: Tobias Häne, Felix Kohler, and Theresia Loy (course during winter term 2014/2015).

Figure 10.1   The process-oriented strategy of the alternative future 'City Region 5.0'

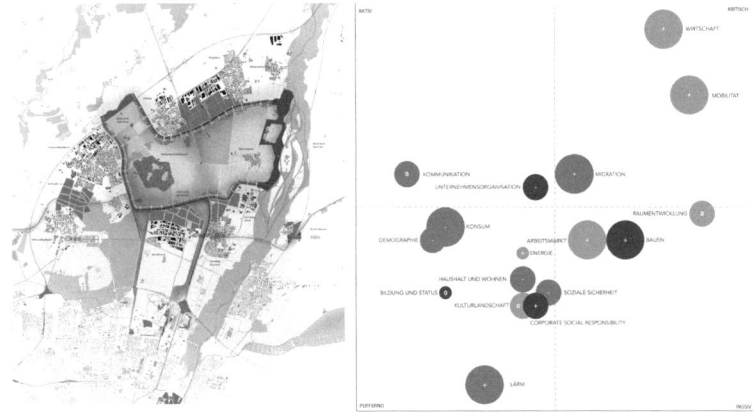

Source: Tobias Häne, Felix Kohler, and Theresia Loy (course during winter term 2014/2015).

*Figure 10.2   The 'Big Plan' mapping (left) and impact analysis (right)
               'City Region 5.0'*

this new understanding, the students are able to synthesize a plausible proposal of a possible and desirable alternative future of the area under investigation.

The trend analysis as a methodological tool connects the problem definition and the problem-solving process. While planners usually think about the future in form of scenarios, we use the term futures in its plural form deliberately. A scenario predicts the development under certain boundary conditions, while alternative futures are educated guesses that are based on connecting the dots between available and intrinsically consistent facts. Vester (2012) calls the latter the art of 'connected thinking'. Due to the fact that cities and regions are complex systems with multiple interdependent variables, we must abandon the idea that science can predict futures. Rather, we believe that well-informed judgments based on trend forecasts are a more suitable way of thinking about the future.

Thinking through several alternative futures rather than one is about testing assumptions and fine-tuning the details during the process. Such an approach is a move away from rational planning models where a government-led agency sets supposedly clear goals based on rigorous analyses and selects proposed interventions based on its presumed ability to achieve those goals. A futures-oriented approach is, rather, a continuous intellectual back and forth that affords room for improvement and acknowledges the necessity of selec-

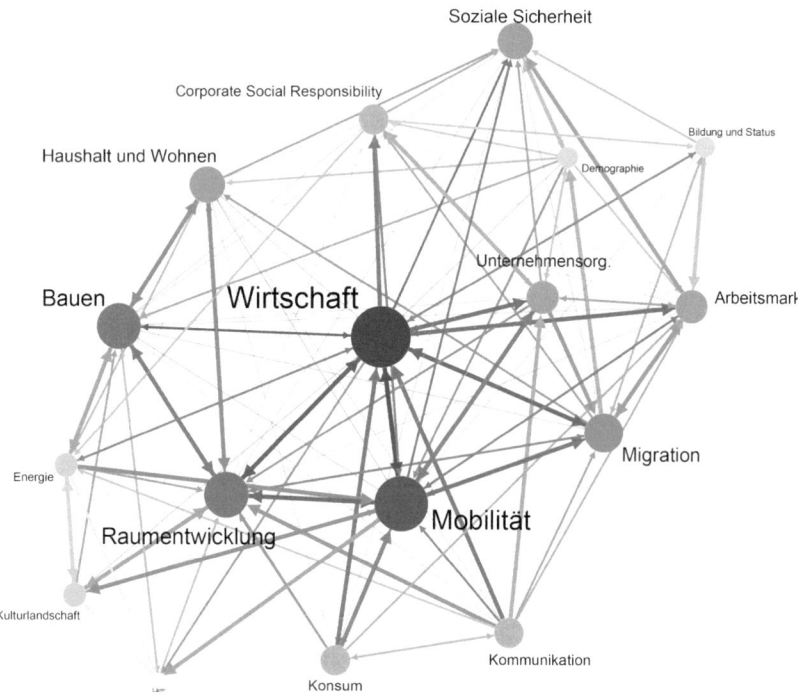

Source: Lucas Schneider Zimmer, Luisa Ehmke and Lukas Ferstl (course during winter term 2017/2018).

Figure 10.3   Visualizations of trends analysis results for the northern district of Munich

tivity in analyses and syntheses. Such an approach can assist in identifying 'the signals amidst the noise' (Silver 2012).

Our trend analysis method is based upon Vester's (2012) sensitivity model (SM). The SM is a form of cross-impact analysis assessing the interrelation of various variables. It is therefore suitable for the analysis of complex urban and regional systems. Various examples of cross-impact analyses in the context of urban development (e.g. Huang et al. 2009; LHM 2016) show intriguing results, but mostly in a non-spatial manner. It is important to keep in mind that the SM is not a 'rationalist' tool for predicting the future. Cross-impact modelling suggests it will provide scientific facts, yet it is indeed limited to the amount of variables that are analysed, largely subjective to assumptions made as part of the modelling process, and in itself not aware of spatial specificities. Thus, we link the systematic analysis of trends and their interrelatedness over a time span of 30 years with regional design thinking. The trend analysis serves as discursive tool allowing students from various disciplines to discuss the interrelation of their perspective on spatial development.

Designing alternative futures for regions becomes plausible due to the transparent process and discourse based on the SM. The identified impacts for regions can be debated and negotiated. Such a process-led perspective has always to bear in mind the contingency of any future. The future, in general, is open – for firms, regions or institutions. The trend analysis enables stakeholders to conceive alternative futures (Alaily-Mattar and Thierstein 2014). Transformation has to be perceived and conceived as an evidence-based creative endeavour.

Execution

Students receive considerable support for the second assignment. Lecturers provide a list of trends. Practically, the list of trends was drawn from a trend report (Ernst-Baseler 2012), which describes various dynamic changes in all areas of society, e.g., demographic, social, environmental, technological, political and economic changes. The quality and especially the timeliness of the trend report is of great importance, because its data are presented as established knowledge. Lecturers also introduce a four-step methodology, alongside instruction of necessary techniques and software skills.

Each student group has to evaluate each trend taking into consideration the trend's local impact direction (positive, neutral or negative), the trend's local dominance (high, medium, low), and the capacity to actively steer the trend on various given territorial scales (municipal, regional, national) (Figure 10.3). The assessment builds on the analytical results of the first assignment and the previous knowledge of the students from their various Bachelor's degrees. In the second step, the student groups identify the opportunities and threats that the area of investigation faces, based on the effects of these trends on the area. Third, using Frederic Vester's model of the paper computer (Vester 2012) the student groups assess the role of these trends within the overall systemic context. A paper computer is basically a matrix that captures the influences of variables on each other. Developed in the 1970s by Vester, it represents a hands-on tool with which one is able to evaluate influences and identify which influences need to be changed in order to achieve a specific result. In the paper computer which we devised for this exercise, the trends are listed on the upper row and left column of the matrix. In each cell of the matrix, the student enters his/her evaluation of the influence of the trend listed in the left column on the trend listed in the upper row. Values ranging between zero and three are entered as values. Zero stands for no influence on each other, three for strong mutual influence.

Students then use this tool to capture their assessment of how strongly the trends influence each other. For example, does the trend 'mobility' have high, medium or no impact on the trend 'regionalism'? Using such a tool is important, because trends are not occurring in isolation, and the students need to understand the systemic context in which trends are operating. The students first fill in the paper computer individually and then crosscheck with the findings of their group. Dissenting assessments are identified and debated until a common evaluation is reached. After filling in the paper computer, and adding the numbers, each student group is able to assess which trends are critical, buffering, active or reactive. Critical trends are those that have a strong effect on and are affected by many other trends. Active trends affect many other trends, reactive trends are affected by many others, and buffering trends do not interrelate much with others at all. In a fourth step, each student group draws a network graphic with the help of the software Gephi that visualizes the interrelations of the trends. The software clusters trends that are more strongly interrelated closer together (Figure 10.3). This formal network analysis of trends enables students to better see and, hence, understand the reciprocal effects of trends.

The laborious trend analysis helps to identify reciprocal effects and the trends that can be actively steered, and to synthesize a plausible development of the future of this area that takes into account the findings of the students' investigations of the future. The trend analysis is a technique that is new to all students. No particular disciplinary group of students claims ownership or expertise. This provides equal grounds for an unbiased discussion. The comprehensive selection of trends further ensures that every relevant topic is discussed, even if students from a particular discipline are more vocal about their concerns.

Implications

The trend analysis is based upon a systemic and relational understanding and shares the benefits and risks of every systemic approach. Systemic thinking helps us to unfold complex interrelations. However, in regard to dynamic spatial development processes, systemic models are often criticized as too simplistic as they usually do not consider the role of space adequately and are limited by the use of static variables. We try to address these issues by using trends – analytical descriptions of change instead of condition – and by accompanying the trend analysis with continuous mapping exercises. By preparing analytical results as spatial trends, the students successfully translate analytical results into spatial interventions and strategies.

A minor shortcoming is that the analytical quality remains dependent on the original catalogue of trends. The used trend report is currently the best on hand – although only applicable to the spatial context of Munich. Using different sets of trends makes the approach adaptable to other areas. Nevertheless, we see a need for translating our analytical research to transformative perspective in order to improve the general evidence base for development trends and planning interventions (Campbell 2012).

The strength of the systemic approach is that it allows students from different disciplines to discuss how their fields of expertise interrelate with each other. It shifts the debate on weighing up between different aspects from normative, often irreconcilable arguments on complex issues to an intersubjective discourse on more tangible connection. Unfolding the complex interrelations of various spatial trends allows to establish a common understanding and to identify key issues for an interdisciplinary spatial strategy. The common understanding reflects the norms and values and the level of knowledge of the students employing the trend analysis. Each group comes to slightly different, but overall similar results. This shows that the trend analysis provides dependable evidence in an intersubjective manner (Healey 1992). Our methodology, overall, necessitates us as lecturers to continuously question ourselves about the plausibility and appropriateness of our didactics.

REFLECTIONS

Opening studio courses for students that are not trained in designing or conceptual thinking introduces some key challenges. As part of our reflections, we want to summarize those challenges and illustrate how our pedagogical approach helps to overcome those.

Interdisciplinary work goes along with the methodological differences of analysing and synthesizing sciences, and the great amount of knowledge from various relevant disciplines that rarely connect into a coherent picture. Students with backgrounds in engineering, planning and architecture tend to draw solutions based on norms and values that educators have imparted during their undergraduate studies. Open-mindedly investigating what is there can be a task that students may need to re-learn. This requires analytical skills, which some students have little experience with. On the other hand, students with a background in social sciences often lack skills of visualization and imagination. Besides missing technical skills, students often fear making decisions that cannot be explicitly deduced from the analysis. Understanding that there are various possible answers to a question requires leaving the comfort zone of empirical work. The trend analysis facilitates a process of convergence between both types of students. The intersubjective nature of the discursive trend analysis sits in between the rationalist, scientific, empirical work of social scientists and the more subjective, creative work of architects and planners.

Another observation was that students quickly felt overwhelmed by the complexity of the task, by engaging with students of other disciplines, and by the ambitious pace of the course. This means that it is crucial to keep students motivated, by asserting repeatedly that there are no rights or wrongs, rather, there is a good and better, bad and worse. Students engaged in this intellectual process operate in unknown territory. Afraid of failure, many fall back on what they are comfortable with. In order to enable students to work outside their comfort zone, relief phases and success experiences are very important to boost morale. Requesting students to rapidly visualize and present their findings at various intervals also assists students in having reality checks as to where they stand in terms of the development of their work. The trend analysis as a strongly guided new methodology also helps to overcome phases of frustration. The rapid gain of information and understanding, and the intermediate, presentable result helps students from the analytical phase to the conceptual phase.

Lastly, a lot of educators 'talk the talk', but only few 'walk the walk'. This means that there are not a lot of precedents and experiences in academia and practice that we can build on. In addition, there is a lot scepticism and discrediting from the applicants of classical planning approaches. To address this, it is helpful to find like-minded institutions and practitioners and show relevant work to the students. We also build on our experience at the institute in teaching this course so far. We get better at it year after year. Again, the trend analysis has been a crucial part of it. Criticizing established methods and instruments of planning practice without providing an alternative can leave students with frustration. Our methodological approach provides an alternative, which might be of value even if the student does not share our critique. (See Box 10.1.)

BOX 10.1 TRANSFERABILITY

Main challenges and suggestions

- One of the main challenges for you as a teacher will be balancing between the complexity of the task and the relevance of the results. Strategic design and planning projects are difficult. Students have limited experience in this domain and the supra-local or even the metropolitan scale is new to them. There is always the potential risk that the students produce results that are far from satisfactory. When setting up the task as well as during supervision some degree of simplification is necessary in order to prevent from being over-complex, but too much can lead to superficial, under-complex and thus irrelevant results.

- The outcomes of the methods used and the added value of using such methods become only visible in the later part of the course. There is a risk of losing momentum midway through the course as the motivation of students who are accustomed to a fast production of deliverables wanes. Teachers have to manage students' impatience and keep the level of motivation as well as the curiosity for the next step high.

Tips for implementation – Dealing with potential challenges

- *Invite relevant practitioners to showcase their work!* Strategic design approaches to urban and regional development are less common activities in day-to-day urban development practice. Students sometimes question the relevance of such approaches. Inviting practitioners that engage in strategic design tasks can exemplify certain use cases and inspire students. If students are asked to show their work, it is usually sufficient to show hand-drawn sketches. These sketches synthesize analytical findings and anchor them in spatial contexts, which allows for profound discussions with experts without spending too much time on visualizing with CAD programs in an early phase of the semester.
- *Do not overload the course with other activities!* Using trend analyses as an interdisciplinary methodology requires a significant amount of time. As a result, the remaining time for the analysis and design of certain aspects is lower than in the case of a traditional, disciplinary studio course. Hence, we recommend keeping the remaining time free of additional other activities, or if necessary organize other activities for the students beforehand, e.g., the field trip or stakeholder engagement events.
- *Discuss, but do not question the methodology during the course!* We openly discuss our methodology with our students as part of the course. It seems important that students do not only learn to apply a certain methodology but also be able to critically reflect upon our reasoning of choosing the method. However, there are stages during the course during which students must stick to the given method in order to reach the course's goal by the end of the semester. If students raise critique during the course of the semester, invite them to a feedback session after grading is complete. In hindsight, students are more informed to engage in a critical discussion.
- *Don't skip the field trip!* Some project areas seem too large for a field trip. You will neither be able to cover the entire area by foot in a reason-

able amount of time, nor do you see many of the non-physical relations of space. However, the field trip is still an essential part. Walking for multiple hours and using public transport – however poorly it may be offered – gives students a feeling of scale and of removing the given barriers of geographical distance. Such an experience quickly shows that strategically designing cannot mean giving answers to each individual plot of land. We recommend visiting local stakeholders, firms, or politicians during the trip to cover aspects students cannot observe.

REFERENCES

Alaily-Mattar, N. and Thierstein, A. (2014) Urban transformation, spatial transformation? Developing alternative futures as a planning methodology. Vortrag, AESOP Annual Conference, Delft.

Butler, J. (1990) *Gender Trouble: Feminism and the Subversion of Identity*. New York: Routledge.

Campbell, H. (2012) Planning to change the world: Between knowledge and action lies synthesis. *Journal of Planning Education and Research* 32(2): 135–146.

EBP Schweiz AG. (2012) *Trend-Report*.

Frank, Andrea I. and Kurth, D. (2010) Planning education in Germany: Impact of the Bologna Agreement. *disP – The Planning Review* 46(182): 25–35.

Frank, A. I., Mironowicz, I., Lourenco, J., Franchini, T., Ache, P., Finka, M., Scholl, B. and Grams, A.. (2014) Educating planners in Europe: A review of 21st century study programmes. *Progress in Planning* 91: 30–94.

Friedmann, J. (1998) Planning theory revisited. *European Planning Studies* 6(3): 245–253.

Gilliard, L. and Thierstein, A. (2016) Competencies revisited. *disP – The Planning Review* 52(1): 42–55.

Harrison, J. (2013) Configuring the new 'regional world': On being caught between territory and networks. *Regional Studies* 47(1): 55–74.

Healey, P. (1992) Planning through debate: The communicative turn in planning theory. *The Town Planning Review* 63(2): 143–162.

Huang, S.-L., Yeh, C.-T., Budd, W. W., and Chen, L.-L. (2009) A Sensitivity Model (SM) approach to analyze urban development in Taiwan based on sustainability indicators. *Environmental Impact Assessment Review* 29: 116–125.

Kegel, U. (2006) Neue Planungsprozesse für die Regionalplanung. In K. Selle (ed.), *Zur räumlichen Entwicklung beitragen. Konzepte. Theorien. Impulse* (pp. 90–100). Dortmund: Dorothea Rohn Verlag.

Kunzmann, K. R. (2000) Strategic spatial development through information and communication. In W. Salet and A. Faludi (eds.), *The Revival of Strategic Spatial Planning* (pp. 259–265). Amsterdam: Royal Netherlands Academy of Arts and Sciences.

Landeshauptstadt München (LHM) (ed.) (2016) *Zukunftsschau München 2040+*. https://www.muenchen.de/rathaus/dam/jcr:d46d2325-619e-4c46-97f8-5883d92c4b10/LHM_Zukunftsschau_Web_01-1.pdf.

Lendi, M. (2008) Raumplanung – ihr politischer Stellenwert in einer veränderten Welt. Angedacht am Beispiel der Schweiz, an einem Sonderfall? *Raumforschung und Raumordnung* 66(5): 383–397.

Rittel, H. W. J. and Webber, M. M. (1973) Dilemmas in a general theory of planning. *Policy Sciences* 3: 155–169.

Rooij, R. and Frank, A. I. (2016) Educating spatial planners for the age of co-creation: The need to risk community, science and practice involvement in planning programmes and curricula. *Planning Practice & Research* 31(5): 473–485.

Sardar, Z. (2010) The namesake: Futures; futures studies; futurology; futuristic; foresight – What's in a name? *Futures* 42: 177–184.

Schönwandt, W. L. (2008) *Planning in Crisis? Theoretical Orientations for Architecture and Planning*. Aldershot: Ashgate.

Schönwandt, W. L. and Jung, W. (2006) Aufgabenstellung, Ergebnisse und Empfehlungen. In W. Schönwandt and W. Jung (eds.), *Ausgewählte Methoden und Instrumente in der räumlichen Planung. Kritische Sondierung als Beitrag zur Diskussion zwischen Planungswissenschaft und -praxis* (pp. 1–25). Hanover: ARL, Akademie für Raumforschung und Landesplanung.

Silver, N. (2012) *The Signal and the Noise: Why Most Predictions Fail – But Some Don't*. New York: Penguin.

Tschirk, W. (2008) Raumplanung neu kommunizieren. Das "Netzwerk Raumplanung" – eine Kommunikationsplattform für PlanerInnen. pnd online. http://www.planung -neu-denken.de/images/stories/pnd/dokumente/pndonline3_2008tschirk.pdf.

Vester, F. (2012) *The Art of Interconnected Thinking: Ideas and Tools for a New Approach to Tackling Complexity*. Munich: MCB Publishing.

Wenger, E. (2000) Communities of practice and social learning systems. *Organization* 7(2): 225–246.

Wiese, A., Förster, A., Gilliard, L. and Thierstein, A. (2014) A spatial strategy for the production of place in two German cities: Urban design interventions as a driver for spatial transformation. *City, Territory and Architecture* 1(13): 1–9.

11. Using theatre and performance for greater reflexivity in planning and design education

Marleen Buizer and Iulian Barba Lata

INTRODUCTION

Scholars of various disciplinary backgrounds increasingly regard the world as relational, as constituted through complex, networked and dynamic flows, and as hardly predictable (e.g., Buser 2012; De Roo and Boelens 2016). Relational thinking has entered spatial planning, urban and landscape design debates from geography since the turn of the century (Allmendinger et al. 2016; Murdoch 2006). The point of departure here is the role relational thinking had in unsettling some of the basic assumptions within spatial planning and design disciplines, thus bearing practical implications for the way research and education activities are organized. In this context, it is fairly commonplace to call for reflexivity and consider what are productive ways of incorporating relational thinking in education and training programmes for upcoming spatial planning and design practitioners.

Unlike positivist approaches that regard researchers as external-objective observers, relational and interpretive approaches regard researchers as immersed in the world they study, as participants and subjects (Healey 2007). While positivist approaches place the researcher in an objective, knowing position, relational and interpretive approaches involve as a key methodological tenet the critical engagement with the researcher's own values and normative frameworks. Here, 'theory' is not used to test and predict, but rather to explore and understand. In addition, while the former approaches pursue legitimacy and social change via outcomes produced from a detached stance, the latter involve the transformation of practice itself as a potential outcome. Therefore, advocates of interpretive research reject the positivist accounts that regard planners as being situated 'above politics' (Davoudi 2012; Healey 2013). Instead, they highlight the political nature of both formal institutional arrangements and informal processes.

As compared with positivism, 'planning spaces' are considered more diverse and less predictable in such relational views. They raise complicated questions about the interplay of formal and informal approaches to area development, and between local and global forces (Allmendinger et al. 2016). Space, in this view, is not just a container of action and decision-making, rather it is socially produced and subject to embodied experience, "something that is (only provisionally) stabilized out of such turbulent processes" (Murdoch 2006, p. 4). Space thus appears as subjective, contested, political, and by no means an empty sheet, with planning and design processes being envisioned as iterative, interpretive, contingent and reflexive.

In a nutshell, the above sketches the conditions that sparked a growing concern with alternative educational approaches. We dwell upon these conditions at length, due to the various questions they raise for planning and design practices: In what ways do practitioners and researchers alike come to appreciate and work with such a diversity of knowledges and spatial imaginaries? What are productive means to stimulate thinking beyond their own disciplinary confines? How do they recognize the role of power in privileging some forms of knowledge over others? What are the possibilities of formulating questions and framing issues in collaboration with local participants, from the initiation of specific planning and design activities throughout their evaluation and transition into new types of activities?

These questions that involve a good deal of introspection are now indeed fairly common. However, there is a longstanding legacy of linear, functionalist thinking in spatial planning that often bypassed such questions. Given the normative assumptions about technical rationality, politics was hardly an issue for planning practices, even upon the emergence of collaborative approaches. The growing emphasis placed on relational thinking has, however, shifted attention to the context-specific character of technical rationality and the fact that planning processes are in every respect bound to power relations (Flyvbjerg 1998). Drawing on Henri Lefebvre's work (e.g., 1991), Davoudi contends that "[t]oo much emphasis on the 'conceived spaces' of planners and systems analysts would undermine the attempts to incorporate 'lived spaces' of imagination and 'perceived spaces' of daily routines" (2012, p. 434). On a similar note, Arjun Appadurai addresses the interplay between the 'ethics of probability' and the 'ethics of possibility', to argue that the dominant concern with the former as an expression of technical rationality should find a better balance with "those ways of thinking, feeling and acting that increase the horizon of hope, that expand the field of the imagination, that produce greater equity" (2013, p. 295). Granted this perspective, we are not advocating here for a complete turnaround towards relational thinking: different research questions require different approaches. Nevertheless, we do think that planning and design for uncertain outcomes and more diverse spaces (including the lived spaces of imagination and the perceived spaces of everyday routines) requires more attention in curricula. In this chapter we present a theoretically inspired teaching methodology that elicits such learning, in order to familiarize planning and design students with the multiplicity of spatial imaginaries.

Building on the previous work of one of the authors on transdisciplinary teamwork in research (Buizer et al. 2015), we will first focus on the use of Participatory Action Research (PAR) and transdisciplinary approaches in teaching. Secondly, we dwell on Goffman's (1959) theatre metaphor, which was developed into a heuristic for reflections on transdisciplinarity in research teams (Boyd et al. 2015). We have since further applied the approach in research and educational settings, and linked it to Judith Butler's (1986) concept of performativity. Lastly, our chapter will introduce two main instances of theatre-based approaches in the classroom (Table 11.1).

The first instance pertains to a course on planning theory and ethics. The course is critical of theory as providing evidence that frontloads research processes, leading to science-based interventions that are putatively the best for solving a predetermined problem. As an alternative, the course supports a relational take on theory, which requires a learning strategy for students to reflect on their own routines and roles, as well as encouraging them to question the rationale behind adopting certain theoretical approaches (Allmendinger 2009). The second instance concerns an MSc course, the 'Atelier Landscape Architecture and Planning', where theatre is used as a heuristic to reflect on the diversity of 'planning spaces' and related routine behaviours, as a means to envision alternatives. The theatre-based approaches are complemented by reflection sessions, which address the critical factors that either enable or constrain the emergence of transformative planning practices.

THEORETICAL INSPIRATIONS

With the current emphasis at our university (and elsewhere, both in academic policy and rhetoric) to deliver 'Science for (societal) Impact', transdisciplinary and participatory methodologies seem to receive more attention. However, Participatory Action Research and transdisciplinarity are also contested, with some arguing that they are mainly benefiting elites and often failing in their pursuit of structural social change (Whitzman 2017). At the same time, they have been recognized for spurring critical reflection on researchers' own responsibility for the places and communities in which they operate (Susskind et al. 2018). They are often invoked in the context of addressing 'wicked problems' such as climate change, food insecurity, poverty and social exclusion (Boyd et al. 2015). PAR approaches represent a necessary addition to the more prominent positivist toolkit of planning and design students, thus enabling

Table 11.1   Two theatre-based approaches in the classroom

Theatre	Theory–practice reflections	Transformative routines	Reflexivity
Course I. BSc Planning Theory (± 30 students, 6 ECTS = 168 hours, of which 42 contact hours, and 126 are self-study hours)	'Playing/ performing theory' as lens	Exploring iteratively the interplay of theory and practice in relation to a common case study area	In what ways do different theoretical lenses render different insights?
Course II. MSc project/ problem-based learning (± 50 students, 9 ECTS = 252 hours, of which 96 contact hours, and 156 are self-study hours)	'Playing/ performing theory' as lens	Exploring iteratively the diversity of 'planning spaces' and envisioning alternatives	What are the factors that enable/constrain the emergence of alternatives?

educational strategies that promote an "attitude of adventure" (Davoudi 2012, p. 432) and exploration, as a viable alternative (Pinel and Urie 2017).

Participatory methodologies are still at the periphery of teaching pro-grammes, and habitually at odds with the routines associated with them. A key issue therefore is to obtain an in-depth understanding of those routines, the conditions and potential impediments for transitioning towards transformative practices. Here, we draw on the work of Goffman (1959), who emphasizes that social actors in everyday interactions 'perform' in a way they think it is expected from them, a process he coins impression management. By managing impressions, actors avoid embarrassment, on their own behalf and on behalf of others. Routines and rituals, established and continuously re-enacted, become normalized through particular behaviours, professions or everyday practices. This does not imply that actors are just managing impressions as merely 'cynical', 'calculative' strategists, but rather that they "protect social continu-ity" (Giddens 1984, p. 70).

With the predominant focus on behaviour and everyday interactions, Goffman's work has only occasionally been associated with the discussion of power relations (Jenkins 2008). His interactional sociology has received some criticism for overemphasizing the role of everyday face-to-face interactions at the expense of structural forces. However, as Jenkins asserts, this is a mis-placed critique that does not sufficiently acknowledge how Goffman's ideas are corresponding with Foucault's attention to power and discourse as part of day-to-day routines. Drawing on Tom Burns's work, Jenkins concludes that "in fact the two theorists (Goffman and Foucault) share a considerable amount of common ground with respect to the normalization of order and the routine everyday ubiquity of power, its mundane invisibility" (Jenkins 2008, p. 158; see also Hacking 2004).

For our translation of Goffman's ideas into a heuristic that elicits reflections on planning and design routines, we argue for a more explicit recognition of the power dimension. Power is thus interpreted as relationally enacted in everyday normalized routines, through specific action repertoires such as sketching, mapping and storytelling. As Alan Read suggests, the "story does not express, describe or illustrate a practice, it makes movement and practice possible in the first place. To move into a place there is the need for a story about it" (1995, p. 153).

In order to consider what are normalized routines and how those might fore-close alternative forms of expression and reflection, theatre-based approaches have proven instrumental for our teaching. We can use the theatre metaphor to ask what is the stage like, whether it is on the same level with the audience, like in street theatre, or at a distance? What props are 'normally' used, and what kind of performer–audience relationships can be imagined? Is there room for improvization and to what extent is such considered desirable? We also habitu-ally question the role of the script writer and director, as well as that of the cast. And is there a backstage of any significance, to reflect on the performance? Alternatively, we can actually 'play' with the metaphor as we did in the two courses that we will present in the next section.

At the same time as gaining an understanding of routine behaviours, one can ask how scrutinizing routines may enable imagining alternatives, and empow-ering participants (students *or* researchers). Indeed, there is much to science practices that is routine, or to use the metaphor of theatre, staged and scripted: the role of the 'knower' as a neutral player that provides 'the science' to support specific interventions, the setting of the university campuses and their buildings, the scripts whereby teachers are expected to transfer knowledge to their 'audience of students' or where scientists are to provide legitimacy to policy decisions. To draw a parallel with Peter Brook's work on theatrical performance, "[t]ruth in theatre is always on the move" (1996, p. 140). In sum, we can easily think of academic teaching and research practices in terms of Goffman's theatre metaphor and come to understand it as 'performed identity'.

The power dimension of performance is more explicitly present in the work of Judith Butler. According to Butler, identities are constructed, performed. She presents the notion of performativity to clarify how the repeated 'doing of gender', *makes* gender, or in paraphrasing Simone de Beauvoir: "one is not born, but rather becomes, a woman" (1986, p. 35). Correspondingly, science is 'performed' by engaging in scientific practices such as conducting research, peer-reviewing, attending conferences and lecturing. Whereas *performance* may be the one-off manifestation of scientific identity via the aforementioned practices, their repetitive character normalizes them into routines and renders them *performative*. The optimistic turn we take with regard to Goffman concerns the use of theatre to reflect on students' own positionality, exposing routine behaviours and evaluating their implications for the emergence of alternatives. This is usually an effective strategy, which enables students to develop new types of routines and to better grasp the interplay between theory and practice.

Course I: (BSc) Learning about Theory through Theatre

When obtaining their University Teaching Qualification (UTQ or BKO), educators at our university are trained to distinguish learning objectives in three distinct domains: the cognitive, affective and sensory domains, focusing respectively on cognitive knowledge, attitudes and practical skills (Anderson et al. 2001). Unsurprisingly, the cognitive domain is prevalent in university curricula. In tune with the overemphasis on expert knowledge, as critically discussed above, the researcher or professional are often depicted as gatekeepers to knowledge, those able to understand, provide the evidence and develop interventions accordingly. The future job of our students! However, this conception of knowledge that renders interventions 'evidence-based' may be at odds with the complex situations our graduates often encounter in practice. Our weekly theatre aims to nurture an open attitude towards the complexity and context-specific character of those situations, the ambivalences and dilemmas of planning and design tasks, as well as the multiple ways in which theory could become meaningful when 'applied' to practice. In the course called 'Planning Theory and Ethics', later renamed 'Concepts and Approaches for Planning Practices', spatial planning theories and concepts are considered as 'sensitizing' (Blumer 1954) and (adjustable) 'lenses', rather than evidence (see Figure 11.1).

The planning-theoretical 'lenses' discussed in the study year 2017–2018 were:

1. Rationalism versus Phronetic Planning Research
2. Discourse and Narrative
3. Formality/Informality and the 'unplanned'
4. New Planners: urban curators and temporality

The course runs for eight weeks (mornings) and started in this with a study trip to a post-industrial site in The Hague (Binckhorst), which is being transformed into an area for living and working. We chose only one case to provide for a shared focus. The study trip consisted of an introduction by several stakeholders to the specific challenges in Binckhorst and a full-day exploration of the area. Thereafter, in a weekly series of activities, the second year bachelor students (specialization in planning, part of a joint programme with landscape architects) read the selected texts and write reviews (after a short e-module 'writing good reviews'), participate in an extended lecture on the 'theoretical lens' of the week, define the key ingredients of the studied theoretical approach and, based on those, they either develop a script for or assess the 'Theory Theatre' performances. The final assignment is an essay in which students need to reflect on the case area by selecting one or two of the theoretical lenses.

By following this sequence, different ways of thinking and learning are mobilized: the more traditional 'reading and summarizing'; working on small classroom activities that explore theory and concepts in light of the case study area; talking and deliberating with other students when preparing the script and rehearsing (a first step that involves theory-practice embodied performance); the performance itself. In this course, we do not provide the Goffman inspired elements of theatre (as we do in the MSc course) but invite students to literally perform theory in relation to an imaginary situation, which unfolds in the case area. By doing so, we 'flip the classroom': students take the lead in developing and sharing the content.

In the Theory Theatre, students work in groups of three to five. Each week, half of the groups perform, while the other half act as a 'jury'. While the performing teams prepare and rehearse their contribution, the jury elaborates the substantive elements from theory that are expected to be included in the performance. The jury also evaluates the performers' skills in conveying their message convincingly, since theory and related concepts often afford a broad range of (creative) translations into the theatre performances. A recurrent point of discussion was whether the performers interpret theory in a normative manner (such that they would use it to prescribe alternative ways of planning/ designing) or as analytical lens (facilitating a more in-depth understanding of a phenomenon). Another important aspect pertained to intentionality and the choice of performance. For instance, some groups opted to convey their message through video materials, while others used poetry, dance and/or music acts. With such a diverse range of performances, we saw that jury-groups started to include elements like 'creativity' and 'participation from the audience' in their evaluation. A short feedback session concluded each performance, in which the jury passed the evaluation and discussed it with the performing team and the audience.

Upon completion of the course, students were able to:

1. Compare different planning theories and practices in a historical and international perspective
2. Distinguish and evaluate the ethical dimensions of the spatial planning profession

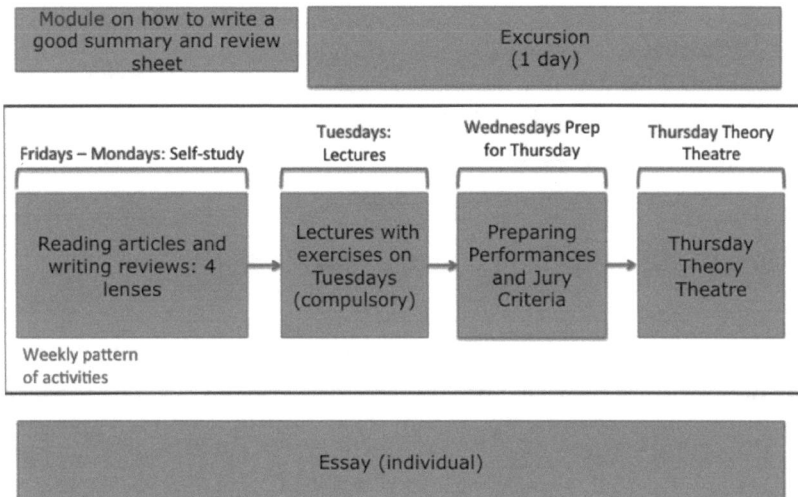

Figure 11.1   The course and its elements

3. Evaluate existing planning situations in the light of theories and ethics of spatial planning
4. Creatively connect theoretical perspectives to practical situations
5. Write reviews and an essay in well-written language

As teachers, our main lessons may be summarized as follows:

1. Adding theatre to the mix of teaching activities as a way to 'flip' the classroom, enables students to actually work with theory and develop new insights when reflecting on practice situations.
2. Students often remain close to their own setting and experiences when translating the theoretical lens to a practice situation. For instance, situations that the students knew well (such as living in student dorms) were more frequently used to explain theory and related concepts than the less-familiar particularities of the case area.
3. In preparing their theatre performances, student teams opted for all sorts of alternative formats: a 'Twister' inspired game that connects theory to practice, a quartet, a route that peers need to explore blindfolded, while following instructions inspired by the theoretical approach. Other formats included quizzes, short films, songs (translating a theory into lyrics and music), poetry, rap with dance, storytelling, a house of commons debate

and even a flash-mob (on one occasion the class decided to perform as a combined group, to the surprise of the teachers).

4. The practice of translating and contrasting theory to practice incorporated interpretations that sometimes remained implicit or obscure to the audience. Having a narrator as part of the performance, could facilitate more focused discussions on how the team evaluated theory.

The course was given for the first time in 2015 and won a student award in 2016, just as the course that we will discuss next.

Course II: (MSc) Reflexivity through Theatre in Project

Landscape architecture and planning are intervention and future-oriented disciplines, which rely to an important extent on the development of creative skills. In our BSc and MSc programs Landscape Architecture and Planning, studio education is important – students create, often by hand, future scenarios or designs. Calls for the programme to frontload those scenarios/designs with 'scientific evidence', demanding a high level of cognitive knowledge, are still strong. We felt a heuristic was needed to critically reflect on this type of learning routines.

The second course in which we work with theatre is the MSc Atelier Landscape Architecture and Planning. Rather than focusing on content (theoretical and practical), significant attention goes to explicit reflections on students' personal development and their teamwork in a context of conducting transdisciplinary research and design work. Not knowing beforehand what will evolve from their process of engagement with local actors, there is an important element of crafting solutions 'on the go', whilst constantly exploring and problematizing dominant problem definitions. There is often an uncomfortable tension between the design practice of 'crafting on the go' and the claims to 'scientific evidence' mentioned above.

The atelier is an intensive, integrative course, which aims to bring together the insights and experience MSc students have gained during the first year of their Master's. It is the last course before they start working on their thesis and internship. With a CV and a motivation letter, students apply to work on a project of their choice. In the months preceding the course, their teachers (called 'coaches') formulate rough outlines in consultation with the commissioners. Students discuss the assignments in more detail with their commissioner during the first two weeks of the course.

Each year, the atelier offers different projects and hosts a variety of project teams under an overarching theme. Research, planning and design activities in the spirit of the designated theme require different approaches, which depend on aspects such as the scale of the project, the people involved, the level and nature of potential contestation or support, and the type of solutions sought.

All projects in the atelier have a research component on the one hand, and a design and planning component on the other. In consultation with their commissioners, who can be as diverse as government officials, NGO representatives, artists or volunteers, students decide on the types of activities required, the outcomes to be achieved and the products to be delivered. Depending on the type of task at hand and the project phase, research activities are balanced with design and planning activities. Usually, the preliminary project phases are defined by more research focused activities, while the later ones tend to rely mainly on intervention-focused activities.

The course is organized before the summer, throughout eight weeks, in order to allow for good field immersion. The students work in groups of five to seven, in one studio space, to allow for cross-group exchanges. The majority consists of landscape architects, one in five is a spatial planner, and there is also a small number of students from other disciplines, such as ecology or urban engineering. Room dividers offer space for displaying their intermediate products.

The learning objectives of this course are summarized as follows:

1. Interpret and investigate the multiple aspects of a landscape challenge
2. Develop a planning and design proposal in response to a landscape challenge, which is supported by research findings and related ethical issues
3. Present the strategy or design in a form that meets the agreements made with the client, whilst offering transparency about the entire process
4. Reflect on the experience of acting in a multi-disciplinary team and the relation of the team to the client, both in an assessment interview and by writing an individual assessment paper
5. Assess the contribution of team members and other stakeholders to the team performance and the execution of project tasks

As part of the course, the students formulate personal development objectives at three levels: individual, team, transdisciplinary. The theatre exercise is organized half-way through the course. After the first four weeks, the students have acquired sufficient experience with teamwork, and most have faced the first hurdles. We then introduce Goffman's work and the theatre metaphor. The students are invited to write a script in two parts, with one part that presents a routine practice, and a second part that envisions a future routine. The groups film their performances, and after each team's performance, the other groups provide feedback. What did they 'see' in the performance? Did they have similar experiences in their own group or when working with commissioners and other social actors? How did they respond? What are their views on the proposed alternative? How does the performing group evaluate the received feedback? We ask the students to summarize their findings in writing.

As coaches, our main findings from the activities are the following:

1. Students generally stay 'close to home' in their performances in the atelier. For example, a recurring topic is 'arriving on time in the mornings', 'taking time for informal coffee breaks' and the timing of meetings. Routines relating to the planning and design profession are more difficult to pinpoint for the students. We expected that doing the exercise mid-way the course (instead of the beginning), would help groups choose routines a little more related to their transdisciplinary fieldwork for example. In their evaluations of the course, the students indicate that their work in the atelier is quite different from the experience of other courses, mainly in terms of the intensity of the engagement with actors in the field, that they are designing for. The fact that they choose to focus on routines in their teams rather than in their engagement with stakeholders in their project areas is probably a result of the lack of experience with such engagement. Perhaps doing a second exercise at the end of the course, giving examples, or asking experienced people to introduce the topic of co-designing, might provide insights that would enable the students to focus more on the transdisciplinary orientation. Yet, the question remains of how effective such an approach would be at this stage of the professional development of students. (A similar observation was made when the exercise was conducted with postdoctoral researchers – their interdisciplinary group work was still such a challenge that they could not think in terms of routines yet, when it came to engagement with non-academic actors.)

2. A second frequent topic is penalties. Groups set informal rules and when these are broken, they may work with penalties like having to bring cake for the others when running late for appointments. In the 'routine' version of the play, they do not have such a system, in the alternative they do.

3. Groups that had more intensive interactions with their commissioners tended to reflect more on those in their performances. For example, one group struggled with a versatile, demanding commissioner, whose views were often not recognized as representing the opinions of people from the community. Here the question of conflicting identities arose – should the group act as consultants and deliver a product in conformance with the demands of their commissioner, or should they prioritize the results of their interviews? To what extent could these two roles be aligned? The performance gave rise to a vivid discussion with other student teams and eventually the group decided to take the lead in responding to the commissioner.

4. In some groups, students have opted to perform the role of their colleagues. This demands a friendly atmosphere and high level of trust within the team, whereby the group could agree, for instance, on exaggerating each other's personas. In this case, theory theatre helped the group to become more open about their group dynamics. Other groups realized the importance of humour as a factor that could help open up a conversation about an otherwise awkward topic.

DISCUSSION AND CONCLUSION

To prepare our graduates to enter an increasingly complex and dynamic world in which uncertainty, struggle and conflict are more common than predictability, consensus and straightforward collaboration, we employed theatre-based approaches in two ways:

- as an exploratory device to evaluate the interplay of theory and practice
- as a heuristic to uncover the diversity of 'planning spaces' and related routines in opening a conversation about alternative behaviours.

In both instances, embodied performance added to the learning experience a layer based on practical skills and a reflexive attitude. In the first instance, 'theory theatre' enabled a playful development of cognitive knowledge and linked the early-curriculum acquaintance with theories, to questions about their meaning for practice situations in which the position of the theorizing explorer also matters. In the second instance, we drew on methodologies such as PAR, and emphasized the role of transdisciplinarity and its challenges. Theatre was used to reflect on the multiple imaginaries and routines that inform planning processes and their broader implications for developing alternatives, i.e., more inclusive and transformative planning practices. We envisioned this would assist in enhancing reflexivity by: (a) involving different researchers, professionals, practitioners and communities throughout the design and planning processes; (b) problematizing (dominant) problem framings; (c) viewing 'knowledge' in terms of 'knowledges' or 'knowledge claims'; and (d) focusing on 'knowledge production' as a verb (Rydin 2005). During the early stages of their performances, students were more concentrated on their teamwork than on their relationship with other societal actors. However, when they did adopt the latter focus, the performances rendered lively discussions that other students could easily relate to.

To facilitate a view/practice of 'science' that embraces a reflexive, 'on the go' learning modality at its core, we presented a teaching strategy inspired by Goffman's imagery of theatre. In attempting to go beyond mere (cognitive) understanding, with students' theatre performances alternatives become actualized through embodied practice. To an extent, change is already enacted. (See Box 11.1.)

BOX 11.1 MAIN CHALLENGES AND SUGGESTIONS

- We found the traditional classroom layout a practical challenge, as before each theory theatre session we had to reshuffle the furniture. In some cases, the classroom furniture was creatively used for the stage setting performances.
- While the theatre-based approaches are quite prominent in the set-up of the two courses, we consider the role of additional assignments (reviewing, jurying, contributions to a course repository, writing a final essay) equally important in meeting the learning objectives (both individual and group ones) assigned to the program and evaluating the proposed learning strategy.
- With the theatre performances it is important to provide enough time for discussing interpretations, whilst challenging the students to debate both form and contents. Using short breaks to transition from performances to reflections with the audience usually allows students to better formulate their questions and comments.
- As the interplay between theory and practice represents a key ingredient of the theatre-based learning strategy, we always relate to a concrete case and its particularities – a common case study area for the BSc course, and the commissioned projects in the MSc atelier.
- Given the interactive format and the load of additional assignments, teamwork is key to a successful preparation of the course. A team of two lecturers and one student assistant would be optimal.

REFERENCES

Allmendinger, P. (2009) *Planning Theory*. Basingstoke: Palgrave Macmillan.

Allmendinger, P., Haughton, G., and Shepherd, E. (2016) Where is planning to be found? Material practices and the multiple spaces of planning. *Environment and Planning C: Government and Policy* 34(1): 38–51.

Anderson, L. W., Krathwohl, D. R., Airasian, P. W., Cruikshank, K. A., Mayer, R. E., Pintrich, P. R., Raths, J. and Wittrock, M. C. (2001) *A Taxonomy for Learning, Teaching, and Assessing: A Revision of Bloom's Taxonomy of Educational Objectives*. New York: Pearson, Allyn & Bacon.

Appadurai A (2013) *The Future as Cultural Fact: Essays on the Global Condition*. London: Verso Books.

Blumer, H. (1954) What is wrong with social theory? *American Sociological Review* 19(1): 3–10.

Boyd, D., Buizer, M., Schibeci, R. and Baudains, C. (2015) Prompting transdisciplinary research: Promising futures for using the performance metaphor in research. *Futures* 65: 175–184.

Brook, P. (1996) *The Empty Space – A Book about the Theatre: Deadly, Holy, Rough, Immediate.* New York: Simon & Schuster.

Buizer, M., Ruthrof, K., Moore, S. A., Veneklaas, E. J., Hardy, G. and Baudains, C. (2015) A critical evaluation of interventions to progress transdisciplinary research. *Society and Natural Resources* 28(6): 670–681.

Buser, M. (2012) The production of space in metropolitan regions: A Lefebvrian analysis of governance and spatial change. *Planning Theory* 11(3): 279–298.

Butler, J. (1986) Sex and gender in Simone de Beauvoir's *Second Sex*. *Yale French Studies* 72: 35–49.

Davoudi, S. (2012) The legacy of positivism and the emergence of interpretive tradition in spatial planning. *Regional Studies* 46(4): 429–441.

de Roo, G. and Boelens, L. (2016) Setting the scene: About planning and a world in change. In G. de Roo and L. Boelens (eds.), *Spatial Planning in a Complex Unpredictable World of Change: Towards a Proactive Co-Evolutionary Type of Planning within the Eurodelta* (pp. 14–27). Groningen: InPlanning.

Flyvbjerg, B. (1998) *Rationality and Power: Democracy in Practice.* Chicago, IL: University of Chicago Press.

Giddens, A. (1984) *The Constitution of Society: Introduction to the Theory of Structuration.* Berkeley, CA: University of California Press.

Goffman, E. (1959) *The Presentation of Self in Everyday Life.* New York: Anchor Books.

Hacking, I. (2004) Between Michel Foucault and Erving Goffman: Between discourse in the abstract and face-to-face interaction. *Economy and Society* 33(3): 277–302.

Healey, P. (2007) *Urban Complexity and Spatial Strategies: Towards a Relational Planning for Our Times.* London: Routledge.

Healey, P. (2013) Circuits of knowledge and techniques: The transnational flow of planning ideas and practices. *International Journal of Urban and Regional Research* 37(5): 1510–1526.

Jenkins, R. (2008) Erving Goffman: A major theorist of power? *Journal of Power* 1(2): 157–168.

Lefebvre, H. (1991) *The Production of Space.* Oxford: Blackwell.

Murdoch, J. (2006) *Post-Structuralist Geography: A Guide to Relational Space.* London: Sage Publications.

Pinel, S. L. and Urie, R. (2017) Learning reflective planning: The application of participatory action research principles to planning studio design and assessment. *Journal of Architectural and Planning Research* 34(1): 32–48.

Read, A. (1995) *Theatre and Everyday Life: An Ethics of Performance.* London: Routledge.

Rydin, Y. (2005) Geographical knowledge and policy: The positive contribution of discourse studies. *Area* 37(1): 73–78.

Susskind, L., Cunningham, D. and Cruxén, I. A. (2018) Teaching participatory action research: The search for pedagogical insights. In L. Susskind, D. Cunningham and I. A. Cruxén (eds.), *(Participatory) Action Research: Principles, Approaches and Applications* (pp. 125–150). New York: Nova Science Publishers.

Whitzman, C. (2017) Participatory action research in affordable housing partnerships: Collaborative rationality, or sleeping with the growth machine? *Planning Practice and Research* 32(5): 495–507.

12. MIKROAKADEMIE: peer learning to enrich the curriculum and enhance participation and self-reflection

Andreas Brück and Angela Million

INTRODUCTION

The MIKROAKADEMIE is a peer-to-peer learning environment for planners, urban designers, architects and students from related fields established at the Technical University (TU) Berlin in 2012/13. It consists of a series of workshops/seminars (approximately five per semester), that reach beyond the scope of standard teaching. Workshops address discourses and contents that would otherwise not be taught. Participants pass on and co-develop their knowledge and learn communication and representation techniques such as hand-drawing, CAD, photography, video-making, remote sensing, cartography (GIS) etc. The concept was developed initially to enhance students' media literacy and to test teaching of new methods in urban design, cartography and presentation techniques. Yet, over time the scope has broadened to include other content and topics as well. Table 12.1 provides an overview of the MIKROAKADEMIE workshops offered over the years. The MIKROAKADEMIE contributes to shaping students' understanding of teaching as a progressive, interactive and recurring process, where one learns 'from each other' (i.e., 'student-to-student') and learns continuously (i.e., flexibly adapting to new situations/resources/technologies, etc.).

The concept of the MIKROAKADEMIE was developed as part of the project 'Innovation in Teaching: Teaching and Learning as a Counter-Current Process' funded by the Stifterverband's 'Fellowship for Innovation in University Teaching'. At its centre was the testing of ideas for (timely and compatible) teaching of methods, tools, skills and techniques for representation, communication of planning information and urban design. The main aim was to encourage development of 'orientational' knowledge that enables navigation through the many possibilities to analyse, represent and convey content. The challenge was not to find new ways of teaching and passing on (fundamental) theoretical and practical knowledge, but rather to encourage students to study (and explore) autonomously creative uses of available resources.

This chapter provides first theoretical considerations and background on the MIKROAKADEMIE's inception. Second, it describes its current state and function. Third, reflections are offered on feedback and lessons learned from implementation. Fourth, the impacts of the MIKROAKADEMIE on TU Berlin's Bachelor and Master's education in Urban Planning and Urban Design are explored, while reflecting on challenges and limitations of the teaching format. Fifth, a brief review of the future potential development of the concept is offered.

MIKROAKADEMIE'S INCEPTION: THEORETICAL CONSIDERATIONS AND PRACTICAL IMPLEMENTATION

City planners are increasingly expected to be able to comprehensively communicate their ideas both verbally and visually. Urban planning and design today take place in the context of far-reaching changes in cities and regions (climate change, socio-cultural and demographic change, digitization, etc.). As the premise of this book stipulates, multiple challenges connected to rapid urbanization, technological advances and societal shifts, global governance and multi-scalar dimensions of policy making, and other factors – all lead to complex situations, wicked problems and difficult institutional settings in which future urban planners and designers will have to operate. Today's didactical approaches for professional education may fall short in providing the necessary skills (Strickland 2017), and novel and innovative pedagogies (Daniels 2012; Freire 1996) will have to be developed to address emergent gaps and weaknesses in our education programmes.

Within this setting, our focus was on communication competencies and the search for novel pedagogies to teach a variety of methods and tools on one hand and offer the necessary depth to master them on the other. As urban design is a process of negotiating very diverse needs and preferences amongst different actors, communication is key, especially as future urban professionals will be required to convey their ideas in participatory ways due to the dramatically heightened interest of the public in co-shaping the environment.

In other words, we sought for teaching formats that enhance skills including techniques for analysis (GIS, mapping, crowd-sourcing, real-time data analysis, etc.), methods of representation (hand sketches, CAD, 3D, graphic design, modelling, interactive models, etc.) and the distribution of content (print media, Web 2.0, social networking, mobile internet, etc.), as well as methods facilitating discussion and feedback – i.e. the involvement of different stakeholders (surveys, moderation, etc.) in planning processes. Due to the increasing

Table 12.1   Overview of MIKROAKADEMIE workshop themes

	Winter Semester (October start)	Summer Semester (April start)
Academic Year 2013/14		– Photography – Art & Public Space – Urban Planning close to Nature – Remote Sensing
Academic Year 2014/15	– GIS Compact – Design Thinking – Remote Sensing	– The French Connection – Berlin–Brandenburg–Berlin Hike – Momentary Archive – Universal Design
Academic Year 2015/16	– Introduction To CAD – Advanced CAD (2d) – Design Thinking – Photo Editing Essentials – Development Plans	– Perspectives, Location Plans, Sections – Image Editing – Photo-Documentation in Urban Planning – Layout of Plans – Urban Games
Academic Year 2016/17	– Text processing & Layout – GIS Intro – CAD Essentials – Spreadsheets for Planners – Urban Games – Vector-graphics Basics	– Roof-Water-Farm – MOOC – Mediation & Non-violent Communication – CAD Essentials – Urban Data Mining
Academic Year 2017/18	– Roof-Water-Farm – MOOC – Mediation & Non-violent Communication – Vector Graphics – Advanced CAD (3D) – Spreadsheets for planners	– Image Editing – Layout of Posters & Brochures – Queer inclusive Planning – Non-formal Education – Design Thinking Boot Camp – Thesis Formatting
Academic Year 2018/19	– Mediation & Non-violent Communication – Layout – Vector-based Illustrations – CAD Basics – Mexican urban design	– Advanced CAD (3D) – CAD – Tips & Tricks – Layout – The Foodbridge – Participatory Urbanism
Academic Year 2019/20	– Free-hand drawing – Audio edit & Podcast-Production – Interactive Online Maps – Critical GIS in Praxis – Intro to Graphics Software	– Conference Organizing – pit2020 Berlin – Soundworkshop – Listen to Corona (in response to the COVID-19 pandemic)

digitalization, there is a multitude of technologies and applications available which are being re-developed/-invented and put into practice in ever more rapid cycles. This means professionals need to constantly learn about new tools, their potentials and limitations, and their practical application.

The MIKROAKADEMIE's format centred, therefore, on testing different ideas for teaching and co-teaching essential skills, while focusing on contents beyond the official curriculum. Although the idea of the tutorial and peer-to-peer learning is not new, it needs to be adapted to current challenges that occur through the rise of much more diverse teaching content which requires continuous revision to retain relevance and actuality as well as through demands for increasing efficiency in teaching in higher education (for categories and type of peer learning see Whitman and Fife 1988, pp. 13–14; Topping 2005).

Hence, the inception of MIKROAKADEMIE was driven by a very practical need to broaden the scope of the curriculum and incorporate students into the teaching and learning experience as this would enhance their communication skills altogether. In parallel, there were theoretical considerations around different implementation options. In the initiation phase, we were mainly driven by two aspects. First, by the aim of creating a 'studio' atmosphere – as we concur with Borden et al. that studio environments offer an "educational benefit in terms of skill development, [that] is greatly superior to that which could be achieved by the individual student working alone" (2010, p. 13). Second, by the urge to allow for more communication skills to be incorporated into the teaching curriculum because we see design as a social process: "Communication with others is at the heart of design just as it is central to teaching and learning" (Vowles et al. 2012).

The MIKROAKADEMIE also tackles media-pedagogical concepts. Yet it does not look at learning new media from the dominating discourse of technology, but from a discourse on meaning and media literacy as part of a general skillset of today's citizens. It is important to use new technologies and methods in a meaningful way while retaining a focus on substantive aspects of urban planning and design. Therefore, all media and computer euphoria aside, it is conveyed that it makes little sense to learn technologies per se, but rather to understand and test application possibilities, and to apply tools in a problem-oriented manner (and possibly even develop them further). By addressing the applicability of technologies and methods, students and teachers are encouraged to break new ground and independently adapt, or further develop technologies and methods to specific urban planning and design needs.

Aside from the content – and contrary to the still common practice of frontal teaching (e.g., in lectures or in the computer lab) and a hierarchical understanding of the wise instructor training the non-knowledgeable student –

the concept behind MIKROAKADEMIE is that of a face-to-face co-learning experience. Just as Topping (2005) discusses different types of peer learning, MIKROAKADEMIE has more characteristics of peer tutoring (vs. cooperative learning). Nevertheless, in our case it is combined with the setting of studio learning and studio culture of design programmes. And while peer tutoring is content wise characterized by a high focus on curriculum content, in our case the content is free flowing. Prior knowledge of students is the base for content and particularly important; we all have knowledge and skills acquired before, after and outside of university education. These skills and knowledges can enrich the formal learning experience by and for fellow students as well as for the teachers. Ideally, learning becomes a symbiosis: The role of the teacher is that of a coach, who accompanies the students in a solution- and goal-oriented manner, activates potentials, encourages performance, continues to develop competencies and promotes the understanding of the subject or matter by encouraging constant review and self-reflection. This way, students are trained in independent thinking, research, problem solving and decision-making.

In addition, teamwork, moderation, visualization and oral presentation are trained; this all serves the purpose of the betterment of students' communication skills. Thus, any student can develop and test new ways of analysis, presentation and communication, and apply these techniques inside and outside the university. Thereby MIKROAKADEMIE opened more space for creative projects and experiments in which teachers and students can actively develop new solutions for real-life planning issues. The philosophy behind this is that design and planning – in the sense of a 'research design' – should not be conveyed as a technically determined solution to problems, but as a process of finding solutions by approaching the problem through trial and error. It is a matter of promoting the solution of complex problems and the development of innovative ideas.

PRESENT PRACTICE: HOW IT WORKS

A major challenge when initiating the MIKROAKADEMIE was to develop a structure that would be flexible enough to test new teaching concepts yet rigid enough to convince everybody that sessions represent a 'proper' university course. In short, a framework was needed that incorporates people teaching each other things into the standards of academic rules and regulations. For this purpose, several aspects were considered (course-hours and workload, accreditation, grading, etc.), which we address while describing the current state, function and acceptance by students, and potential future directions of the MIKROAKADEMIE.

To encourage participation, it was key that course participants would get something out of the course that is worth more than the knowledge gained itself; in the sense of experience on one side (i.e., it is more enjoyable than e.g. watching a YouTube tutorial at home), and in the sense of certification on the other (i.e., there is a proof of participation and/or knowledge gained). Hence, one of the utmost important challenges was to incorporate the MIKROAKADEMIE and its courses into the curriculum of urban design and planning studies replete with credit points (CP) for participation. It is for this reason that a regular course in the MIKROAKADEMIE consists of two full days of instruction (approx. 15 teaching hours / 2 × 7.5h class time) plus homework intended to repeat and recapitulate content (which is calculated with the same number of hours). Assuming students spend as much time on the exercises outside of class, participation in a course cumulates to workload of 25–30 teaching hours, which accounts for 1 CP according to European Credit Transfer System (ECTS, EU 2015, p. 77). Awards are pass/fail. If participants are not interested in earning CPs, they can also opt for a printed certificate that confirms their participation.

In a peer-to-peer setting, there is another group that needs to be taken care of: the instructors! The most intriguing question was: Why would somebody choose to prepare a small class and stand in front of a crowd and teach them something? An idea was to pay tutors for their efforts; yet, in a university setting where there is no money allocated for such activities this was not an option. Looking for solutions for how to honour MIKROAKADEMIE instructors, we opted for a pragmatic solution. Student-tutors, who are recruited from the BA and MA programmes and volunteer to prepare and conduct a course, receive two CPs for their work. Using CPs to 'pay' tutors has proven to be successful for several reasons. First, and most importantly, it is preferable to paying money as it draws a clear separation between regular teaching and lecturing and does not lead to a structure of low-wage, non-permanent contracts. Instead, it accentuates the learning character (teaching is something one needs to learn) of giving a course in the MIKROAKADEMIE and at the same time rewards the efforts of preparing and conducting a course. Second, at least for some, it works as an incentive to lead a course. Such certification of abilities by a university body (i.e., through the credit points statement in the degree transcript or through a certificate stating that a course was held) is often preferred to earning money in the short-term.

Another issue was the identification and recruiting of instructors for the courses – i.e., to find people that could deliver high-quality teaching as they really are 'experts' in a field. To secure quality courses taught within the framework of the MIKROAKADEMIE, interested instructors need to apply specifying their field of experience and knowledge – e.g., by providing a CV or portfolio as well as providing a course description, outline, exercises, etc. and potential date(s) for the course. A team from the University then selects instructors based on knowledge and/or skills and the relevance of the proposed content. A consultation process is used to refine the scope of the course and make adaptations to guarantee general standards. This managerial intervention ensures that there is no overlap of contents (i.e., two very similar courses in one semester), that courses take place in a distributed manner across the semester and that the setting up of courses starts at minimum two weeks prior to the scheduled date. Also, help in regard to equipment (e.g., soft- and hardware, flipcharts, materials) is offered and a teaching location is guaranteed (e.g., the studio, a computer lab or other facilities). While student-instructors are made responsible for preparation and delivery of the content, administrative tasks – including the announcement of courses, inscription of participants and certification – are handled by university staff (requiring an input of approximately 5 hours per course). Thence, the role of the academic staff supervising the MIKROAKADEMIE becomes that of a manager – responsible for the community of participants – who ensures the courses run smoothly and the offer is attractive.

To sum up the character of MIKROAKADEMIE as a peer-learning format the organizational variables provided by Topping (2005, pp. 633–634) are helpful:

1. Curriculum content in our MIKROAKADEMIE courses vary widely and can be on virtually every imaginable subject related to methods and tools for urban planning and design.
2. Contact constellation – one student-teacher is working with a group of peers, which can vary in size from three to ten, seldom more; sometimes academic staff and PhD students become also learners in the MIKROAKADEMIE.
3. Within and between institutions – most MIKROAKADEMIE courses take place within the same institution, but student-teachers also come from other institutions (e.g., Hasso Plattner Institute, alumni of TU Berlin), and sometimes students taking part in the MIKROAKADEMIE come from other universities in Berlin.
4. Year of study – helpers (in our case student-teachers) and helped (in our case students who are participants in the MIKROAKADEMIE) may be from the same or different years of study.
5. Ability – most MIKROAKADEMIES operate on a cross-ability basis even if students are the same age and from the same year. Here it can be that student-teachers have 'superior' mastery of only a very small portion of the curriculum, or all might be of equal ability but working towards a shared, deeper, and hopefully correct understanding. Instances of 'Meta-ignorance' can be a problem – the helper doesn't know that they don't know the correct facts (Topping 2005, p. 633). Thus, we always

tutor our MIKROAKADEMIE teachers to get an idea about their knowledge level.

6. Time – MIKROAKADEMIE is scheduled in combination of regular class contact time and outside of this (sometimes it happens on Saturdays, which is not a regular teaching day at TU Berlin).
7. Place – MIKROAKADEMIE can vary in location of operation, but studio settings are favoured.
8. Voluntary or compulsory – in our case the MIKROAKADEMIE is voluntary as student-teachers and student participants self-select, but one has to note that students have to select a number of elective courses to fulfil credit requirements.
9. Reinforcement – MIKROAKADEMIE involves extrinsic reinforcement for the student-teachers and the student participants in the sense, that students need credits to fulfil their study programmes. Without doubt there is also intrinsic motivation, such as getting social praise and expertise acknowledgement. These are further discussed below.

PEER ASSESSMENT AND LESSONS LEARNED

With any innovation it is important to reflect on benefits, challenges and limitations of the teaching format and discuss how students perceive MIKROAKADEMIE courses. Since the beginning the courses were constantly monitored, evaluated and results documented and referenced for the ongoing development of the format using questionnaires and discussion rounds. This allowed us to build on students' opinions and reflections to improve the organization and management of the courses. We also wanted to assess the MIKROAKADEMIE's impact on TU Berlin's BA and MA in Urban Planning and Urban Design. In the future, the space for MIKRO-Courses will be broadened and the transferability/customization of the idea to other areas of study and their specific requirements tested. Yet, before we examine potential future developments, we want to discuss the peer-learning format and its development – from the initial pilot to the now well-established course – and critically reflect on the concept in the light of peer education approaches in higher education.

Overall, the MIKRAOAKADEMIE can be seen as successful in tackling the need for more (varied/specialized) courses on methods and tools for urban planners and designers. Not only was the innovative approach acknowledged by the Stifterverband's fellowship but students praise the courses and approve its quality by attendance. Hundreds of students took the opportunity to participate in elective (and core) seminars as 'learners' and/or 'teachers', thanks to changed examination regulations at the BA and MA Urban and Regional Planning at the Institute of Urban and Regional Planning (ISR), as well as in the interdisciplinary MA Urban Design (IfA, ISR, ILAUP, IfS).[1] Over the years, the MIKROAKADEMIE has become an established concept and accredited teaching format at TU Berlin (i.e., it has been incorporated into the official curriculum of several BA/MA studies); which can also be seen as one of the main drivers behind the MIKROAKADEMIE's success as courses are legitimized.

Evaluation of participant's experience and the overall resonance to the courses is very positive: A big majority of participants are very happy with both the course options (topics and content) as well as with the frequency and scope of the teaching. Especially the flexibility of the programme (i.e., in registration and participation), as well as the consensus about course contents (i.e., 'important' topics decided upon by demand) and the ability to choose from a broader variety of topics are often named as specifically positive (when compared to other courses). Another positive aspect highlighted by many is the atmosphere in the sessions and the experience of the studio setting as a 'learning experience' (Vowles et al. 2012). For many, learning in a course setting (with other students/peer pressure) is preferable to learning alone; and the human interface tops the online video tutorial and other self-teaching instruments (and/or, they complement each other). The situation in which students teach students leads to low hierarchies and feeling of equality among participants; which again lowers barriers in participation and involvement in class. Students feel confident to ask extra questions or ask for solutions to specific problems they encounter – which altogether leads to a more proactive and creative learning environment. Also, the feeling that trial and error is lived (not only proclaimed) is highlighted by participants when reflecting on their experience. Many associate the freedom to fail with the fact that the MIKROAKADEMIE is not graded (as by university law students cannot grade other students), hence there is no pressure to succeed but rather a freedom to experiment. Such 'free-range' courses are secured by law at public universities in Berlin, where 25% of all courses are not to be graded and therefore do not influence the final degree qualification of the Bachelor's or Master's degree.

Thence, while the MIKROAKADEMIE has become a field for experimentation and exchange of ideas, it also has become an institution of sorts, or at least a sought-after resource by students to not only gain knowledge, but also showcase and prove their skills and abilities. The success of the programme is greatly based on the fact that credit points can be gained and that the efforts put into learning are rewarded – as opposed to training yourself at home, with friends or via online tutorials. On top, participants from other universities, graduates and others that cannot or do not need to get credit points for their engagement with the MIKROAKADEMIE are offered certificates stating that they did participate or lead a certain course. Both credit points and certificates ensure that students' work is valued and put on record; and both are perceived as an opportunity to show what they are capable of (e.g., in CVs or during job interviews) as one holds proof from an acknowledged university of having led a specific course or being knowledgeable in the use of a certain software, etc.

An additional benefit is that the MIKROAKADEMIE ensures community. Thanks to the structure of a module – at TU Berlin one has to accumulate 3 CPs to complete a module – participants are prompted to attend several micro-courses, either as participants or as instructors. This leads to students knowing each other and their colleagues' skills and knowledge level in certain areas and discussing certain course contents also outside of the regular course hours. Therefore, not only a sense of give-and-take is assured – people sharing their knowledge and ideas – but also a more general feeling of ownership and community. Although it might be hard to measure such intangibles, the constantly growing number of participants and courses offered each semester could be taken as a sign for the growing engagement with the teaching format. Given the fact that students are repetitive participants – and often do more than three courses – we can confidently assume that there is a positive perception of MIKROAKADEMIE, and that students like to take part also as part of a community of people with common goals.

On the downside, what is criticized is that the quality of courses differs depending on the instructor (but so do 'official' university courses). Participants acknowledge, that the 'teacher-students' go through a process of learning by doing; and that one can learn how to teach by attending MIKROAKADEMIE courses and looking at other people's techniques and abilities when communicating contents. Often enough, participants are encouraged to impart a course by themselves only after having attended one or two sessions as participants and realizing that teaching is not that complicated. The other, more fundamental critique is that the high demand for certain courses is leaving people out (i.e., not being able to take the course they want in the specific semester they desire to do it). The fact that we are closing course-inscription at a maximum of 20 participants is triggering demands for higher frequency or for repetition of courses that are in high demand. The problem here though, lies in the ability to find 'new' course instructors; teacher-students who already gave a certain course are normally not interested in repeating it – plus it is not encouraged by the MIKROAKADEMIE programme, as it runs against the initial concept of *not* wanting to replace standard courses with student-taught peer formats. Instead, the demand for certain course contents (e.g., mediation or design thinking) is taken as democratically decided upon assurance, that these topics might need to be incorporated into the standard curriculum of the BA and MA studies in Urban Planning and Design.

FUTURE PERSPECTIVES AND OUTLOOK

We introduced the MIKROAKADEMIE at TU Berlin as a peer-to-peer learning platform devoted to increase future professionals' abilities to comprehensively communicate their urban design ideas through different means. Although this has always been part of design teaching, we see a growing demand for communication skills on various levels. This is in part due to the increasing digitalization, and the growing number of technologies and applications, as well as the speed at which they are being re-developed/-invented and the consequent need to update skills. This is true of the area of analysis (GIS, mapping, crowdsourcing, real-time-data analysis, etc.), representation (hand-drawing, CAD, 3D, graphic design, model-making, interactive modelling, etc.), as well as preparation of content (printed media, Web 2.0, social networks, mobile internet, etc.). And while the MIKROAKADEMIE's inception was clearly driven by very specific needs at the time at TU Berlin, we want to discuss the concept's transferability to other educational settings as well as its pedagogical innovations and developments in the field of education for spatial planning in general.

In our opinion, the education of future urbanists and planners needs to be seen as a social learning process especially in the context of planning where one has to be able to work and communicate across lay and professional boundaries. So, Million and Parnell (2017) asked: What is the position of knowledge in this context? How might planners learn to bring their knowledge in those processes across not only as moderator but as educator? "A framework is needed to guide the educative planner's development of appropriate knowledge, skills and attitudes: setting out, for example, potential learning- and teaching-related roles, such as mentor, facilitator, councillor, entertainer, advocate, critical friend, more experienced participant and knowledge holder" (Million and Parnell 2017, p. 79). The MIKROAKADEMIE is providing such a framework, but may not be enough.

We need an urban design and planning education that embraces critical teaching, learning and reflection as well as research and teaching methodologies for critical design, which can be weapons of choice for communication and understanding consequences of e.g. digitalization, economic policy and other schemes in cities and of bold engagement in shaping urban tomorrows. As Brück (2017, p. 155) argues, future urban planners should internalize asking divergent questions that follow dynamic inquiry methods and create variations, alternative answers, and scenarios of possible procedures, rather than being fixated on static knowledge and 'end products'. The MIKROAKADEMIE can be seen as a chance to explore the need for new skills and knowledge and could help to foster the transformation of planning education from the bottom-up.

Furthermore, the main concept behind the MIKROAKADEMIE platform is not only to broaden the dissemination of technical skills; rather, it also contributes to shaping understandings of learning as a progressive, interactive and recurring process where one learns 'from each other' and flexibly shares knowledge – an example of self-learning environments (SLEs).[2] In the foreground is the encouragement of autonomous, life-long learning; an 'orientational' knowledge that enables navigation through the many possibilities to analyse, represent and convey content.

As proposed by the editors of this book, future pedagogies for planners will need to help prepare students for uncertain futures, social responsibility and working with different collaborators across sectors in an interdisciplinary and creative manner to effect change and create healthy, equitable, high quality communities and places. If everything is becoming more fluid, less permanent, in constant adaptation, then education of urban designers and planners needs to follow suit. And it is: the flexibilization of curricula and learning environments is happening. Planning students evolve from a receiver of education to a provider of knowledge, becoming educative planners and active contributors to curriculum development. In parallel, the entire city is gaining recognition as a learning platform as teaching is breaking out of the confinement of the academic ivory tower. This might be seen as critical when discussing the potential future role and status of universities: while one could argue that the function of a university as knowledge provider is endangered by P2P concepts and other fluid formats, the experience from the MIKRAOAKADEMIE shows that academic institutions are still regarded as quality guarantors and therefore a self-taught course in such a setting is still valued higher than an internet video tutorial or non-accredited course.

There are already positive experiences in urban planning of coaching (design consultations / competition participation) and problem-based learning (project work), which are now to be extended to other areas of teaching like peer-to-peer learning formats (e.g. Grant and Manuel 1995; Oonk et al. 2016). Like the MIKROAKADEMIE, workshops, summer-schools, and other teaching formats are making academia fluid, enabling proximities to real-life tasks, connecting theory and practice, and are sharing knowledge, knowledge creation, and knowledge applications. By reshaping and re-conceptualizing current university roles and missions, such innovative pedagogies contribute to both: enhancing students' learning and promoting 21st century competencies for urban designers and planners.

A vital question is then how could the MIKROAKADMIE's format and concept be transferred to other institutions and how could it be further developed? When looking at potential futures for our teaching – in the urban design and planning programmes at TU Berlin in general, and of the MIKROAKADEMIE format in particular – two issues arise: (1) practical to do's and organizational variables and ideas concerning core aspects of the teaching like content, modus operandi, time, objectives, etc. that we would like to try out and experiment with, and (2) theoretical and contemplative aspects in relation to a wider perspective and research on peer learning (i.e., the observation and interpretation of our own doing).

When it comes to the practical suggestions and developments, it seems obvious that MIKROAKADEMIE will need to further widen its focus by adding topics and course types. This has already happened over the last couple of semesters and we foresee it continuing; examples being experiments with MOOCs[3] or courses that resemble excursions and hands-on workshops in the city (erasing the confinement of the classroom). With this widening of the offer we expect a parallel expansion of the target group[4] (meaning participants: instructors as well as learners) – also a trend we have been observing already in the past years. The MIKROAKADEMIE is seen as a format that should have options to give more extensive/longer courses (including more credit points) – at least in regard to specific topics that might need more than two sessions to cover, as well as course concepts that need a longer extent (in time) to be fruitful. Such demands are being discussed, and the future might bring a variety of formats including three to five day workshops or excursions, as well as more stratified course contents (e.g., more theoretical and/or practical courses). The challenge in the expansion of focus lies in the framework through which the MIKROAKADEMIE functions, which means being flexible enough to incorporate new ideas, while at the same time not losing its character and functionality. Monitoring and evaluation – as a continued peer assessment and 'community management' – will eventually become more important (e.g., to assess effects of changes/innovations on the existing structure). Meanwhile, as the 'community' grows, the management of people, topics, quality, etc. becomes more complex – triggering a need for streamlined processes and automatization of management. We have for example rationalized the course proposal process and simplified the registration using online forms/processes in order to lower the administrative workload.

Considering the MIKROAKADEMIE as a research arena offers an opportunity to investigate needs and trends in future urban design and planning education. As a peer assisted learning format and peer tutoring the content of courses is 'fluid' and studio culture (as setting) can function as an experimental testbed for 'trend setting' in planning education. As it reflects the needs and wants of contemporary students ('Generation Y'), it has the potential of understanding changes in perception and fostering a bottom-up development of curriculum content – for the benefit of tutors/helpers and students/helped alike. Therefore, we are eager to explore causes and/or (perceived) needs for specific skills and knowledge demanded to be incorporated into the curriculum or generally thought as essential by participants. The evaluation of the MIKROAKADEMIE could help foster the transformation of planning education as it can provide guidance of what new methods and tools for analysis, design, visualization, communication, participation, etc. could/should be incorporated into the standard curriculum of every urban designer and planner. This research will go on. (See Box 12.1.)

BOX 12.1 KEY CHALLENGES AND SUGGESTIONS

- The main challenge remains in setting up a structure flexible enough to test new teaching concepts, yet rigid enough to comply with university regulations. Finding a framework that incorporates people teaching each other things into the standards of academic regulations will likely vary from institution to institution.
- MIKROAKADEMIE engenders community, as participants are prompted to attend several micro-courses, either as participants or as instructors. Understanding this community and their needs through constant evaluation is vital as only this will allow for regular adaptation of the courses and their contents.
- Course instructors ('teacher-students') need guidance as they go through a process of learning by doing in relation to teaching. Tutoring the tutors becomes an important task in setting up the courses. Yet, one can also learn how to teach by attending MIKROAKADEMIE courses and looking at other instructors' techniques and approaches.
- Optimum class size has been around 10 to 15 (minimum five and maximum 20). High demand for certain courses in combination with relatively small group sizes might trigger demands for higher frequency and the repetition of courses. The problem here lies in the ability to find 'new' course instructors.

NOTES

1. The international Master's programme 'Urban Design' at TU Berlin is a joint, interdisciplinary programme run collaboratively between the Institute of Architecture (IfA), the Institute of Urban & Regional Planning (ISR), the Institute of Landscape Architecture and Environmental Planning (ILAUP), and the Institute of Sociology (IfS).
2. See Sugata Mitra and his 'School in the Cloud' – www.theschoolinthecloud.org.
3. For example, in 2017 on Productive Cities; based on findings from the research project 'Roof-Water-Farm' http://www.roofwaterfarm.com.
4. For example, international students (coupled with the demand for English – or other languages – as instruction language), participants from different backgrounds and studies within TU Berlin (e.g., architecture, ecology, engineering) as well as participants from outside TU Berlin (e.g., professionals).

REFERENCES

Borden, I. et al. (2010) *Subject Benchmark Statement: Architecture*. Gloucester: The Quality Assurance Agency for Higher Education.

Brück, A. (2017) *Urban Tomorrows 2030: Visions & Counter-Visions for Future Cities*. Doctoral thesis, TU Berlin.

Daniels, H. (2012) *An Introduction to Vygotsky*. New York: Routledge.

EU (2015) *ECTS Users' Guide*. European Union Publications Office. https://ec .europa.eu/education/sites/education/files/ects-users-guide_en.pdf (retrieved May 2018). See also: http://ec.europa.eu/education/resources/european-credit-transfer -accumulation-system_en.

Freire, P. (1996) *Pedagogy of the Oppressed*. Harmondsworth: Penguin.

Grant, J. and Manuel, P. (1995) Using a peer resource learning model in planning education. *Journal of Planning Education and Research* 15(1): 51–57.

Million, A. and Parnell, R. (2017) The educative planner. *disP – The Planning Review* 53(2): 78–79.

Oonk, C., Gulikers, J. and Mulder, M. (2016) Educating collaborative planners: Strengthening evidence for the learning potential of multi-stakeholder regional learning environments. *Planning Practice & Research* 31(5): 533–551.

Strickland, R. (2017) Editorial: Ten recommendations for enhancing urban design teaching and learning. *Urban Design and Planning* 170: 93–95.

Topping, K. J. (2005) Trends in peer-learning. *Educational Psychology* 26(6): 631–645.

Vowles, H., Low, J. and Doron, H. (2012) Investigating architecture studio culture in the UK: A progress report. *Journal for Education in the Built Environment* 7(2): 26–49.

Whitman, N. and Fife, J. (1988) *Peer Teaching: To Teach is to Learn Twice*. ASHE-ERIC Higher Education Report No. 4.

Additional Resources.

Webpage MIKROAKADEMIE: https://labor-k.org/home-en/courses/#mika.

PART IV

Further education and life-long capacity building

13. Online, but not isolated: addressing a key challenge of digital distance learning

Adam Sheppard

INTRODUCTION

In the middle of the 1980s the Royal Town Planning Institute (RTPI) was reflecting upon routes to professional membership. Pondering to discontinue professional examinations which allowed a practice-based route into membership alongside the traditional academic qualification model, the challenge was to retain a viable pathway for future members for whom the traditional educational option was either not viable or appropriate. The answer was to create a distance learning programme, the MA Town and Country Planning, which enrolled the first cohort in 1985. The programme ran successfully until its replacement in 2015 with a revised version – the MSc Urban and Rural Planning. This programme was delivered by the Joint Distance Learning Consortium (JDLC) comprising in 2015 of UWE Bristol, Leeds Beckett University, London South Bank University, Dundee University, and the Open University as an external provider of materials that enable both an open access study pathway for students without the required educational background for direct entry as well as a series of modules specifically selected to support the RTPI specialism route offered as part of the programme.

Theory and practice concerning pedagogy evolves over time. Furthermore, education programmes also need to align with national and professional narratives and policies concerning widening participation and enhanced opportunities for those unable to access traditional contact-based courses. In the context of the original MA Town and Country Planning the passage of time and the associated changes in academia and practice resulted in the need for significant reform; the growing emphasis upon student-centred learning was central to this and the need to reimagine the manner in which effective student-centred learning is enabled through a distance learning planning programme drove the reform which is presented and discussed in this chapter.

Although the redesign's lead institution UWE Bristol has longstanding experience in distance learning, this programme redesign represented a step-change in the delivery of distance learning. The programme needed to enable soft skills development within its offer, reflecting the recognized demands of planning and related professions as well as the broader growing emphasis upon this within higher education. This was ultimately facilitated with the assistance of the university's Learning Innovation Unit (LIU) and a creative use of ICT at the heart of this re-imagination of planning education. The resultant programme, the MSc Urban and Rural Planning, represented a transformation in teaching practices for the JDLC. In fact, these innovative approaches have subsequently informed the next generation of distance learning programmes in planning education more widely.

SEEDS FOR CHANGE IN A PIONEERING PROGRAMME

The initial MA Town and Country planning which was established in 1985 was presented as a distance learning course, but this proposition can be challenged based upon the actual delivery approach. Learning at a distance was initially delivered on this programme through hard copy, and from 2008 onward by digital materials. Content was throughout delivered in a passive manner with limited opportunity for student interactions. Critically though, the programme also included face to face contact including a residential Spring School, a residential Summer School, induction events, and final year dissertation study days. These compulsory contact-based sessions were vital to enable cohort development, interaction, assessment, and a quality student experience.

Following Moore et al.'s definition of *distance learning* as an "effort of providing access to learning for those who are geographically distant" (2011, p. 129), the MA Town and Country Planning did therefore offer an element of distance learning, but it would perhaps be better described as blended learning. As noted by Garrison and Vaughan (2008, p. 6): "Attaining the threshold of blended learning means replacing aspects of face-to-face learning with appropriate online learning experiences ...". In other words, the MA Town and Country Planning was really a blended learning experience with students undertaking a learning journey supported by both materials to enable distance learning and (compulsory) contact experiences. This history is important as a driver for how the subsequent replacement programme, the MSc Urban and Rural Planning, emerged.

By the beginning of the second decade of the 21st century it was clear that the programme required significant revision. This was due in part to two key changes; the first was the finances of higher education which created an environment where the previously delivered arrangements were no longer viable from a resource perspective, particularly the contact elements of the programme. The second key change was in the attitude of students which was evolving notably and expecting an experience the MA course was incapable of delivering. This latter dynamic sits within a wider and significant context of change within higher education; the move towards more student-centred learning approaches, alongside ICT developments and a widening participation drive, together with the need to create a quality student experience with strong cohort identity. This contextual evolution is driving change within academia in a number of respects, but for distance learning the added challenge is how to create best practice for students who are geographically disparate and interacting online.

Consultation with the then student body indicated a need to remove the contact elements of the programme, thereby shifting the approach of the replacement MSc from a blended learning model to a pure distance learning model with flexible asynchronous learning but also offering modern 'virtual' meeting and collaboration / communication spaces. The student feedback was interesting on two levels; not only did they not wish to have *compulsory contact* events within the programme, they also wished to avoid being required to be *online* at a fixed date and time. This is understandable given the student cohort's diversity in terms of age and educational background and their situation with a majority in full time work and/or managing demanding home lives. The added complexity to the student feedback however was that students did wish to have opportunities for meaningful *interaction* with each other.

ADVANTAGES AND CHALLENGES OF DISTANCE LEARNING

Study via distance learning can have multiple advantages for students; it can enable learning where this otherwise may not be viable. Challenges around location, transport, availability of time, flexibility of time, family and employment circumstances can all limit access to education and through distance learning it is possible for them to be managed (Croft et al. 2010; Lake 1999). Distance learning, however, has drawbacks as well:

> Providing online activities has particular challenges, including difficulty of encouraging participation (Gibson et al., 2001), anxiety of students (Hughes and Daykin, 2002), difficulty of creating successful critical/analytical dialogue (Hughes and Daykin, 2002), potential for mistaken beliefs to be generated and shared (Weller, 2002), difficulty of tutor facilitation of online debate (Hughes and Daykin, 2002) and ability of the tutor to answer queries promptly. (Croft et al. 2010, p. 31)

Croft et al. go on to state that learner isolation, and the need for effective inter-action, are critical. It is of note that the provision of passive materials only is equally challenged based on the inadequacy of this to actively enable learning.

In the context of programme revisions, the educators needed to be aware of the learner isolation challenge and overcome this, together with the need to enable active learning. But the design team were equally aware of the student preferences around learning approaches, meaning many commonly used approaches such as webinars were not suitable given the need for these to be timed events. Another challenge in the context of distance learning is the delivery of soft skills on which there is a growing emphasis placed in higher education as of late:

> universities are putting greater emphasis on developing competencies that were tra-ditionally marginalized for highly valued "hard" skills. It has been well established throughout the literature the significance of proving professional development skills concurrently with graduate programming. (Gauvreau et al. 2016, p. 92)

Town planning and related professions place traditionally a strong emphasis on such skills in association with professional body accreditation, reflecting the need for planners to develop such skills to operate effectively in inter- and multi-disciplinary environments – a trait that is becoming even more relevant in the context of contemporary society. Thus, for the MSc Urban and Rural Planning the requirement for soft skill development to be embraced was par-ticularly acute given their significance to professional practice.

REDESIGNING DISTANCE LEARNING

The re-imagined MSc Urban and Rural Planning was launched in 2015 as a replacement for the MA Town and Country planning. Like its predecessor, this three-year distance learning programme was accredited by the Royal Town Planning Institute (RTPI), the professional body for town planning in the UK, as a 'Combined Award'.[1] As before, the core content was designed to be delivered by the JDLC member Planning Schools, with the Open University continuing to offer selected modules to enable both entry options onto the programme, and also modules for the RTPI Specialism programme element alongside the guided dissertation. To enhance flexibility, a variety of exit points were introduced with the ability for students to exit at year one (PG Certificate), year two (PGDip and RTPI Spatial Award), or complete year three and secure the full Combined Award (Figure 13.1).

Overall management and administration of the programme is undertaken by a designated lead institution (Leeds Beckett University since 2020), while the

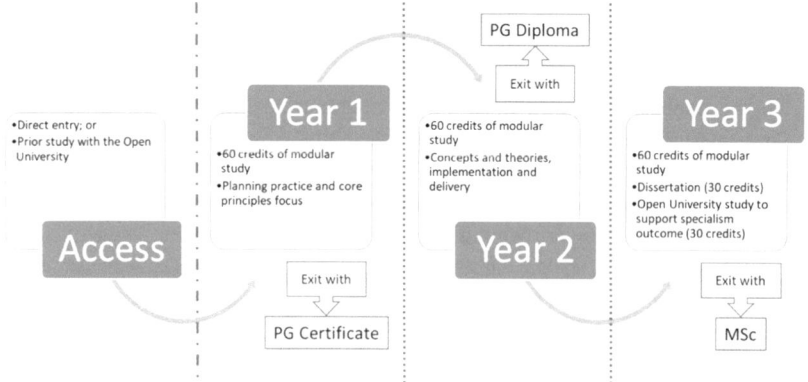

Source: Author.

Figure 13.1   Programme concept structure

delivery of the programme is shared, with each institution taking responsibility for identified modules.

The programme review did also create an opportunity for a content refresh, but the broad structural approach remained. Some change was introduced following discussions with the RTPI; the desire was to create maximum choice and opportunity through the specialism options and as such three pathways were created based around (i) Environmental Decision Making, (ii) Social Policy, and (iii) Management, Decision Making and Leadership. Embedded within this was a longstanding support for onwards learning. These were enabled via options for further study with the Open University, such as the option of a Masters of Business Administration (MBA) module which could be studied within the MSc programme but then transferred into the Open University MBA offer. The overall programme structure is presented in Figure 13.2.

RE-IMAGINING DISTANCE LEARNING

The aim to transition to a 'pure' distance learning model was the key principle that guided the programme design and approach. While the MA utilized a blended learning approach to overcome learner isolation, create interaction opportunities, and support the learning of the students, reinforcing and clarifying knowledge and experience, the online experience was broadly a passive one. Although, there were some self-managed study exercises available to students, the consultation demonstrated clearly that students did not engage

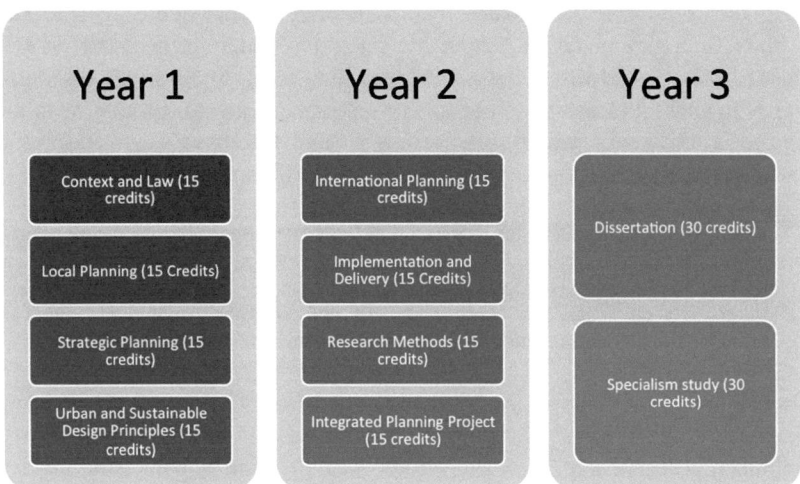

Figure 13.2   Programme modular structure

with these and consumed the provided materials in a passive manner only. Critically, outside of the provided contact events there was no facilitated online student interaction during periods of remote study, indeed in most instances there was no interaction, beyond occasional student-led network development through email and, more recently, Facebook, WhatsApp, etc. The transition to a 'pure' online learning approach therefore needed to embrace an approach which enabled effective student interaction, addressing both effective online learning and addressing the wider challenges associated with learner isolation.

At its heart the approach of the MSc was the application of online collaborative learning theory. This is a constructivist teaching approach which is based upon the principle of student collaboration to solve problems and learn through interaction, rather than a passive consumption of provided materials. Further, Harasim postulated that:

> The principle of collaborative learning may be the single most important concept for online networked learning, since this principle addresses the strong socio-affective and cognitive power of learning on the Web. The Web's asynchronous nature both enables and requires collaborative learning: collaboration provides the social glue of a community that engages learners and motivates them to participate. (2000, p. 53)

As such the approach demands an active learning leader (lecturer/tutor) who both facilitates and participates in the learning journey with the students. Although passive materials remain available and underpin the provided evidence base for students to draw upon, enabling engagement in the discourse is key to enabling learning to occur. The discourse is key to learning, with the student's active engagement with not only the materials but also with peers and the associated discussion, central to students' development:

> Articulation is a cognitive act in which the student presents, defends, develops, and refines ideas. To articulate their ideas, students must organize their thoughts and information into knowledge structures. Active learner participation leads to multiple perspectives on issues, a divergence of ideas, and positions that students must sort through to find meaning and convergence. (Harasim 2000, p. 53)

From a pedagogy perspective student-centred learning, with active student learners, mutual respect, interdependence, and autonomy underpinning the approach (O'Neill and McMahon 2005) can be aligned with collaborative learning theory and allows for clarity in the conceptual understanding of the desired programme approach. In the delivery approach a triangulation therefore needed to occur, with interactions taking place between the learning

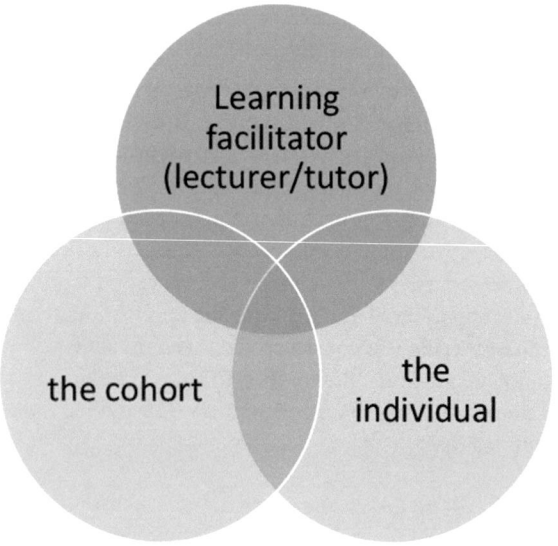

Source: Author.

Figure 13.3   *Triangulation required to enable online collaborative learning*

facilitator, the individual student, and the wider cohort with both directly/ exclusive and wider group interaction provided for within the context of the learning journey (Figure 13.3).

Furthermore, learning isolation creates challenges beyond the ability of the student to undertake the knowledge and understanding journey effectively as a result of the lack of opportunity to articulate thought and interact in discourse. There is also the matter of learner well-being. The psychological implications of remote and isolated study, due to the lack of a peer group for wider social interaction and support are highlighted by the higher than average dropout rates associated with online learning (Croft et al. 2010).

There is an added layer of complexity here; student study approaches are varied and thus a flexible methodology to the enabling of learning is required to maximize the effectiveness of the student experience and success. As discussed by Croft et al. (2010), isolated learning is not a consistent challenge, it will vary between students and by circumstance. Compulsory interaction also created variable responses from students (Croft et al. 2010), a phenomenon corroborated by the student consultation exercise where a clear position was taken on the desire to create genuine flexibility in learning such that students did not need to be online at any specified date and time, maximizing their ability to engage in their learning as and when convenient to them. The characteristics and diversity of the student body associated with the MSc heightened this dynamic, with a significant diversity of scenarios (and geographical locations) having an impact.

RE-CREATING THE LEARNING ENVIRONMENT

As a result, the design team created a concept tagged the 'classroom to coffee shop' derived from the idea of creating an online campus. The online campus is not focused on creating a virtual campus, but rather considered the role of different spaces and scenarios of interaction and the extent to which these could be recreated online. The intention was to create 'spaces' which enabled an online collaborative learning approach and allowed students to engage with their peers, learning facilities, and the wider university support and learning infrastructure. Direct comparison was made with the contact-based campus learning environment; here, several scenarios occur for the student in the context of their student life, including:

1. Structured delivery of materials through lectures;
2. Structured student-centred learning through seminars, etc.;
3. Structured social interactions through organized events;
4. Unstructured student-centred learning through informal interactions;
5. Unstructured social interactions through student-led interactions.

Within the campus based working day, the above occurs in a number of key spaces:

1. Lecture theatres;
2. Seminar rooms and other teaching spaces;
3. Other provided learning spaces, including the library;
4. Student facilities, including cafés and communal spaces.

The MSc endeavoured to create online spaces where these scenarios could occur, but there was also consideration of control and ownership; a number of the spaces and activities above are student controlled and orchestrated, with students choosing location, timing, agenda, culture, and characteristics. This placed additional demands and challenges to the aspirations of the programme design team.

The 2015 redesign was underpinned by the UWE Bristol online platforms, with 'MyUWE' providing students with access to their records, timetabling information, key information, and access to additional information and support, and Blackboard™ acting as the main learning space. Blackboard™ has many positive attributes as a Virtual Learning Environment (VLE) but is distinctly a university controlled and managed space and there is little opportunity to change this. As a result, the need for a 'third space' was identified which could be a genuinely shared space within which students felt a sense of control and influence; this was critical to completing the ranges of spaces considered necessary to form an online campus. The chosen platform was the Piazza education forum. This is an 'external' platform which can be linked into Blackboard™ but stands as a separate and non-institutional space. A fourth space, Facebook, was also used; a university moderated space for less formal, but still appropriate, interactions to take place. Bringing MyUWE, Blackboard, Facebook, and Piazza together provided the range of spaces to operationalize the classroom to coffee shop concept (Figure 13.4).

Of these spaces, it is Piazza which is most significant in some respects to the delivery of effective distance learning. The core learning materials, typically e-book based with associated wider reading and links to video / audio content, are delivered in Blackboard to create resources for students to engage with, but it is in Piazza where the online collaborative learning and student-centred experience can be enacted. Blackboard does allow student collaboration to occur, but Piazza addresses the challenge of control of spaces and the student behaviour associated with different degrees of control.

As a final comment it merits emphasizing that this was created in a resource constrained context. Delivery assumed a comparable resource to a contact-based module time demand. An initial investment is required in the creation of the written learning materials, but once this has been undertaken it

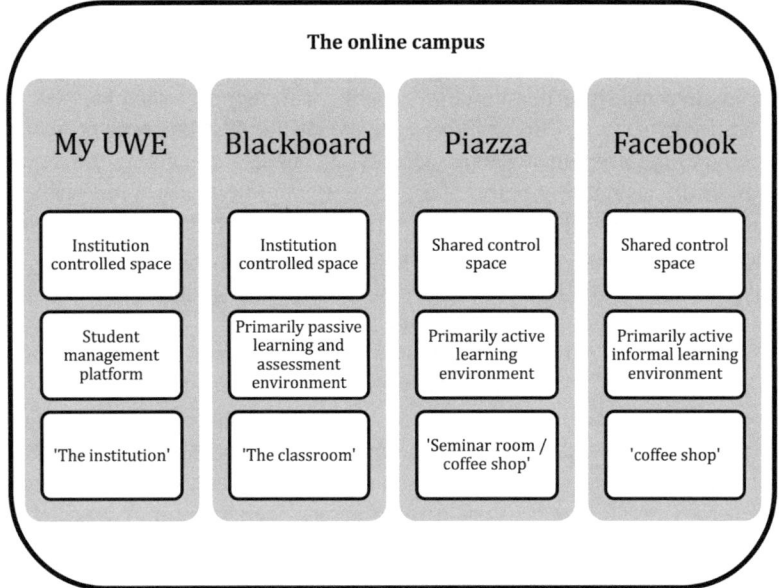

Source: Author.

Figure 13.4   Classroom to coffee shop concept

requires update and evolution rather than recreation in line with the resources employed in a contact-based module. The online campus does not need to be an expensive creation.

OPERATIONALIZING THE PROGRAMME

On the MSc, modules were designed to run sequentially with materials made available at the point at which the module becomes live. This allows students to engage with the materials at their own convenience; a key requirement based upon student feedback. Conceptually the teaching team distinguishes between active and passive spaces.

Blackboard is the passive space, where materials are prepared, structured into learning unit and presented to students for engagement at their convenience. The Blackboard Learning Units effectively allow the creation of e-books inclusive of embedded imagery, video, audio, and links to wider resources. The space is therefore passive in the sense that the student is engaging in an individual and solo learning journey through the units, but the spaces can be dynamic and can include degrees of interaction for the learner. Content creation is in line with a contact-based approach, with the materials mapped against the time implications of interacting with them. The provision of the complete set of Learning Units associated with a module also allows for effective time management and study planning for students. A further important element was the ability to submit a diversity of assessment outputs; this was critical for the programme from an academic perspective but also in meeting the requirements of the accrediting body. Not only is there a need to submit academic essays, practice reports, portfolios etc, but also presentations. Through using linked software,[2] it is possible to upload student recorded presentations into Blackboard without a size limit. This allows a full spectrum of assessment to be realized without required attendance.

Piazza represents the active space where meaningful online collaborative learning can occur. Within Piazza, year groups are created, replicating the real-world year cohort experience. The Piazza space therefore transcends the contained module runs, meaning the space is interacted with over the course of the full academic year. This equally allows individual interaction threads to run across the full year. As students progress, their space moves with them allowing the creation of a rich resource covering the entire student journey over the course of the three years of study. To enhance the collaborative potential, sub-groups can also be created within the year groups. Within this Piazza space, interactions can occur in two ways: (1) learning facilitator enabled, and (2) student enabled.

The learning facilitator interaction will occur in different ways, but typically involves setting tasks or providing discussion points for students to respond to. These will be linked to the module learning or wider skills and knowledge development. These are opportunities created by the programme team with the intention of stimulating discussion and articulation concerning the discourses relevant to the present point of the student journey, creating a progressive structure to the learning journey and narrative, and supporting the development of learning in a linear and coordinated manner alongside the planned module journey. Interactions will also create a shared resource for students to draw upon and further support their learning and assessments. Interactions are encouraged, but are not compulsory, allowing student choice and flexibility.

The student enabled interactions occur in the same space, with students able to create new 'conversations', share materials, and develop interactive opportunities for their peers. Although student enabled, the learning facilitators are also able to engage with these interactions and maximize their potential value as online collaborative learning occurrences.

Piazza is a valuable platform for a diversity of activity types, but a particularly important element is group working. As noted above, facilitator interactions can be based around a requirement for group interactions. This can extend to group assessments. The ability to offer group interactions in this manner was not only important for pedagogical and cohort development reasons, but also because of the requirements of the RTPI; enabling meaningful group working, particularly being mindful of evidenced soft skill development, was the only area of concern (alongside the ability to include presentations) expressed by the Institute upon presentation of the new programme model. A further benefit of Piazza is the ability to create group spaces with external parties; in the case of the new MSc programme a dedicated space was created to allow student feedback and discussion to occur with the accrediting body – the RTPI. To enable students to provide confidential feedback to the RTPI, the space was created to exclude access by the academic teaching team.

The final space is Facebook, which was introduced to be used with more of a social purpose, creating an informal space for interactions. Such spaces are commonplace across programmes of all types at university, and the programme design team felt such an 'approved' Facebook group would still have value; a key reason for this is that membership can extend beyond year groups and active students, creating a single space for all current students, alumni, and future students. This space can have a particular dynamic, with a more informal and inclusive area to share things of interest, including job and event opportunities and media/open access items of interest. Although overlap with Piazza activity can occur, the experience of the MSc has been that discussion can be less constrained and wider in scope. Thus far, no inappropriate behaviour has been observed in this, the least managed space associated with the programme.

The significance to planning education of the JDLC's MSc lies not so much in the content, as in the delivery approach. Access to planning education underpins the educational philosophy and indeed purpose of the JDLC. For some, a full-time or part-time residential course simply isn't viable. This can be for a range of reasons as mentioned earlier in this chapter. The fact that the JDLC MSc was designed as a 'pure' distance learning programme therefore is central to its significance; a genuinely distance learning offering maximizes the opportunity to study the course, irrespective of location and, broadly, circumstance. Delivery in this manner within planning education remains rare, meaning that for the profession it is an important provision. Critically though, it is considered that *how* the programme is offered and delivered is of equal significance; creating the ability to undertake student-centred online collaborative learning means students on this programme are able to experience distance learning without the full implications of remote/isolated learner experience. Meaning interactions can occur, cohorts can be formed, relationships can develop, and enhanced learning can occur. This is further reinforced by the module requirements, with several of the modules requiring student interactions and group work, either in formative activities or assessments.

OUTCOMES

Since the release of the online MSc programme there has been evolution in how the learning spaces that underpin the classroom to coffee shop concept are utilized. Experience has highlighted the following:

1. *Consistency* – In the initial cycles different staff members within the team engaged within the Piazza space differently, and to different degrees. This created an uneven experience for students, which can be problematic if a perception or reality of a variation in quality of service emerges from this. A key challenge is therefore how to create consistency in the user experience, a matter which can only be achieved through programme team agreement.
2. *Balance of interactions* – The consistency challenge above is not a matter of everyone engaging more regularly; student feedback has highlighted the implications of over-interacting as a learning facilitator, creating pressure to interact. Emphasizing the voluntary nature of the interactions is therefore important, but so too is an awareness and understanding of the appropriate level, timing, demand implication, and requirements associated with created interactions.
3. *Study time* – Linked to this is the need to plan overall interactions including the study time associated with a given module. Creating the learning units can be planned based on projected interaction time, but time within the shared space (Piazza) equally needs management. Student enabled interactions are external to this, mirroring student interactions outside of timetabled sessions in a contact-based programme, but the staff enabled interactions should be considered and managed.
4. *Wider support* – Creating interactions with the programme team was the focus on the MSc approach, but experience showed that students then had an aspiration for wider support to also be available through the platform, i.e., advice from support services. The response to this was a combination of either bringing support team colleagues into the Piazza space where resources allowed this to be offered, or alternatively ensuring clarity to students in relation to how to access wider support across the university.
5. *Flexibility of access* – This challenge is currently associated with both Blackboard and Piazza when students are unable to directly export the written materials from the Blackboard learning units, or the Piazza spaces, as PDFs. This means students need to be online to access the materials. Though rarely an issue, some students have noted the advantage of hard copy materials, including when travelling. Conversely, the Piazza space has proven effective and useable by tablet and via phone app, enhancing

the ability of the student to engage in learning in a diversity of locations and scenarios.

6. *Resources* – Resource implications were a slight unknown when the MSc was first opened. Experience has shown a mixed picture. One side of the coin is that Piazza can reduce email traffic; questions posed by students in Piazza, or responses to an emailed question, reduce further email traffic through a shared answer being available to the whole year cohort. Encouraging students to pose questions, unless personal/sensitive in nature, through Piazza reinforces this pattern. The flip side of the coin is that with the students able to interact 24/7, there is an expectation in relation to the level of staff interaction and response times. This requires learning facilitator workload planning and managing student expectations.

7. *Contact* – The discussion in this chapter is focused on the use of a 'pure' model of distance learning and the ability of this to function as an effective educational/learner experience with the learner isolation minimized. The fact remains however, that student feedback continues to demand some level of contact for some learners. Delivering this as an optional opportunity, where students who wish no contact will not be disadvantaged but the contact experience is meaningful and impactful, is challenging. Providing such opportunities, based on the programme team experience, do add value for selected students in the context of cohort building and the sense of belonging and attachment that can be supported. As such the programme continues to offer selected, optional, events focused on networking and cohort building rather than the delivery of academic content.

IMPACTS

The MSc Urban and Rural Planning was introduced in 2015 and since commencement student feedback has been secured from each year group every cycle. The response to the programme has been overwhelmingly positive. Of particular note has been Piazza; based upon student feedback the creation of a shared space successfully enabled student-led interaction, student-centred learning, cohort development, and helped to overcome learner isolation. The feedback further suggests that flexible asynchronous learning has been enabled. Piazza can be used to help support soft skills development. Student satisfaction levels for the programme were high, and recruitment increased from mid-teens to mid-thirties during the period 2015–2020 when UWE Bristol led the consortium.

A measure of success for this programme must be its ability to deliver planning education best practice through distance learning. It is suggested that the programme can be considered successful in this respect; hard and soft skills and content are delivered, interaction occurs, student-centred learning is enabled, and the challenging requirements of the RTPI are met, including enabling student presentations and evidencing of interpersonal skills development. External Examiner reporting, supported by student feedback, points to a programme offering 'Access for all to a quality Town and Country Planning education' in line with the guiding principle of the JDLC Planning School philosophy.

A further significant effect of this programme has been the institutional impact within the 2015 redesign on the lead institution, UWE Bristol, and the Consortium more widely. Leadership of the JDLC has now passed to Leeds Beckett University, who continue to progress the evolution of this offer to reflect the constant nature of change in distance learning delivery. New and exciting changes will no doubt come forward in the coming years. The innovations associated with this programme have been highlighted through academic conference papers and university level discussion. The conceptual approach, together with the ICT implications, have informed the development of new programmes at UWE Bristol; the 2015 MSc Urban and Rural Planning programme was a trailblazer which, moving on from this offering, is now shaping the future online offer from the UWE Bristol Planning School – most notably the MSc Planning and Urban Leadership, newly launched in 2020 as online only programme – and is impacting more widely across the university.

In addition, the RTPI has developed online resources for universities, including video career / professional development talks, which online planning programmes can take advantage of.

FINAL THOUGHTS

The MSc Urban and Rural Planning programme was developed to use selected platforms to deliver a concept. A key message here is that the concept is important, not the use of the same software platforms. The four spaces which constitute the online campus and 'classroom to coffee shop' concept shown in Figure 13.4 were selected based upon institutional arrangements, availability, and resources. Other platforms and structural approaches could be utilized. Most important is the creation of the spaces and associated options for control and ownership. It is suggested that a platform with a degree of separation from the central institutional platforms is desirable, such as Piazza or similar; this creates a separation from the institutionally controlled space, supporting the perception and reality of a shared area of influence.

Creating the spaces, and then aligning the spaces with an online collaborative learning approach which embraces student-centred learning is what underpinned the JDLC's approach and MSc offer; distance learning has very particular and significant challenges associated with it for both students and educational providers, but these can be addressed to varying degrees through an approach which creates such an active, collaborative, and shared (virtual) world. The challenge is how this can be delivered in a manner which is viable from a resource perspective, and which creates consistency in experience. It is suggested that a lead university, responsible for all ICT, quality assurance, strategic management, and central support, can ensure a stable core, but delivering a consistent learner experience whilst allowing for individuality of approach by educators remains difficult. This is true for all forms of education but requires perhaps greater diligence when working in a distance learning environment due to intermittent and asynchronous interactions that make it more difficult to overcome miscommunications. (See Box 13.1.)

BOX 13.1 IMPLEMENTATION TIPS

- Ensure a robust core ICT infrastructure.
- Ensure effective ICT support, operationalization, and investment into appropriate platforms with due consideration to the diversity of devices that will be used to engage with the materials.
- Ensure a holistic approach to teaching and learning, including support from 'central' teams including library and student support. Such infrastructure may be designed with a degree of assumption of contact; adaption in support approaches may therefore be required.
- Effective leadership, functional structures and approaches to programme management and governance are critical; this will require careful consideration of partnership scenarios.
- Ensure an agreed approach and consistency to the defining characteristics of module delivery across the programme, and ensure students understand, expect, and appreciate variation where this occurs.
- Ensure consistency in interaction to avoid 'peaks and troughs' in student experience. This doesn't need to be constant interaction, but consistency and planning allows students to have security and understanding of the learning approach.
- Ensure standard programme approaches, such as Student Representatives, are adaptable and available.
- Consider the diversity of learner requirements in the delivery of content, including disabilities.
- Finally, don't underestimate the desire (and sometimes need) of students to download and print online materials.

NOTES

1. The RTPI accredits programmes based on delivering core material ('Spatial') or specific subject focused content ('Specialism'), or both ('Combined').
2. The JDLC at UWE uses Kaltura, but other software exists.

REFERENCES

Croft, N., Dalton, A. and Grant, M (2010) Overcoming isolation in distance learning: Building a learning community through time and space. *Journal for Education in the Built Environment* 5(1): 27–64.

Garrison, D. and Vaughan, N. (2008) *Blended Learning in Higher Education: Framework, Principles, and Guidelines*. San Francisco: Wiley & Sons.

Gauvreau, S. A., Hurst, D., Cleveland-Innes, M. and Hawranik, P. (2016) Online professional skills workshops: Perspectives from distance education graduate students. *International Review of Research in Open and Distance Learning* 17(5).

Gibson, J. W., Tesone, D. V. and Blackwell, C. W. (2001) The journey to cyberspace: Reflections from three online business professors. *SAM Advanced Management Journal* 66(1): 30–34.

Harasim, L. (2000) Shift happens: Online education as a new paradigm in learning. *The Internet and Higher Education* 3(1–2): 41–61.

Hughes, M. and Daykin, N. (2002) Towards constructivism: Investigating students' perceptions and learning as a result of using an online environment. *Innovations in Education and Teaching International* 39(3): 217–223.

Lake, D. (1999) Reducing isolation for distance students: An on-line initiative. *Open Learning* 14(3): 14–23.

Moore, J. L., Dickson-Deane, C. and Galyen, K. (2011) e-Learning, online learning, and distance learning environments: Are they the same? *The Internet and Higher Education* 14(2): 129–135.

O'Neill, G. and McMahon, T. (2005) Student-centred learning: What does it mean for students and lecturers? In G. O'Neill, S. Moore and B. McMullin (eds.), *Emerging Issues in the Practice of University Learning and Teaching* (pp. 27–36). Dublin: AISHE.

Weller, M. (2002) *Delivering Learning on the Net: The Why, What & How of Online Education*. London: Routledge Falmer.

14. A problem-based and process-oriented curriculum in continuing education

Anita Grams

INTRODUCTION

The continuing education programme, MAS in Spatial Planning offered at the ETH Zurich, responds to specific requirements associated with Swiss planning practice. Switzerland's territorial fragmentation into 26 federal states (called cantons) and its land-locked location entail that many spatial planning problems become trans-cantonal or transnational. Thus, it is not easy to develop recommendations for decision-makers on how limited resources might best be used to solve any current or future spatial problem. Moreover, implementing spatial plans will require formal instruments and procedures, and considering regulations and legislation which will inevitably vary between cantons and between cantons and the nation states bordering Switzerland. Therefore, for spatial planning education, it hardly makes sense to focus on imparting expertise on exactly *which* formal instruments and procedures are to be applied in different administrative units. Instead, planning education programmes ought to focus on developing methodological expertise on *how* problems can be solved in a limited time. Said differently, it is far more meaningful, albeit not generally accepted practice in Switzerland, to train experts to understand planning primarily as an action-oriented, problem-solving and complex decision-making process.

Conceptualizing spatial planning as an action-oriented discipline, then, requires a focus on problem exploration and problem clarification (or definition) as basis for developing solutions for difficult, unsolved spatial issues, on addressing spatial conflicts and on envisioning scenarios for desirable future developments. As solutions to spatial planning problems are inherently associated with long-term, future dimensions, clarification processes must be able to adroitly handle circumstantial changes linked to uncertainties, such as changing political priorities or shrinking financial resources. Modelling and perfecting forecasting methods alone will be insufficient for appropriately dealing with the degree of uncertainty associated with most planning processes. Rather, what is needed are methods that consider uncertainties, as well as desired and undesired effects of decisions in solution-finding processes.

The theories underpinning this approach urge to thoroughly examine the initial starting point of a spatially relevant problem (Rittel 1972, p. 392, Schönwandt 2011, pp. 295–300; Schönwandt and Jung 2005, p. 790). A universally valid method for exploring, clarifying and solving future spatially relevant problems cannot be prescribed; instead, Scholl (2011, p. 279) has argued that methods depend on a given task, and must be tailored to the problem situation. Moreover, what underlies most difficult, unsolved tasks is a decision-making problem (Behn and Vaupel 1982, pp. 40f.), which in turn triggers subsequent action. As such, approaches for

1.   exploring and clarifying problems, and
2.   preparing decisions and actions

can be considered as core of the planning discipline and therefore ought to take centre-stage in research as well as *teaching* of spatial planning. Teaching on the MAS in Spatial Planning at the ETH is further based on the belief that solutions for planning issues

3.   require experts to work in interdisciplinary settings, and
4.   that handling uncertainty in planning processes can be learned.

To optimally prepare students for developing solutions for ill-defined problems, the continuing education programme for spatial planning at the ETH Zurich in Switzerland[1] employs pedagogies that focus primarily on imparting skills in problem definition as well as process expertise with simulations and study projects taking centre stage in the curriculum. Simulations are used for testing actions and decisions. Work on difficult, unsolved tasks can be understood as a method to sensitize students to uncertainties in planning processes. By internalizing problem-solving processes graduates are then conditioned to take on leadership roles for complex spatial planning tasks.

This focused and specialized approach is in line with the characteristics of an advanced studies programme in Switzerland. The MAS has stringent entry requirements, i.e., applicants must hold a Master's degree in a spatially relevant discipline such as architecture, geography or environmental sciences and have a minimum of two years' professional experience in a leading position in a private planning office, government administration or other relevant institution as prerequisite of being accepted into the programme. This allows educators to draw on prior knowledge and different disciplinary expertise of students when teaching. With its conceptualization of continuing (advanced) education in spatial planning, Switzerland occupies a unique position compared to the rest of Europe (Frank et al. 2014) but the problem-based, process-oriented teaching and learning is nevertheless transferable and can be replicated in other contexts.

A PROBLEM-BASED AND PROCESS-ORIENTED CURRICULUM

Curriculum Structure

The curriculum of the MAS comprises four key learning units: one simulation in the form of a group exercise labelled *experimental simulation* and three *study projects* (which simulate real problems) at different spatial scales and in different spatial contexts (Figure 14.1). These learning units are complemented by a thesis and sixteen one-week modules each focussing on a specific topic in the field of spatial planning. The one-week modules provide additional input to the study projects, imparting factual knowledge and introducing new methods to be tested in the study projects.

The MAS being a continuing education programme, students study part-time. Students attend all-day sessions for one week out of each month over a period of two years. For project work this means that students work one week together in teams at university and three weeks remotely using an online platform for exchanges and communication. During the three off-site weeks they typically work part-time in professional practice as for example project manager, head of an office or as self-employed expert.

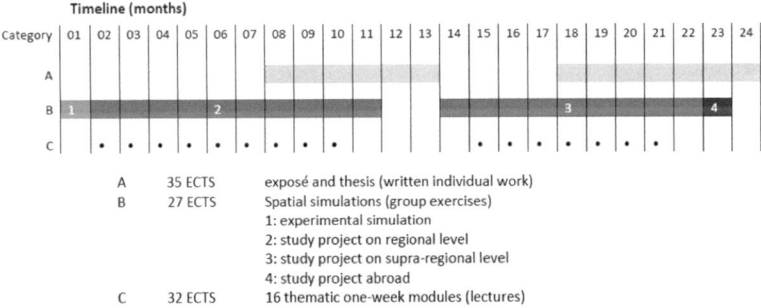

Figure 14.1   *Overview of learning units in the MAS programme in spatial planning at ETH Zurich*

Learning unit 1: experimental simulation of a test planning procedure
The experimental simulation exercise is used to simulate the clarification and decision-making process of a *test-planning* procedure (Scholl 2011, p. 330).

Test-planning is an informal planning approach typically used for large-scale complex projects in Austria and Switzerland, comprising a process where different stakeholders (e.g., land owner, community, government ministries, municipal planning officers, NGOs, etc.) meet over a period of approximately one year in regular intervals under the guidance of an independent facilitator to discuss and subsequently develop possible solutions to a planning problem.[2] The simulation follows the organizational and operational structure common for this kind of informal procedure but in a highly condensed time frame. In contrast to study projects (which also embrace the test-planning method), the experimental simulation does not focus on developing a spatial strategy but instead on the negotiation process in an interdisciplinary group with diverse interests. This exercise is implemented and performed preferably before working on study projects (Figure 14.1). It helps students become aware of the political and social dimensions of spatial planning.

Experimental simulations can be conceptualized as thought experiments in which students assume the roles of different actors and stakeholders of a planning procedure through role play, representing their respective aims and reasoning. The learning objective is to explore possible decisions and actions in general. Over the course of several role-playing cycles, the students take on

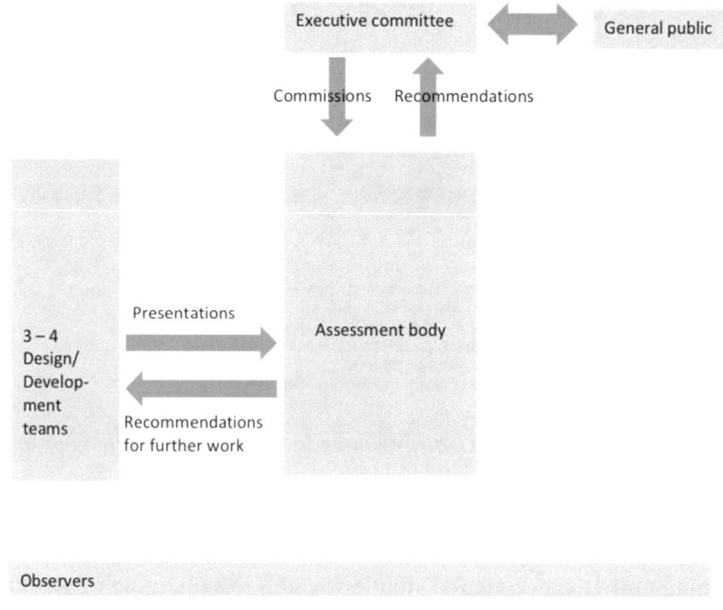

Figure 14.2   Roles in the experimental simulation exercise

Table 14.1   Roles and tasks of actors in a process simulation

Role	Task	Group size
Assessment body, incl. chairperson	• Responsibility for correct implementation of the test planning procedure • Assessment of team contributions based on task formulation and assessment criteria • Conduct of dialogue with the teams • Proposal with recommendations addressed to the executive committee for the next procedural step	5–7
Executive committee	• Overall supervision of the procedure • Responsible for strategic decisions • Appraisal of design proposals put forth by teams	3–5
3–4 Design teams	• Preparation of drafts • Presentation of findings • Revision of drafts based on the recommendations of the assessment body	16–20
Observers	• Continuous process observation • Regular report to the assessment body	3–4
General public	• Critique of final recommendations from the viewpoint of the general public	4–5
Total		**30–40 Students**

various roles in different settings. By combining their own daily work experiences with the presumed aims of the respective actors, they practice reasoning skills, and how to respond in messy, contentious situations where a given problem is not at all clear. For this reason, experimental simulations tend to be most powerful as a teaching tool in continuing education where students already have a certain professional background and experience. A typical set-up of actor groups, including roles and responsibilities used for these experimental simulations is outlined in Table 14.1 and Figure 14.2.

The first role, labelled 'assessment body', is staffed by five to seven students; it provides quality assurance in the test-planning procedure. One of its tasks is to strive for decisions by consensus. The 'assessment body' is led by an unanimously elected chairperson. The following representatives constitute the 'assessment body': representation of property owners; experts from the fields of urban development, transportation, economics, open space and green space planning, and social issues.

The second role is the 'executive committee'. This constitutes the commissioning authority which oversees the test-planning procedure. The commissioning authority is informed of the stage of the work progress by the chairperson of the assessment body subsequent to presentations of the design teams. The executive committee has also the opportunity to pose questions to the assessment body and to provide information about changes in political conditions.

The third role type are different interdisciplinary design/development 'teams' consisting of experts in urban development, open space planning, transportation, and economics. Each design/development team is led by an urban development representative which is preferably an architect or spatial planner.

The fourth role is a group of 'observers'. They analyse the learning process and give feedback at the concluding discussion of the exercise. This ensures that the didactic objective is met. Fifth, and finally, the 'general public' too is represented within the simulation, including representatives of associations, owners of adjacent properties and potential investors. Likewise, representatives of the media are to be included in this group.[34]

The operational structure of the experimental simulation exercise follows a realistic negotiation and encompasses several cycles. For teaching purposes, three cycles on three consecutive days have proven effective. On the fourth day, the exercise is concluded with a media conference. The media conference allows subject matters which have not yet been covered to be addressed, also by teaching staff.

The experimental simulation is prepared, performed and assessed in close collaboration with key actors of the real planning process which is emulated. Their assessment is vital for the evaluation of students' performance. The learning objectives for the experimental simulation are similar to those of the study projects (described next) but have the aim to specifically develop argumentation and negotiation skills.

Learning units 2–4: study projects at different scales and in different contexts

Although the problems for the study projects and associated tasks are drawn from actual planning situations, the projects are not 'live projects'; they purely serve didactic purposes. Students must develop solutions to complex tasks in spatial development based on a clarification process of the given spatial, factual and operative conditions. The projects provide the students first with opportunities to apply and bring together knowledge from their prior professional experiences, and second, to supplement and deepen the knowledge and skills acquired during the advanced programme. Third, the study projects allow students to reflect on various professional viewpoints and fourth, as stu-

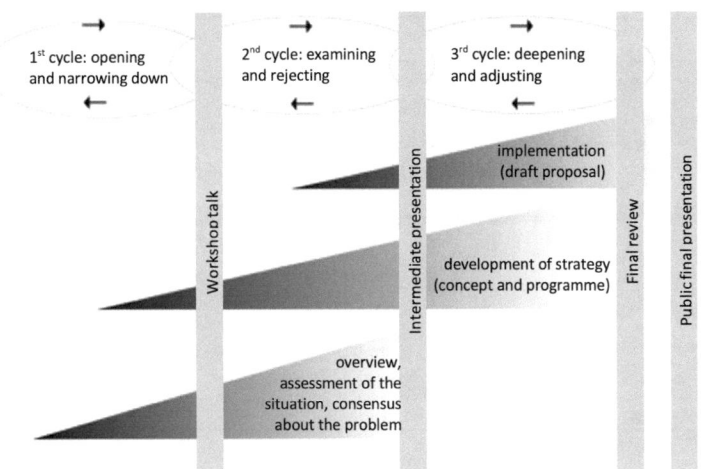

Figure 14.3   Phases of the clarification process in process-oriented learning

dents continue to acquire new knowledge from their scholarship and research, this can inform, in turn, their professional practice instantly.

Study projects within the framework of the MAS in spatial planning basically simulate the method of test-planning (Scholl 2011, p. 330) as outlined previously. The organization of study projects presupposes a few albeit important rules, such as division of students into competing teams, limited time for implementation and a clear structure of the learning process. Though the groups simultaneously work on the same assignment, each of them focuses on a specific component deemed essential based on the group's selected strategy. The group will for example consider the feasibility of the selected approach with respect to costs, time constraints, and other important parameters. It is expected that students hold already elementary knowledge in fields such as project management, knowledge of formal procedures and instruments or skills such as the application of programmes for processing large amounts of geodata.

Competing, interdisciplinary teams work on a task within a limited time period while being regularly subjected to criticism by a team of experts from the project field. Working on problem-solving in three cycles with different foci leads to robust reasoning, which finally culminates in a recommendation to relevant actors. In the first cycle, an overview of the main influencing factors and an assessment of the situation is made (Figure 14.3). At the end

Table 14.2   Features of study projects of MAS in spatial planning at ETH

	Regional project	Supra-regional project	Project abroad
Scope of consideration	City and its agglomeration	Functional space	City and its agglomeration
Work parameters	As given in the assignment	Freely selectable, based on thematic focus	As given in the assignment
Focus decree	Spatial	Theme-specific	Spatial
Process time	10 months	9 months	1 week
Number of students	20–24	20–24	30–40
Number of teams	4	4	6–7
Number of students per team	5–6	5–6	5–6
Number of teaching staff	6	8	10–12
Language of instruction	German	German	English

of this 'opening and narrowing down' phase, a statement determines which problem is to be solved from the viewpoint of the students. In a subsequent second cycle, this statement is re-examined and developed into a concept. In conjunction with temporal structuring which divides the individual elements of the problem-solving process into short-, medium-, and long-term measures, the concept turns into a strategy. This forms the core of the clarification process. The third cycle serves to deepen and adjust the results, culminating in a draft proposal presented to relevant actors.

Over the course of the MAS, students will work on three different projects (Table 14.2); yet, for each project these three procedural phases are applied regardless whether the project lasts several months or only one week. Likewise, the learning objectives for study projects remain broadly the same. They consist of being able to:

- Detect, assess and classify the main conflicts of spatial development;
- Define the need for planning action;
- Efficiently manage the time and human resources for the project;
- Evaluate different solutions and demonstrate their feasibility exemplarily;
- Recognize possibilities and limits of formal and informal planning;
- Efficiently work in interdisciplinary groups, optimally using individual knowledge and skills of each group member.

At the beginning of the programme, students work first on a regionally focused project, which is usually a city and its agglomeration, such as the city of Winterthur (population 100,000), with a substantial potential of inward development due to existing inner-city brownfields. They will work in several competing interdisciplinary teams. Many students are familiar with this project scale due to their professional experience in planning practice as project leaders. The major challenge consists of arguing conclusively and taking common decisions in a team. An expert for working methods supports the students if conflicts arise due to difficult group dynamics. For the second project, the territorial scope is extended and includes a functional space such as a metropolitan region. The learning objective is to force the students to find a thematic focus that includes the most promising approach to solve the identified spatial problem.

After successfully completing two projects, the students work on a third project under more difficult conditions abroad typically focusing on a city and its agglomeration. In the past students worked on projects in the City of Athens (Greece) or Isfahan (Iran), for example. Pedagogically, one goal is to examine whether students have internalized problem-orientation as an approach. Thematically, the focus lies on coordinating development around related and/or potentially conflicting tasks such as urban and railway development. Students face challenges insofar as, firstly, the project abroad is conducted in only a week; secondly, the groups are interdisciplinary and intercultural (i.e., they include students from the partnering institution); and thirdly, the work is conducted in English.

Teaching study projects is resource intensive as it involves substantial preparation, supervision and assessment tasks. The instructor–student ratios for the MAS stand at 1:4 or 1:5, differing significantly to the 1:40 teacher–student ratio average at undergraduate level in Switzerland. The evaluation of student proposals is conducted by experts who have a wide range of experiences in practice and who closely supervise the learning process during monthly personal coaching sessions. The teaching does not only involve teachers from academia but also practitioners occupying leading positions in industry such as directors of planning departments or heads of private planning companies. The scope for consideration and associated therewith the number of problems that have to be coordinated, defines the number of experts involved in the learning unit. It has proven effective to organize students in maximum seven teams in order to assess the results of the study projects in a final internal and public review lasting each one day.

SPATIAL SIMULATIONS AS A TEACHING METHOD IN CONTINUING EDUCATION IN SPATIAL PLANNING

As the experiences over the last few years have shown, problem-oriented teaching utilizing spatial simulations is a major challenge for students but also for educators. Process orientation, in contrast to product orientation, is unfamiliar to most students at the start of the MAS. Only through intensive engagement of teachers with experience in the problem-solving approach do students achieve solid reasoning skills. In particular, the combination of study projects and experimental simulations of negotiation processes leads to an intensification of learning. Skills are developed which allow students to maintain an overview even under difficult conditions and with ill-defined problems. To exercise reasoning skills in different cultural contexts fosters furthermore the collaboration in interdisciplinary groups. Spatial simulations especially encourage students who intend to handle difficult, unsolved tasks in an international context in their subsequent career and to take on leadership roles. The experience gathered in the continuing education programme in spatial planning at ETH Zurich has led to the identification of several factors determining the probabilities of success and failure of simulations as a teaching method.

First, the impartation of methodological knowledge to already experienced professionals by means of difficult, unsolved tasks places significantly different demands on teachers compared to instructions in standard undergraduate programmes. It is vital that lecturers have first-hand experience in the actual process which is being used as an example for the simulation. This means that the educators responsible for the course are participating in cooperation projects in practice and have preferably even developed and led them. Problem-orientation in spatial planning at university level cannot be taken for granted, though future problems in planning demonstrate that it is precisely problem-orientation that is needed to attain new knowledge in research and teaching (Grams 2018, p. 144; Scholl 2012).

Second, the application of simulations in teaching requires more preparation time than is conventionally available for teaching on a day-to-day basis. An effective approach is to start drafting the brief already during an actual procedure in order to identify critical milestones in the procedural process at an early stage and to productively imbibe them in teaching. Moreover, a study trip to the site of a completed or ongoing test-planning procedure following the simulation has proven valuable. As such, students can get an idea of the circumstances on site and look back on the procedure while being engaged in discussion with important process-specific actors. Questions which may have arisen during the simulation, can be answered by the actual actors. This dramatically enhances the learning experience.

Third, structuring and timing tasks appropriately and carefully is important. For the experimental simulation (learning unit 1) approximately one condensed week works well with approximately 50% of the time devoted to self-study and 50% to group work. Self-study time is important in order to allow for a thorough familiarization of students with their assigned roles in the simulation, particularly as students typically change roles three times over the time of the exercise. The learning effect is maximized if these role changes occur on consecutive days, with a new distribution of roles performed at the start of each day. The ability to teach the experimental simulation en bloc in a week is thus essential to maximize learning. It should be highlighted that not all roles are equal in their level of responsibility and roles such as the chairperson for the assessment body should be assigned to students with a managerial background or leadership experience, if possible, to maximize the exercise's effectiveness.

There should also be sufficient time scheduled for the regional and supra-regional study projects to allow students to develop in-depth understanding of both the conditions and the processes and get to know other team members. Given the part-time nature of the MAS, running each project over two semesters has worked well.

Fourth, a precondition for enhanced learning by spatial simulations and study projects is a good level of prior experience, *from students*, in handling problem-solving processes in practice. If initial experience in real planning processes is lacking, study projects may not contribute to knowledge enhancement at the same level. Moreover, experimental simulation exercises risk being reduced to mere role plays. This can lead to frustration not only among students but also teachers. Therefore, continuing education in spatial planning is particularly suited for applying study projects and experimental simulations as a learning method.

In conclusion, the preparation and implementation of process-oriented learning methods such as experimental simulations and study projects require more teaching staff than is the case for conventional exercises and lectures. It has proven to be beneficial to have two to three research assistants for formulating project tasks, of which at least one must have participated in a procedure in practice and is at doctorate or postdoctorate level.

RECOMMENDATIONS FOR FURTHER DEVELOPMENT OF TEACHING METHODS IN CONTINUING EDUCATION IN SPATIAL PLANNING

In continuing education in spatial planning, it is useful to focus on imparting methodological knowledge on how difficult tasks can be addressed. By confronting the students with actual planning problems in combination with their own prior knowledge and intuition, they can simulate problem-solving and gain insights from contrasting these simulated solutions and processes with those experienced in their workplaces. Learning units such as study projects and experimental simulations strengthen the skills of working in interdisciplinary groups and therefore focus on integrative decision-making.

Students are motivated to take over leading positions in difficult planning tasks. A spatial planner is not only responsible for supplying ideas at a very early stage of a planning process, but also for balancing interests and initiating interactions among actors. This constitutes a major challenge, all the more so, considering planning's political dimensions. Planners must carefully assess ideas, interests and interactions. As such, planners are also exposed to social and economic constraints making planning – and the teaching of spatial planning – extremely demanding.

The didactic approach of problem-orientation allows to transfer spatial simulations to other contexts and other planning levels. As the experience in the continuing education programme shows, some core elements for the implementation are crucial. First of all, students have to possess work experience to maximize learning by combining their own existing tacit knowledge from practice with the newly acquired knowledge through group work during the course. In addition to this, an advanced degree such as a Master's in a spatially relevant discipline such as geography, architecture or environmental science is advantageous (and in the case of the MAS at the ETH it is a prerequisite for enrolment in the programme). To have maximum impact on interdisciplinary group work, students from social and political sciences should be admitted to the programme. For an experimental simulation exercise less teaching staff is needed than for study projects. The latter must be prepared and conducted both by academics who supervise the process methodologically and experts from planning practice who support the students in an efficient problem-solving process. While an experimental simulation can be prepared in a relatively short time, the task brief for study projects is prepared by teaching staff over approximately one year. This includes interviews with experts outside academia, testing own hypotheses for spatial strategies or editing of available geodata sets. This means that study projects are costly, time-consuming and personnel intensive learning units. In continuing education programmes these costs can be passed on in the form of student tuition fees, while in undergraduate courses this is often not possible. An aggravating factor lies in a certain reasonable upper limit of the number of students participating in process-oriented learning units. A limiting factor is the time needed for reviews with the participation of all students and teachers. These reviews should take place over one day to keep the best overview over the different contributions of the teams to compare and finally assess them. A rhythm of 20 minutes for presentation, 20 minutes for questions and 20 minutes for feedback has proved useful in the MAS programme in spatial planning at ETH Zurich.

Process-oriented learning units bring vitality and pragmatism to the process. Illustrating a planning process by means of experimental simulations can most aptly be described by the term 'enactment'. This also makes clear that careful adherence to role differentiation in the exercise enhances the learning effect. This results in the recommendation to focus more on the simulation of processes in continuing education in spatial planning. By combining study projects on different levels and in different contexts with experimental simulations to foster negotiation skills, innovative solutions for unsolved problems can arise via an interdisciplinary clarification process. Designing and testing arguments in a negotiation process that feels 'real' can greatly enhance personal motivation and the sense of discovery in students. They are able to strengthen their competencies by learning to cope with opposition and criticism. At the same time, this method fosters an enthusiasm and a fascination for planning problems. This is important since planning efforts and interventions may have lasting impacts for many decades or even generations. A strong interest in testing, experimenting, and of course solving problems should be a basic requirement for future planners. Training of these skills is highly stimulated by spatial simulations. (See Box 14.1.)

BOX 14.1 TIPS FOR IMPLEMENTING A PROCESS-ORIENTED CURRICULUM IN CONTINUING EDUCATION

- **Teaching staff with practical experience:** The educators responsible for the programme must have practical experience in cooperation projects and preferably even have developed and led such activities as a basis for developing realistic and precise task descriptions. Whenever possible, actors and stakeholders involved in the actual site development should be involved as discussants, coaches or experts.
- **Precise task description:** A solid task brief is the starting point of the learning process. It should combine an overview of the most important indicators with an assessment of the situation prepared by the teaching staff so that the problem-solving process can commence immediately. Preparing a task brief for a regional and supra-regional study project takes approximately one year and must include hypotheses on what is the spatially relevant problem.
- **Adequate time for project tasks:** Given the part-time nature of the programme allocating sufficient time to projects is vital. Experience suggests that projects carried out over two semesters in sequence of about 3 months work well.
- **Sequences of self-study and group work in study projects:** Equal time should be devoted to self-study and group work.
- **Interdisciplinary group configuration:** Teams for study projects or spatial simulations should comprise different, relevant disciplines such as architecture, geography, sociology, environmental sciences, etc. A good mix of quantitative and qualitative skills per team is also advisable with at least one of them having experience with graphic presentation and spatial analysis software (GIS, AutoCAD or similar).

- **Group size and teaching staff ratio for study projects:** Team sizes of four to seven members have proven successful. To ensure adequate time to discuss teams' different contributions in the plenary four to six groups per day is practicable. Each group should be coached by one experienced professional.

NOTES

1.   http://www.masraumplanung.ethz.ch.
2.   A more detailed description of the method can be found in the MAS instruction movie: The pearl along the Aare. Part 1: Test Planning as a method for dealing with complex planning problems <https://masraumplanung.ethz.ch/forschung/ lehrfilme.html>.
3.   The main features of the experimental simulation exercise can be seen in the MAS instruction movie: The pearl along the Aare. Part 3: Spatial planning to design spaces suitable to live in <https://masraumplanung.ethz.ch/forschung/lehrfilme .html>.

REFERENCES

Behn, R. and Vaupel, J. (1982) *Quick Analysis for Busy Decision Makers.* New York: Basic Books.

Frank, A., Mironowicz, I., Lourenco, J., Franchini, T., Ache, P., Finka, M., Scholl, B. and Grams, A. (2014) Educating planners in Europe: A review of 21st century study programmes. *Progress in Planning* 91: 30–94.

Grams, A. (2018) *Playing with Density: The Compass for Inward Development as a Problem-Focused Methodology for Densification in Small and Medium-Sized Communes.* Zürich: vdf Hochschulverlag AG at the ETH Zurich.

Rittel, H. (1972) On the planning crises: Systems analysis of the "first and second generations". *Bedriftsøkonmen* 8: 390–396.

Scholl, B. (2011) Die Methode der Testplanung. Exemplarische Veranschaulichung für die Auswahl und den Einsatz von Methoden in Klärungsprozessen. In Akademie für Raumforschung und Landesplanung (ed.), *Grundriss der Raumordnung und Raumentwicklung* (pp. 330–346). Hanover: Akademie für Raumforschung und Landesplanung.

Scholl, B. (ed.) (2012) *HESP. Higher Education in Spatial Planning: Positions and Reflections.* Zürich: vdf Hochschulverlag AG at the ETH Zurich.

Schönwandt, W. (2011) Probleme als Ausgangspunkt für die Auswahl und den Einsatz von Methoden. In Akademie für Raumforschung und Landesplanung (ed.), *Grundriss der Raumordnung und Raumentwicklung* (pp. 291–310). Hanover: Akademie für Raumforschung und Landesplanung.

Schönwandt, W. and Jung, W. (2005) Planungstheorie. In: Akademie für Raumforschung und Landesplanung (Ed.), *Handwörterbuch der Raumordnung* (pp. 789–797). Hanover: Akademie für Raumforschung und Landesplanung.

15. Professional training for social responsibility: fundamentals and practice of a residency programme in architecture and urbanism

Maria L. Refinetti Martins and Paula Custódio de Oliveira

PLANNING IN THE 'SOUTH': THE STATE OF CITIES IN BRAZIL

Brazil is amongst the countries that experienced rapid urbanization, entailing roughly a doubling of the proportion of population living in urban settings in half a century. Urbanization levels went from 31% in 1940, to 56% in 1970, and reached 84% in 2010 equalling an urban population of 209 million inhabitants.[1] In a country where the public sector's provision is insufficient and the majority of the population has no resources to access housing via the market, most of this urbanization occurred informally and thereby creating considerable instability and legal insecurities. Informal settlements can be found practically in all Brazilian cities. They are characterized by the precarious nature of housing, lack of infrastructure, no access to services, and their location mainly in the peripheral regions. These settlements are developed with no formal technical knowledge and do not count on any public or private funding.

To this day the informal city is growing at a faster rate than the formal city despite the considerable volume of homes built during the last decade by the *My House, My Life* (Minha Casa, Minha Vida) programme. It is evident that the housing market and the public housing programme cannot serve parts of the population – a situation no different from what can be seen in other countries in Latin America, Africa and parts of Asia.

The most common precarious settlements found in Brazilian cities are self-built properties in areas with irregularities regarding land licensing and clandestine properties (with no licence application); settlements with no planning or design (such as the *favelas*) or slums located in consolidated but rather old areas, objects of total neglect, with no maintenance whatsoever, in a state of disrepair.

BACKGROUND AND CONCEPTS

It is in the context of these large self-built settlements that the FAUUSP residency programme emerged. Its reference points are:

- the practice of extension and outreach activities promoted by universities in the undergraduate courses of Architecture and Urbanism;
- the practice of technical support provided by young professionals from these programmes in association with social movements in their fight for the right to housing; and
- proposals from professional sectors of Architecture and Urbanism with a view to expanding their professional scope to self-built homes in precarious settlements.

The practice of university extension and outreach was consolidated in the academic environment since the 1990s spontaneously and independently from the formal curriculum, through the experiences of academic housing laboratories, which emerged in different units and provided opportunities for experimentation that supported housing movements, enabling their self-managed initiatives, providing assistance, quality design, and highly specialized knowledge. This led to the concept of the 'Right to Architecture', in addition to the 'Right to the City', with several experiences of the creation of public policies in participatory municipal administrations, and of local actions being supported by NGOs. From this emerged the idea that academic and research paths could be transformed in professional concepts and practices. Following this line of thought, several activities emerged throughout Brazil in academia, initially small but with a critical and analytical approach at the basis of all their projects, programmes, plans and managerial proposals for the real city, aiming at social inclusion and at a more inclusive perception of the public interest. Several housing laboratories were created in federal and state universities, as well as in some religious universities. In a context of the adoption of a new constitution which included new social rights, this kind of academic activity gained momentum in the field of Architecture and Urban Planning.

In 1997, the Faculty of Architecture of the University of São Paulo – FAUUSP – created the Housing and Human Settlements Laboratory – LABHAB,[2] whose experience was important for the creation of the Residency Programme (LABHAB 2004–2017; Martins 2014; Martins and Bittencourt 2017). More specifically, in 2003, one of the LABHAB activities focused on the development of a Housing and Urban Action Plan for Risk Areas of

Socioeconomic Exclusion and Violence – the Jardim Angela Neighbourhood. Using concepts and methodologies different from the traditional Municipal Master Plans, LABHAB carried out extensive analysis and dialogue with local representatives, developing proposals, including the design for specific areas. Well-articulated, the proposal involved a course for the Development of Urban Projects of Social Interest, held in the same neighbourhood of M'Boi Mirim, engaging government officials, healthcare workers, and the community, resulting in a series of collectively developed local projects and programmes. It also resulted in a set of opportunities for immediate action to be taken by officials and from their privileged learning space, by various undergraduate and postgraduate students who participated in the process. This experience, regarding its content and design, was in some ways the inception of the Residency Programme in Architecture and Urbanism developed a few years later.

Another relevant experience was the research project on Management of Rainwaters in Urban Environments, carried out by a network of 16 Brazilian universities (2012–2016). Here LABHAB proposed unconventional solutions for urban sanitation and drainage problems to be adapted for the physical configuration of poor settlements, also coming up with recommendations for urban environmental regulations. These solutions aimed mainly at spaces of collective use in the settlements, and in situations of environmental risk associated with slope areas and banks of streams. Alternative construction systems were tested at construction sites of the university campus, and also in the municipality of São Bernardo do Campo, São Paulo Metropolitan Region. The research team was composed of members of the association of residents, undergraduate and postgraduate students, and students and teachers from the state's secondary school in the neighbourhood. In the course of the debate, student involvement facilitated the visualization of technical parameters to engender better qualified physical and territorial solutions than those usually practised by authorities and contracted companies. In this sense, the activity also opened a door with the local City Hall, holding workshops for the discussion of the theme with local officials, managers and contractors.

Since 2017, LABHAB has developed another Research and Outreach Programme based on the features of a Brazilian planning instrument called PEUC, which stands for 'Compulsory Subdivision, Construction and Utilization of Land'.[3] The programme aimed at identifying the morphology, typology and current use of notified properties through field research, analysing the impact of PEUC and the feasibility of using such properties for social housing.

Last but not least, the Residency Programme is also inspired by a national law which provides for public and free technical support to social housing dwellers and explicitly states that in addition to ensuring the right to housing, the goal of the technical support is to: "optimize and qualify the rational use of the built space and its surroundings, regulate the building and its settlement, avoid the occupation of risk areas and of environmental interest". The law is the result of the endeavour of professional bodies willing to promote the social value of Architecture, Engineering and Urban Planning. Public debates were held by these organizations in the 1990s and they resulted in the drafting and enactment of this law. It also establishes that "technical assistance services are subject to an agreement or term of partnership with the Union, State, Federal District, or Municipality and must be provided by professionals from the fields of architecture, urban planning, and engineering acting as: public servants, members of non-profit NGOs, professionals enrolled in residency programs, and teachers in outreach activities" (BRASIL Lei n° 11,888/2008).

This was the context under which the FAUUSP Residency Programme was established, supported by the Faculty Administration and the LABHAB. Its basis was the concept of the Urban Project of Social Interest – as a counterpoint to the movement that saw the city as a form of financial investment, thus increasing territorial inequalities. As such the programme seeks to foster the dialogue with the local governments[4] and to train professionals able to operate in the much-entangled legal administrative field, envisaging alternatives for a more inclusive city.

NATURE, AIMS AND INSTITUTIONAL DESIGN OF THE PROGRAMME

The 1988 Constitution establishes that universities abide by the principle of inseparability between teaching, research and university extension and outreach. This is reiterated by the Law of the Guidelines and Bases of the National Education, from 1996, which states that the goals and the principles of higher education include the combination of teaching, practice and research grounded in one single pedagogical process (BRASIL. Lei n° 9,394/1996). Moreover, Architecture and Planning in Brazil are considered applied social sciences and gaining practical experience in the form of a placement in a private office or in a public institution is part of the degree's minimum national curriculum, according to a Ministry of Education Resolution from 2007.

Going beyond this, some institutions have started at the undergraduate level not only to include placements in a public or private company or institution but also university outreach and extension activities focused on the external community. The inclusion of these types of activity in undergraduate courses of the Urban Planning curriculum is – while not standard – nevertheless a successful practice as documented by international experiences in e.g., New Zealand (Rosier 1999), the United States (Brooks et al. 2002), Australia (Freestone et al. 2006) and the United Kingdom (Frank 2010).

Rosier (1999) theorizes on the efforts to develop a reflective practice, one that takes into consideration the evolution of knowledge as well as institutional issues brought to light by professional practice, and where academic supervision ensures that the knowledge is applicable to the practice: "these (practical) skills could be best gained through personal experience in the field, under the guidance of a practitioner who is able to link theoretical ideas and experience in developing as a reflective practitioner" (Rosier 1999, p. 143). A reflective practice presupposes knowledge about the current practices in the real world, reflection about the knowledge acquired in the classroom, and, from this reflection new skills are developed to deal with the issues of the professional practice. The wider role of the university is therefore to "educate the people to fulfil societal needs" (Rosier 1999, p. 145). In their description of the placements' application these authors (Brooks et al. 2002; Frank 2010; Freestone et al. 2006; Rosier 1999) also emphasize the importance of the university's support for the adaptation of students to professional environments, validating the knowledge acquired in the classroom and to be put into practice at work.

While the Residency Programme shares the understanding of joining practical experience and theoretical content in coordinated stages supported by the university, it presents a marked difference and departure from placements embedded in curricula aimed at facilitating an initial professional experience prior to graduation. Firstly, the Residency Programme is aimed at professionals already graduated and qualified. As such it bears greater resemblance to the residencies for healthcare professionals or those for the preparation of professionals in public service – such as for the position of 'public manager' in Brazilian ministries, or the position of 'senior manager of civil engineering in the field of urban and regional planning' in the German government (BTW 2014). In these cases, the focus is on training individuals in higher public administration, with competencies tested by an exam. And secondly, in the Brazilian case – in contrast to, for example, the German postgraduation trainee programme – the FAUUSP Residency has a decidedly social focus seeking to fill gaps where public policies fall short of societal needs.

In Brazil there are several agents among the university and professional bodies involved in offering a public service focusing on the improvement of districts and housing. This includes the National Federation of Architects – FNA (trade union), the Architecture and Urbanism Council – CAU (the profession's professional association akin to the RTPI in the UK) seeking to increase professionals' contribution to improving cities, and the universities' extension and outreach departments, whose work is in the field of continuing education and who attempt to increase professional training with a social bias.

Specifically, in Brazil, the intention and hope therefore is not only to train professionals for a market that already exists but rather to develop a labour market and public policies, at the same time. In other words, the goal is to train people to foster positions and a career in public service (and therefore outside strict market rules), but not necessarily as part of the state. This is an important and very positive difference of the Residency Programme; one which also makes it difficult to be implemented, as it requires a programming and a coordination that are difficult to obtain.

As a body of ideas, the scope of the Residency Programme originates from principles such as Urban Reform and Right to the City, commitments of the Brazilian Constitution, but in a current context of emergence of public services such as the OS or Social Organizations,[5] which are not state-managed (Azevedo 2014; Braga Ponte 2015).

To some extent, the Architecture and Urbanism Residency's reference model in Brazil is the Residency in the Healthcare Sector instituted at national level as a postgraduate diploma that consists of learning experience, but that also enhances the public service offer to the population. Residency, then, is defined as a "modality of postgraduate education lato sensu focused on in-service education, targeted at professionals from the healthcare sector" (BRASIL Lei n° 11,129/2005). It clearly states that the residency is a programme for the promotion of qualified young health professionals in the labour market, notably in priority areas of the Brazilian National Unified Health System (SUS).[6] It establishes that "residency requires full-time dedication and is carried out both under pedagogical and medical supervision, a joint responsibility between the Education and the Healthcare sectors" (BRASIL Lei n° 11,129/2005). The Residency in this area is managed by the Ministries of Education and Health. It is from the latter that the resources for its functioning are provided, as part of the National Unified Health System (SUS). Residents, in their in-service training, are responsible for part of the medical care.

The FAUUSP Residency Programme 2015–2016 expanded the concept of a Residency Programme to include the fields of urban settlements and management, keeping the same fundamentals, and correspondence, associating the Education and Urban Development (Planning) sectors. The difference from the healthcare sector is that, despite the existence of a law that provides for the provision of services in housing and habitat, there is no national housing and habitat system. The existing law for this area does not make it compulsory to apply resources; it only stipulates that technical assistance to Housing of Social Interest must be effected through the financial support from the Union, the States, the Federal District or the Municipalities. This technical support in the fields of architecture, urban planning and engineering, can be either direct assistance or through Residency Programmes. Thus, the inception and implementation of Residency Programmes depends on the initiative of various levels of government and in 2015–2016, funding was allocated at the municipal level. The Residency Programme was the form proposed by FAUUSP in the face of the interest expressed by the Municipal Department of Urban

Development – SMDU, of the city of São Paulo, to approach the universities to promote debates and contributions on the planning and development of urban settlements. As such, the proposal of the Residency was built through a dialogue between FAUUSP and SMDU.

The format that was agreed upon meant that the residents engaged in a full-time programme during one year, and received a scholarship salary (of similar value to the Master's degree scholarship), participating in both academic and practical activities which were agreed with the São Paulo City Department of Urban Development (SMDU–PMSP). This meant students took part in the development of regional masterplans for São Paulo regional city halls.[7]

PROGRAMME STRUCTURE

As stated above, the Residency in Architecture and Urbanism Programme includes theoretical and practical activities. It is a graduate Lato Sensu programme at the level of specialization. The course's duration is 1,920 hours, composed of 360 hours of theoretical activities in the classroom, 188 hours of seminars, 1,272 hours of supervised practical activity and 100 hours of development of individual monographs under the guidance of a supervisor.

The programme offered in 2015–2016 was structured in three modules of four months each: the first two modules have classroom activities (two full weekdays) and practical field activities (three full weekdays). The third module focuses on the conclusion and presentation of the individual practical work of each student that must be based on or developed as a result of the work of the entire period, pedagogically speaking. Supervision and guidance were provided by 12 professors from FAUUSP and 17 tutors from the São Paulo City Hall. The topics offered in the programme aimed at providing theoretical, technical and managerial support for the development of projects and plans of a local nature for the various Regional City Halls within the São Paulo city. For this purpose, each of the different Regional City Halls was assigned one student.

Each module, composed of two topics, linked theoretical content to a specific type of practice. This is visualized in Table 15.1. The subjects offered were: Processes and Methods of Urban Planning and Management; Urban Processes, Plans, and Projects of São Paulo City (Module 1), Local Management and Urban Qualification; Contracts and Public Management (Module 2), State and the Public Sphere, Projects and Monographs Orientation (Module 3).

In the supervised practice activities, residents worked together with the various Departments (Housing, Transportation, Health, Education, Social Assistance, Public Works, Municipal Services), the Regional City Halls, and the Councils of Representatives.

Table 15.1   *Correlations between educational content and practical work in each module*

	1st module 4 months	2nd module 4 months	3rd module 4 months
FAUUSP Disciplinary Field:	Planning / Urbanism	Public Management and Administration	State and Public Sphere Proposals
Theoretical classes	Processes and Methods of Urban Planning and Management Urban Processes, Plans, and Projects of São Paulo	Local Management and Urban Qualification Contracts and Public Management	State and the Public Sphere Projects and Monographs orientation
Products	Monographs on each Regional City Hall	Exercises: Reflection and deepening the theme of the classes	Individual projects of residents: Reflection / Proposition
Regional City Halls / SMDU Works	Surveys and interaction with sectors and regional city halls	Articulation with the sectors and Regional Councils City conference Participation	Feedback to the Councils Final articulation with the Working Groups
Synthesis	Synthesis Maps Problematization	Formatting for the participatory process Systematization and processing	Maps review
Products	Preliminary proposals (developed for each regional city hall in groups composed of residents, technicians from the various secretariats, and working groups from the regional City Hall WGs)	Preliminary proposals made available Revised language Quino (internal database)	Formatting proposals (Proposals Notebook) for the Regional Plans Dialogue for drafting the Regional Plan Act

To pass, students had to participate both in the classroom and in the practical activities. The minimum grade for approval is seven (7.0), with 85% attendance required. The practical activities proportionally demand the same attendance in addition to a report of the activities to be submitted to the tutor, who makes an assessment (pass / fail) at the end of each module. The final work is equivalent to the disciplines in terms of weighting in the overall mark, and consists of a project proposal, urban intervention, sectorial policy, public policy management or administrative action of the student's free choice. Each resident has an academic supervisor, and the final work is presented to and evaluated by a panel composed of three members: the supervisor, one faculty professor, and one public administration professional.

By combining 'academic' and 'professional' time, the Residency Programme allows the graduates to conduct, on one hand, a broader and freer research, and on the other hand, gives them an understanding of the pressures and constraints of public management regarding legal, administrative and financial conditions, in real-life situations. In this sense it differs from a professional internship (or placement), where the practice often ends up independent and disconnected from the academic contribution. It is also different from professional Master's degrees even when such degrees offer considerable professional and practical content. As the programme's nature of interaction with society derived its inspiration from the outreach activities developed in the institution by research groups and laboratories, particularly the Housing and Human Settlements Laboratory (Laboratório de Habitação e Assentamentos Humanos – LABHAB) it features a close association to the real city, taking into consideration the daily lives of the inhabitants of each region, in a close dialogue with the Local Councils. The practical work supports the development of the Regional Plans for the Regional City Halls, in alignment with the Master Plan, and, in this way the programme fosters multi-level dialogue among master plan, public policies, physical intervention, and local management of equipment or services. Parameters for the development of the Regional Plans were designed by those in charge of the SMDU, and the theoretical framework and academic references were drawn from previous experiences developed at FAUUSP.

PROGRAMME EVALUATION

The Residency Programme attracted considerable interest amongst early career professionals. Following a call for applicants holding an Architecture and Urbanism degree (obtained between 1 August 2010 and 25 September 2015), a total of 290 applications were received for the offered 32 places.

Moreover, there was not only strong interest, but the programme can also be seen as quite successful. Students – upon completion – indicated their satisfaction, recommended the programme to colleagues, and insisted that new iterations of the programme should be run, through private messages and on the faculty's Facebook page: Residência FAUUSP.[8]

All students who completed the programme were asked to provide an evaluation of the programme – through an electronic questionnaire, which is standard for the academic aspect of all programmes at the University of São Paulo. The response rate was 50–70% of the students, with slight variations between the six courses of the programme, and the ratings were mostly 'good' and 'very good', with only a small percentage of the 400 items given a 'poor' rating.

However, as this standard questionnaire focuses on academic issues such as interest in the content, bibliography and clarity and objectivity of the faculty member and the grade assignment criteria, the evaluation failed to capture the quality and learning from practical elements of the Residency Programme.

To gain a deeper understanding of the impact of the programme on students' learning (including on their careers and professional development), the instructor team contacted students by email. Feedback from this supplementary survey suggests that approximately half of them were successful securing jobs in the public sector or setting up a Technical Advisory Service, and the other half were accepted to a Master's or PhD programme. It is hard to appreciate the significance of this data because as the programme was coming to its end, Brazil suffered a political setback and was plunged into deep economic crisis with high levels of unemployment.

Among the municipal staff who were Residency tutors, there were several positive manifestations but only on an informal basis. Although the programme has ended, the local communities (Councils of Representatives) frequently communicate with former programme participants to consult them on technical issues, or when in need of maps or information on their neighbourhoods.

At this point one could question what could be the motivation for professionals to sign up and participate in this extra training programme, earning merely a scholarship for their full-time involvement, instead of entering the professional market. There are many reasons, one could say, and among them, the lack of courses with such profile, both practical and academic, the opportunity to get to know the public sector and work in it, which can be hard for recent graduates, a considerable level of lack of good and motivating job offerings, and certainly, an enthusiasm for working in the field of social interest, something really rare in the existing labour market.

INSTITUTIONAL CHALLENGES AND PERSPECTIVES

The Residency Programme in bringing together public agents, organized society, and university students to develop knowledge and technical assets is a process in which everyone learns and which in turn increases the probability that the proposed projects are effectively implemented.

Until the first decade of this century, urban improvement projects relied on the socio-political and economic context, which included, in Brazil, the process of constitutionalizing new rights, the design of new urban-legal instruments, a new concept of housing deficit and housing of social interest, the *My House, My Life* programme, with its chapter III, related to Regulations of Housing of Social Interest, the coming onto the scene of environmental issues, the specific laws for the Guarapiranga and Billings basins, and the municipality being considered a federated entity.

Throughout this period, the dialogue between social movements, democratic municipal administrations, popular mandates, NGOs, trade unions, and academia pointed to the potential of building new knowledge. It was from these new paradigms that so many proposals of public policies have emerged, initially implemented at the municipal level and then by the Ministry of Cities. However, from 2016 onward, this pattern seemed to have reached its limit in a time of profound changes in the world and in Brazil, with setbacks in social policies, changes in labour regulations, the dominance of rentism over production, and the increase in concentration of income.

In the field of Urban Policy and Planning, new management models tend to transfer many urban development initiatives from public authorities to the private sector. Different forms of contracts are being used in urban development, such as the consortium urban operations and public–private partnerships. To meet the new challenges that arise, new designs and proposals are needed, and it is precisely in this context that a less market-oriented activity can bring about opportunities to be explored. This moment of learning may also be a space for urban interventions that favour the public interest. Creating these windows of opportunities is a big challenge but it is hoped that this new offer of the Residency Programme in Urbanism and Architecture could make a contribution in this regard.

The 2015–2016 programme was made feasible by a set of very specific circumstances: a municipal administration that invested in dialogue and partnership with universities and which was developing local Urban Development Plans for each one of the sub-municipalities, as required by the Municipal Master Plan. Within these conditions, the partnership was put in place. The municipality awarded scholarships to the residents in exchange for full-time involvement. The Residents received scholarships with the condition of being approved on the course and to offer the expected services to the sub-municipalities and community councils.

However, to repeat this format depends on creating these opportunities in São Paulo or in other municipalities, which is dependent on a mayor's decision and priorities, and on the availability of resources. A new alternative arose in 2018, in the form of a Professionalizing Practice in 'Technical Assistance to Housing of Social Interest', which started in January 2019 in collaboration with an NGO. It is a much shorter programme with fewer hours – a total of 270 over five months. It is also a free course, but without scholarships, for 25 students. Activities take place only three days a week: all day on Fridays (theory classes at the university) and on weekends at informal and precarious neighbourhoods, for which projects of physical improvement and landholding regularization will be developed in cooperation with the local community. The programme includes teaching time by faculty members (university extension and outreach are part of their contractual requirements), with a small amount of financial aid provided by the Undergraduate and the Outreach Deans' Offices, which will make resources available for the transportation and for two scholarships for participating undergraduate students.

Some other experiences of Residency in Architecture and Urban Planning, in other formats can be found at the Federal Universities of Bahia, Brasilia, Paraiba and Pelotas. Recently a new proposal is being developed at the University of São Paulo, São Carlos campus, consisting of an agreement with a municipality in the region.

CONCLUDING REMARKS

A crucial issue remains. While the experience may contribute to create a specialization for training a new type of professional, a university student who is now able to deal with the problem of precarious settlements in the Brazilian cities or their many counterparts in Latin America, Africa and parts of Asia where most of the space is produced without professional intervention, we must acknowledge that technical knowledge itself is only part of the challenge. The main challenge is to attract public funds which are currently more available to sectors within the market than to promote social welfare through projects with the scope of those that such outreach programmes develop. In this sense, the projects elaborated by the residents and directed by their tutors and professors can represent elements that facilitate the search for resources by communities or local administrations.[9] They may also encourage new – and not necessarily governmental – forms of producing public policies, i.e., developed not with a government agency but with organized communities.[10]

Therefore, the key objectives of the Residency Programme are clearly focused on the formation of cadres and in designing public policies that aim at expanding support to upgrade the self-construction praxis and the improvement of the precarious settlements. While initially not at the forefront of the academic concerns when setting up the programme, the special learning experiences accrued through this programme are clearly leading to the development of new knowledges and values bridging theory and practice and thus improving the professional training in Architecture and Urbanism. (See Box 15.1.)

BOX 15.1 IMPLEMENTATION TIPS

In order to implement a programme like the Residency Programme, a plan of action and much determination to make it happen are required. A good assessment of the national and local contexts and knowledge of the guidelines and rules governing higher education and the profession are vital. Some particular challenges are:

- Creating institutional formats that make the proposals technically viable as well as academically formal, and to follow the rigour of the professional field.
- Identifying entities – like municipalities, NGOs, departments, within existing institutional structures that may accommodate part of the programme, making available human, economic and non-monetary resources.
- Organizing partnerships and procedures to select the cases to work on.
- Devising a timetable including theoretical classes and practical work that is feasible for professionals, students and the community (including evenings or weekends).
- Being flexible with programme length and intensity – e.g., creating also options for part-time modes which respect workable hours but in turn do not depend on the availability of scholarships.

NOTES

1. IBGE Portal e Censo demográfico 1940–2010.
2. LABHAB is a laboratory of the Department of Architecture and Architecture of FAU-USP, created by Prof. Erminia Maricato. It began its activities in 1997, with the proposal of interconnecting teaching, research and university outreach activities in the same space, giving priority to the formulation of alternatives for housing, urban and environmental demands aimed at social inclusion. Experimentation and practice in real situations are part of the theoretical construction.
3. The instrument of PEUC follows from the provisions of the Brazilian Constitution on the social function of property (Art. 182). In order to avoid the retention of unoccupied properties, the municipal public authority may notify owners to promote their proper use, under penalty of a progressive property tax over time or expropriation with payment of public debt securities with redemption up to ten years.
4. Municipalities and, in the case of São Paulo, with its subdivisions: Regional City Halls. There are 32 in this city, which has over 11 million inhabitants.
5. In Brazilian law, a Social Organization (OS) is a category that the administration assigns to a not-for-profit private body, so that it can execute its objectives in the interest of the community. It is a new form of partnership, in which the so-called third sector – that is, services in the public interest but not necessarily provided directly by government bodies – is embraced. The requisites to meet these criteria are: non-profit operation; a social objective in any of the areas provided in the law: teaching, health, culture, science, technology, or the environment; collegiate governing bodies with representatives from public authorities and the community; advertisement of its activities; submission to the Court of Auditors for purposes of control; a management contract with public authorities regarding goals to be achieved and control of results. Although there are criticisms, the model has been widely adopted, particularly in public hospitals and primary care management by public administrations of the most diverse political fields.

6. Public health system, under responsibility of the three levels of government, in an articulated and complementary manner.
7. Coordination at FAUUSP: Maria Cristina Silva Leme (Institutional Coordinator) and Maria Lucia Refinetti Martins (Academic Coordinator); Coordination at SMDU-PMSP: Carolina Heldt D'Almeida (Institutional Coordinator) and Fábio Mariz Gonçalves (Technical Coordinator).
8. https://www.facebook.com/residenciafauusp/?_tn_=%2Cd%2CP-R&eid =ARC4FPBTauOle1ur0nzrkDiobsR-BFgIgoxizD0UgHQRFUD9ly2g _GZarRIe7hrJWTMqXd6fEULaaWKG.
9. A report of the experience and the collection of final works provided by the group of Residents may be found in a two-volume book: *Residência em Arquitetura e Urbanismo na Universidade de São Paulo* (São Paulo: FAUUSP), 2 vols: http://www.fau.usp.br/cultura-e-extensao/residencia/.
10. Information about this programme can be seen at: http://www.fau.usp.br/cultura-e -extensao/cursos/.

REFERENCES

Azevedo, E. de Andrade (2014) Organização Social. http://www.pge.sp.gov.br/ centrodeestudos/revistaspge/revista5/5rev6.htm.
Braga Ponte, C. (2015) Controle no Terceiro Setor: Organizações Sociais – OS e Organizações da Sociedade Civil de Interesse Público – OSCIP. *Revista da Escola Superior da Procuradoria Geral do Estado de São Paulo* 6(1): 27–50.
BRASIL. Lei nº 9,394/1996. National Education Guidelines and Bases.
BRASIL. Lei nº 11,129/2005. Young Apprentice and Residency in the Healthcare Area.
BRASIL. Lei nº 11,888/2008. Provides for Public and Free Technical Assistance to Social Housing.
Brooks, K. R., Nocks, B. C., Farris, J. T. and Cunningham, M. G. (2002) Teaching for practice: Implementing a process to integrate work experience in an MCRP curriculum. *Journal of Planning Education and Research* 22: 188–200.
BTW (Ministerium für Wirtschaft, Arbeit und Wohnungsbau Baden-Württemberg) (2014) *Merkblatt Baureferendariat – Städtebau und Raumordnung.*
Frank, A. (2010) Making a case for complementarity of student learning from year-long work-based placements in town planning. *Learning and Teaching in Higher Education* 4(2): 21–54.
Freestone, R., Thompson, S. and Williams, P. (2006) Student experiences of work-based learning in planning education. *Journal of Planning Education and Research* 26: 237–249.
Laboratório de Habitação e Assentamentos Humanos (LABHAB) (2004–2017) *Relatório Anual.* São Paulo: FAUUSP.
Martins, M. L. R. (2014) Experiência de Assistência Técnica no LABHAB-FAUUSP – pesquisa e participação na construção do conhecimento Anais do III Encontro Nacional da Associação de Pesquisa e Pós-Graduação em Arquitetura e Urbanismo, 2014, São Paulo, UPM-PUCCampinas, 2014.v.1. pp.1–11.

Martins, M. L. R. and Bittencourt, S. (2017) Challenges and innovation in the Architecture and Urbanism Residency: Working to overcome the gap between planning and implementation. AESOP Annual Congress Proceedings, Lisbon.

Rosier, D. J. (1999) The three-year undergraduate planning program and … practice, practice, practice. *Australian Planner* 36(3): 142–145.

16. A student workshop on tactical urbanism: one day to change the 100th year neighbourhood?

Duygu Cihanger Ribeiro

INTRODUCTION

The Chamber of City Planners of Turkey organizes an annual urbanism colloquium that brings together planners and planning students with diverse educational backgrounds. In November 2016, this colloquium was held in Ankara at Middle East Technical University (METU) under the theme of planning education. The urbanism colloquium provides an excellent learning environment for urban planning professionals and affords interaction with urban planning students. Students attend academic presentations but are also engaged in urban design and photography competitions and in discussions on their expectations from university programmes, the Chamber and planning education. In addition, the Chamber organizes a student workshop generally with the help of the host university before each urbanism colloquium to which students from different universities are invited. This chapter presents and critically reviews the development, aims and success of the 2016 workshop which comprised pedagogical innovations on various levels. On one hand the workshop represents a pedagogical experiment where different actors (Chamber, community, instructors) enable the process and as such the workshop forms an innovative, extracurricular, co-learning environment. On the other hand, a new perspective on urban planning (tactical urbanism) was introduced which inspired teaching that substantially differs from standard planning education pedagogies in Turkey.

While the Chamber is nominally the organizational lead, the local host university's contribution is crucial for reaching out to urban planners from other institutions and cities in Turkey. Workshop instructors, typically drawn from the local host institution, are in charge of defining a suitable topic, introduce theory and possible real-life implications, and lastly organize and lead students throughout the process. If relevant for the workshop theme, local municipalities and associations are consulted for content development. Student participants are selected based on an application to the Chamber in which students need to explain why they are interested in participating in the workshop. Applications are evaluated by the Chamber's organizing committee and the workshop instructors. In our case, the students were selected based on their motivational statement, as well as diversity and gender equality criteria.

As an extracurricular activity, the workshop represents an opportunity to experiment with novel ideas and in 2016 METU instructors chose the topic of 'tactical urbanism'. The diversity of the student group, the limited time frame and budget all seemed appropriate to introduce this trending topic. In general, 'tactical urbanism' calls for a *long-term change with a short-term action* by including a range of actors from governments and non-profit organizations to citizen groups. Projects under this mantle promote an efficient use of financial and temporal resources for unleashing the creative potential of community groups (Lydon and Garcia 2015). 'Tactical urbanism' stands in stark contrast to master planning with its spatial, temporal scope and actor definition. Introducing the topic to students required a novel pedagogical approach and different to those commonly applied in planning education in Turkey.

Even though the initial aim of the workshop was to engage students with a somewhat manageable and exciting topic, the process reveals new possibilities to learn about innovative approaches in urban planning, both for instructors and students. There was an emphasis on students' active involvement in everyday activities of the workshop, letting them explore and develop their own interpretations of the theme. While some students engaged in intense and structured interactions with representatives of local residents, others became involved in many daily and spontaneous encounters with local residents; however, there were also some students who preferred to deduce their individual understanding from the workshop focusing only on their own ideas and observations.

The chapter's first section on *background* gives an overview of the theoretical grounding of the workshop theme and describes planning education pedagogies typical for the Turkish context using the example of the Department of City and Regional Planning at METU. This is followed by a description of the *process* that includes the motivation and realization of the workshop and elaborates on its alternative pedagogical approach. Lastly, reflections from students and a discussion on pedagogies for planning education in the future are presented in the *aftermath* section.

BACKGROUND

Urban planners need to be highly attentive regarding the conditions and transformations of the societies we live in. Together with technical skills in modelling, computer software use, drawing and design skills, this societal focus might be one of the most significant and peculiar aspects for urban planning professionals. Therefore, to take our gaze at the street, where everyday life and social practices prevail, is meaningful and good practice in the context of planning education. Through a human-centred perspective, urban planners and planning students can gain insights into the ongoing social and spatial transformations in cities. Urban planning history features several important human-centric studies despite the dominance of top-down planning approaches. The examples range from the opposition of Team 10 to the rationality of modernism during the 1950s (Risselada and Heuvel 2005) to Jane Jacobs's (1961) attention to the ordinary life of citizens and their living spaces in the 1960s. These studies contributed to the development of advocacy, participatory and inclusive planning and design perspectives. More recently, we see an increase in the action-oriented, short-term and inclusive projects which Barnett (2011) defines as collective urbanism. Temporary Urbanism, Pop-Up Cities, Tactical Urbanism, Guerrilla Urbanism, D(o).I(t).Y(ourself) Urbanism are some frequently used terms in a growing body of literature, all referring variably to the notion of everyday urbanism (Bishop and Williams 2012; Chase et al. 2008; Hou 2010; Lydon and Garcia 2015; Oswalt et al. 2013).

A commonality amongst these approaches is their focus on the value of the community's self-interventions on already laid-out urban plans as a way to circumvent exclusion from the planning processes or to avoid being trapped in the aesthetics of design (Carmona 2014, p. 5). They focus on the inhabitants' roles and responsibilities in creating physical spaces aside from the formal urban planning schemes. Therefore, tactical urban projects call for the broader inclusion of people, while operating in a limited space and focus on a well-defined urban problem for efficient use of time and the participating human capital. Examples range from the famous PARK(ing)[1] day events to pop-up concerts and sports activities. There is no doubt that these alternative perspectives for doing urbanism attract significant attention as evidenced in the 2014 exhibition 'Uneven Growth: Tactical Urbanisms for Expanding Megacities' curated by the Museum of Modern Arts (MOMA) in New York. This interest is highly significant since these approaches claim to present an alternative to conventional top-down, expensive, static, comprehensive and long-lasting urban planning approaches. Still, as this trend grows, the questions increase on its political and spatial contexts[2] (Webb 2017). These approaches are not templates to fit in every urban context due to the different planning laws and regulations, not to mention the role of planning education. For instance, it is harder to relate their relevancy to urban planning education since there are few independent initiatives organizing direct urban interventions to date.

Planning Education System in a Nutshell

These concerns on the relevancy and practicality of a tactical project in Turkey and its adaptability to urban planning education are best revealed through an illustration from a long-standing education programme. The City and Regional Planning (CRP) Department at METU illustrates the typical planning education framework in Turkey. Its urban planning education programme profoundly focuses on studio pedagogy to transfer basic planning skills to students (Lang 1983). To start, students are introduced to a standard planning process that involves an initial analysis and site visit, followed by a further detailed analysis of the site. Following this approach, which Patrick Geddes (1911) referred to as *civic survey*, students develop a large-scale plan proposal (1:100.000 and 1:25.000), a master plan proposal (1:5.000) and an urban design project (1:1.000). All steps are accompanied by regular and frequent studio critiques that are either one-to-one or group based. Overall, the studio process goes beyond lecturing, allowing students to think and evaluate problems and their solutions themselves. The site visits and the following urban analysis engage students deeply with a city and place, and their profession. They also develop strong ties among peers due to the time they spend together, working and sharing their knowledge, feelings and ideas.

Throughout the programme's existence, academics at METU have expansively discussed the department's educational approach as early as the 1980s reflecting shifts in politics and society filtering through to departmental policies, plans and programmes (Bademli and Akışık 1979). At the time, the department chose to pursue a particular educational approach with alterations in the theoretical courses and the content of studio but without any continuous interactions with local actors. Nevertheless, further discussions and future reforms are inevitable in planning education programmes due to the changing conditions of urban contexts and planning approaches.

As such, the emerging discussions of late, on complexity sciences for cities, and flexible urban design have not been incorporated in Turkish planning education curricula as yet. This is due to practical reasons such as a shortage in staff with research backgrounds in different allied fields and excess in class size as well as a political context which dictates that teaching in planning education aligns with the processes and procedures of the actual planning system and regulations. Tactical urbanism stands apart since it defends the indeterminacy of urban futures and focuses on alternative time, actors and spatial structures. Therefore, trying out a workshop for planning students designed to sharply differ from what they are being taught at school stimulates excitement, bringing out new opportunities but also concerns.

PROCESS

Motivation: Setting Up the Theme

The fundamental aim of the workshop was to highlight a real-life urban problem and to make students excited, committed and interested in the subject throughout the four-day workshop. Within the context of 'tactical urbanism', spatial problems are addressed which students can live in, see, touch and internalize before proposing solutions. The 100th Year Neighbourhood, that is adjacent to the METU Campus provided an opportunity to conduct this workshop. Called also the 'workers' housing blocks', this neighbourhood has a sense of community and willingness to be active to improve public space. The workshop title 'Neighbourhood Atelier: Thinking on Urban Space, Instant, On-the-Spot, Collective' avoided jargon to appeal to lay people and residents but encapsulated tactical urbanism principles. Moreover, the title was inspired by the existing neighbourhood initiative that has a house for community gatherings and a production place, which they named 'neighbourhood atelier'.

Prior to the workshop, a meeting was organized with representatives of the neighbourhood initiative as well as other residents of the area to frame the perceived problems in the area in an inclusive and broad manner as possible. The twenty students from eleven different universities were informed only about the title of the workshop but not its aims and thus the first step of the workshop was to provide an introductory presentation on the workshop theme, the theoretical frame on the increasing the role of the inhabitant as a designer (Alexander 1979) and on the inquiries into new design approaches focusing on compositional yet partial collage, catalysts on urban developments and small-scale designs (Lerner 2015; Oswalt et al. 2013; Rowe and Koetter 1978). These theoretical frameworks are built on recently emerging concepts such as temporary urban spaces (Haydn and Temel 2006), second-hand spaces (Ziehl and Osswald 2012), and handmade urbanism (Rosa and Weiland 2013). Other crucial aspects for fulfilling the aim of the workshop were posed as questions:

- Authorship: Who designs/makes the city?
- Scale: What is the smallest scale(s) of urban planning and design?
- Temporality: What is the temporal dimension, aim or quality of urban planning and design?
- Design Quality: Can we walk about any design qualities in a space that are produced instantly, on-the-spot and collectively?
- Political Authority: What is the role of formal planning authority in these processes?

These questions fostered a mutual discussion between the workshop instructors and students. They are critical concepts in formulating any urban planning approach and the very possibility of having different answers would inevitably lead to questioning what is taught in university departments at present. If we change the temporality and spatial scale, the focus shifts towards particular spatial processes such as coexistence, parasitism and integration instead of a long-term master plan. At the same time, the changing answers require new tools and media that would help these processes to come alive. Thus, the students were encouraged to explore video making, photography-collage, i.e. new technological tools in urban planning (Evans-Cowley 2018) together with conventional methods such as installations, small-scale construction, and event organization.

Opportunities: Interaction with People and Space

Tactical urbanism includes a five-step approach to design consisting of (1) empathizing with the target group to (2) defining specific problems and opportunities, (3) ideating research, (4) planning a prototype and (5) testing it (Lydon and Garcia 2015, p. 172). Although the programme followed a similar flow, adaptations were needed for the site-specific conditions due to the state of emergency (declared 20 July 2016) that the country was in at the time of the workshop which created limitations in terms of conducting a study in public space.

As part of the first step of empathizing with the target group, a meeting was organized with the neighbourhood initiative before the workshop. Although there was an idea to get in contact with the local municipality since we were planning to intervene in the public realm, this idea was not welcome by the Chamber. And since students were expected to develop a rather amateurish, everyday user perspective to the problems, no urban planning practitioners from academia, public or private sector were invited for the workshop.

To define specific problems and opportunities, we agreed on preserving the existing social life of the neighbourhood through incrementally and sensibly developing the physical layout especially by addressing deficits through small-scale designs. This requires making students familiar with the peculiarities of the neighbourhood to make use of the students' time and effort in a concrete and useful manner within an ongoing and real-life urban condition. Following a short theoretical discussion, a photograph series underlining the peculiarity and some of the spatial problems of the 100th Year Neighbourhood was developed. The neighbourhood initiative participated in presenting their works on the site and students had a chance to meet with the volunteers that work for the social and spatial betterment of the neighbourhood. In the context of a planning education programme, this approach differs significantly from conventional assignments in Turkey. First, the problem definition was developed in direct coordination with the residents' support and without any professional guidance or steering. Introducing the volunteer group to students as one of the first events in the workshop aimed to illustrate the actual actors and people who would be affected by the interventions. This way, we started not with a stereotype or already given decisions on a project, but with the ideas coming from the residents. Secondly, throughout the ideation and research, a site visit in which the theoretical discussion topics are shown with real-life examples is conducted and, thirdly, free working time is given to the students to formulate research ideas. Finally, they were responsible for the implementation of their own proposals.

Realization: Unexpected Encounters

During the site visit, students discovered hidden corners, design values in the self-made gardens, wall writings and noted their ideas and concerns as we walked. From then on, they were left to work independently on their project ideas. With only a minimum of guidance they worked in four groups of five students each. There was no direct instruction process to let them express their spontaneity and creativity (Kipper 2006). This approach not only allowed students to become aware of the fundamental problems of the site in line with the introductory presentations and guided tour explanations, but also provided opportunities for them to raise new subjects by using the advantage of being an outsider and therefore being able to think freely and see without prejudice. After they presented their sketch drawings, keywords and talked about their ideas, it became clear that some of the groups sought to fulfil the initiative's requests (Group A, Group C), while others developed entirely new ideas which were inspired by their field observations and experiences (Group B, Group D).

The following two days of the workshop were devoted to the realization of these projects (see Figure 16.1). Especially, finding and collecting the necessary materials to complete the project was time consuming and required unexpected skills. There was a need to find construction materials for the bus stop seats (pipes, nails), plants to decorate it or source things for the outdoor living room. However, the tasks entailed making contact and interacting with the local shopkeeper community. Visiting the variety store, hardware shop, stationers, market, second-hand shop and florist and talking to them created an interest for all parties. This direct integration with the inhabitants of the neighbourhood gave excitement to the workshop participants as well as informing more people in the neighbourhood about our intention. Throughout this process, the Chamber of City Planners provided financial and moral support to buy and transport the materials, not to forget the provision of wooden pallets and tools by the neighbourhood initiative. Later, groups dispersed to their project site after the gathering of all necessary materials and equipment. We have encountered the most exciting outcome of the workshop after the finalization of the projects. The students were open to improvizations since almost nothing goes the way it is planned, and this created a challenge to see hardships and surprises for both tactical urbanism trials and its reflections of an education programme.

Source: Cihanger (2016).

Figure 16.1   From initial idea sketch to implementation

Two projects (Groups A and B) aimed to foster change through the physical transformation at small scales. Group A named their project 'Bus Stop Seat' proposing to build seating in front of a transformer station which has a memorial wall painted by the neighbourhood initiative commemorating the Soma Mine Disaster.[3] This project responded to the initiative's request to make something that would refine and organize the space in front of the wall to attract more attention and present respect to their work. While the group initially intended to better define the memorial wall through building multiple seats, they ended up making only one seat due to time and material limitations. Although the project has not finished in the way it was intended, the seat created a charming and functional urban corner. Students observed how people used the seat as a table to leave their bags while waiting for the bus.

Group B offered to create an outdoor living room that approximates a Do It Yourself project. This started from admiration of both the aesthetic beauty and enclosure of an urban niche they encountered during our walk. As they pursued a sensitive re-touch to the urban corner, Group B developed close ties with the residents living adjacent to their project area. While they were decorating the fences of that apartment, some of the residents showed great interest and support.

In contrast Group C pursued a project named 'Bus Stop Awaits You' and designed a portable bus stop cover that calls attention to the lack of sheltered bus stops in the neighbourhood via an activity. This design was conceived as a mobile cover which the students aimed to carry themselves almost as a flash mob to attract more attention. The time-lapse video they produced shows the residents' interactions and reactions to the impromptu shelter during the morning rush hour. The group members asserted that a few persons asked their purpose and one of them even wondered ironically if the mayor had sent them there. Even if only temporarily, they have pointed to a hidden but significant everyday life problem with a sense of humour through their interventions.

Lastly, Group D formulated a multi-step approach by merging the problem definitions of the neighbourhood initiative and their observations regarding the collective garden. The group members were astonished by the existence and significance of the collective neighbourhood garden as well as finding it problematic that no indications, signs or clear image would show the place of this garden. For this, they came up with a comprehensive gaming and decorating approach in and around the garden. They designed a hopscotch-like play/street game that would attract attention towards this garden while providing a fun moment for people and especially for children, as well as easing the wayfinding to this site. This game attracted many children's attention and as residents saw the students in action, they commented that "it is great that somebody tries to do something positive for our neighbourhood" (Figure 16.1).

The students presented their projects in the colloquium as the last task of the workshop. Pedagogically, letting students decide the content and foci of their presentations reinforced creativity and their autonomy. Each group selected a representative who spoke to a crowd of urban planners and planning students with their own media preferences. These included time-lapse videos, photo collages, videos, and models. The students exhibited a high level of confidence in their work which was reflected in the positive and constructive reaction of the audience. For education purposes this process was an achievement in bringing different stakeholders together, making students from different universities work collectively through hands-on experience in an urban living space. However, its pedagogical implications do not end as the presentations end. As the educational purpose merges with an urbanism try-out, the process turned out to be a dual educational task. Therefore, the workshop aftermath exhibits stimulating issues on tactical urbanism and their impact on students' understanding of urban planning and design.

AFTERMATH

The design thinking process of tactical urbanism includes five steps: empathize, define, ideate, prototype, and test (Lydon and Garcia 2015, p. 173). The workshop closely followed a similar flow yet after the last step of 'testing', most of the projects vanished shortly after their realization. If we focus on the end product of this education process, it might suggest that we have failed. However, in the context of planning education, this was an experimental yet highly influential and informative education and a pedagogical experience. Being one of the initial attempts in Turkey, the workshop has been a positive learning process for the diverse mix of students from different planning departments and class years. These participants experienced a new approach to urbanism which consists of learning-by-doing through a hands-on process that nevertheless allows personal reflections on theory while at the same time there is collaboration with peers and interaction with different stakeholders. This opportunity to leave the studios and try out a trending urbanism approach within our own spatial, financial and political limits in the city of Ankara raised many topics to discuss. Maybe the 'short-term action' did not result in 'long-term change' as it is claimed in the motto of tactical urbanism; instead, this workshop experience with limited time and budget with a highly spontaneous and inclusive process impacted the participants more than the physical space.

Reflections from the Students

This educational experiment has been extended with a short open-ended questionnaire administered a few months later to collect students' thoughts and reflections on the workshop experience. Their responses highlight three central insights pertaining to (1) being on site, (2) implementing their ideas instantaneously and (3) talking to the residents. The feedback unveiled a surprising awareness of students towards their profession and the significance of this experience as can be seen from one student stating:

> In the context of our country, this kind of new approach is meaningful since there is mistrust for our profession.

Leaving the university and working immersively on the actual site seem to enable another way of enacting their profession and engage with the concerns of other people. Furthermore, changing the working environment to be on the site with other students from different universities fostered participants' creativity, since "the greatest ideas pop up spontaneously" as one of the participants confessed. The workshop programme was highly flexible with no official definition of their submission, no outline for the workflow and no projection date for the implementation of their projects. This process accelerated new thoughts as we look at an urban problem from an opposite temporal and scalar direction. Students experience a way of urban planning and design that is implemented in the short-term and with a limited spatial scale. It is true that their initial design ideas did not completely work out once they started to implement them in urban space. However, attempting to realize their ideas in the neighbourhood, influencing the residents, might have helped students in terms of their educational insights rather than the success of tactical urbanism and the durability of their projects in the long-term. A student clarifies this as follows:

> This experience showed us that planning is not only about papers, long-term plans, scales, and formalities. It was significant to see what we thought as realized in space instantaneously.

Still, to provide ground for interaction with the residents is probably the most favourable outcome of the study. There were no structured interviews but informal encounters and talks among the students and the residents. This natural mode of interaction seems to excite students and make them feel they are doing something that might improve some of these people's lives. Most of the students agreed upon the positivity of this outcome:

> It was important to talk with the residents, the actual users of our small projects to see and respect their ideas. This is a good chance to observe and decide the benefits of a project without any cost.

> Planners, in this context, can be the organizers, negotiators in this kind of perspective by making room for the ordinary user to be more added to the process.

When students were asked to define their feelings about this experience, they used stimulating terms such as "solution, participation, think-produce-do, awareness, uniqueness, innovative, creative, attractive, small touches – no drawing sheets". These words are not overvalued at the expense of conventional planning education in universities. However, independent of their content and theme, the inclusion of different learning processes such as workshops in addition to the studio programmes creates space for students to interact and produce work in a more limited time period. If these workshops are arranged together with students from different universities or departments as well as with NGOs and community organizations, urban planning education will contribute to developing the social engagement skills of students. Through this collaboration, novel ideas are likely to develop, not to mention the provision of university–community engagement (Frank and Silver 2018) in planning education and the chance to increase the sense of social responsibility of students.

FUTURE IDEAS FOR A FLEXIBLE (PLANNING) APPROACH AND RELATED PEDAGOGIES?

Due to the complexity of cities and societies, it is not easy or even possible to predict a precise future for the field of planning (Portugali 2011) and planning education (Barnett 2007). However, accepting this indeterminacy, we should embrace flexible, collaborative pedagogies to teach urban planning and design. To test this proposition, the workshop on the theme of tactical urbanism aimed to prepare students as well as the instructors for an emerging perspective that influences the theoretical and practical dimensions of urban planning. The findings challenge conventional concerns since a more encompassing *authorship* and levels of spatial *scales* are of importance as well as the inclusion of different rhythms and *temporalities* in the design consideration in addition to a sole future orientation. These shifts require urban planners and designers to regard even the most ordinary and personal spatial solutions as *design qualities* that are unveiled by the inhabitants. Still, these emerging studies stand in between being a forerunner of the future of planning and indicating a tailored political, economic idea that defines the role of *political authority*. We should remember that the popularity of these small-scale projects after the 1990s is mostly as a result of the withdrawal of government from producing "large-scale planning as well as local service provision" (Boer and Minkjan 2016). Despite the shortcomings in respect to long-term impact, visibility and the realities of tactical urbanism in all geographies, it carries the belief that life can be changed through changing space and societal inclusion (Zeiger 2011). Within our context, the workshop did not entirely follow the course of tactical urbanism, at least not in the way it is stated in theory and books. The projects became partial and even ephemeral. Despite the fact that the projects did not solve the problem at hand, they have highlighted issues and made them visible as one of the participants stated in the feedback survey:

> I have noticed how to implement what we discuss on paper as a planner. Although this way was not offering permanent solutions to what we have named as problems, I have learned that to point out the problem creates a significant awareness.

Within the context of working instantaneously, on the spot, and collectively, the students had an opportunity to develop solutions to everyday problems and experience the spontaneous responses from the residents. Leaving their planning studios, sketch papers and long working hours from time to time supports the student to be more receptive to ongoing urban issues especially in their close surroundings. Meanwhile, maybe the most crucial responsibility goes to the instructors for they are required to be open to the operational shortcomings, the partial failures of their programmes. If they claim to pursue this reflexive and collaborative manner in their pedagogies, they should welcome the spontaneous nature of complexity in cities, in planning, as well as in education.

The workshop process reveals possible methods such as not wholly structuring the problem definition, learning from local actors, giving the voice first to students as well as giving them space to develop their ideas instead of starting with lectures and a specific theoretical grounding. These proposals do not mean the abandonment of being thorough in planning education, but to embrace being tactical in it. Still, in a more inclusive perspective, the local administrations, urban practitioners and residents should be included throughout any tactical urbanism study, which was not completely fulfilled here due to the aims and short working time of the presented workshop. Especially, gathering prior knowledge from the residents before defining the project would certainly bring a more grounded approach to urban planning practices as provided in this workshop thanks to the volunteers of the neighbourhood initiative. Furthermore, the most significant contribution to urban planning education is to continuously remind students and show them the communities they work for, the unique and crucial ideas they might see in the niches of everyday life and space. (See Box 16.1.)

BOX 16.1 REPLICATION AND IMPLEMENTATION TIPS

The following explains the workshop framework for introducing 'tactical urbanism' in planning education to aid replication and implementation. Key learning outcomes for students and instructors:

- becoming familiar with emerging theories and new planning method;
- enhancing student creativity through changing their working environments, conditions and time frame to solve an ongoing urban problem that they experience in real life and urban setting;
- broadening perspectives on societal problems by working with local residents, groups, related urban professionals and associations;

- fostering independent learning and taking ownership of the learning process as students are tasked to assume responsibility of the entire learning process with only subtle interventions and coaching from the instructors;
- developing and practising new approaches of co-learning.

Possible formats:

- The tactical urbanism workshop is one blocked week as part of the regular semester and realized for an urban site which is known to the students, where they can experience daily problems and interact with residents.
- The tactical urbanism workshop is conceived as an extracurricular teaching event, e.g., as part of a summer school or an international student workshop.

Assessment:

- The assessment should comply with the aim of the workshop, that is, empowering students' involvement and activity in the process not to mention its reverberations for the local setting and residents. Each group can comment on every project and evaluate the results while the residents or local associations could be consulted on the success or necessity of any intervention.

Challenges of changing the setting:

- In order to ensure availability of in-depth contextual knowledge of local urban problems, it is advisable and useful to work closely with local urban practitioners. Ideally such practitioners should be given a chance to conduct the workshop after conveying theoretical principles and the framework of the workshop such as aim, duration, and expected outcomes. Local municipalities need to be contacted prior to the workshop to prevent any problems during the implementation of projects.

ACKNOWLEDGEMENTS

This workshop would not have been possible without the support of the Chamber of City Planners of Turkey and the enthusiastic participation of the students. Special thanks go to Oya Memlük Çobanoğlu for her continuous support throughout and after the workshop.

NOTES

1. For more information on the PARK(ing) Day, see https://www.citylab.com/life/ 2017/09/from-parking-to-parklet/539952/.
2. For more information on the political and economic concerns related to tactical urbanism see Neil Brenner's essay entitled 'Is "tactical urbanism" an alternative to neoliberal urbanism?' http://post.at.moma.org/content_items/587-is-tactical -urbanism-an-alternative-to-neoliberal-urbanism.
3. "On 13 May 2014, an explosion at a coal mine in Soma, Manisa, Turkey, caused an underground mine fire, which burned until 15 May. In total, 301 people were killed in what was the worst mine disaster in Turkey's history." See https://en .wikipedia.org/wiki/Soma_mine_disaster.

REFERENCES

Alexander, C. (1979) *The Timeless Way of Building*. New York, Oxford University Press.

Bademli, R. and Akışık, S. (eds.) (1979) *The Seminar on Developing Planning Education Program-1*. Occasional Paper Series, METU Faculty of Architecture, Ankara, Turkey.

Barnett, R. (2007) Learning for an unknown future. *Higher Education Research & Development* 23(3): 247–260.

Barnett, J. (2011) A short guide to 60 of the newest urbanisms. *Planning* 77(4): 19–22.

Bishop, P. and Williams, L. (eds.) (2012) *The Temporary City*. London: Routledge.

Carmona, M. (2014) The place-shaping continuum: A theory of urban design process. *Journal of Urban Design* 19(1): 2–36.

Chase, J., Crawford, M. and Kaliski, J. (eds.) (2008) *Everyday Urbanism: Expanded*. New York: Monacelli Press.

Evans-Cowley, J. (2018) Planning education with and through technologies. In A. Frank and C. Silver (eds.), *Urban Planning Education: Beginnings, Global Movement and Future Prospects* (pp. 293–307). Cham: Springer International.

Frank, A. and Silver, C. (eds.) (2018) *Urban Planning Education: Beginnings, Global Movement and Future Prospects*. Cham: Springer International.

Geddes, P. (1911) *Civic Survey of Edinburgh*. Edinburgh: Civics Department.

Haydn, F. and Temel, R. (eds.) (2006) *Temporary Urban Spaces: Concepts for the Use of City Spaces*. Basel: Birkhäuser.

Hou, J. (ed.) (2010) *Insurgent Public Space: Guerrilla Urbanism and the Remaking of Contemporary Cities*. New York: Routledge.

Jacobs, J. (1961) *The Death and Life of Great American Cities*. New York: Random House.

Kipper, D. A. (2006) The canon of spontaneity – creativity revisited: The effect of empirical findings. *Journal of Group Psychotherapy Psychodrama & Sociometry* 59(3): 117–126.

Lang, J. (1983) Teaching planning to city planning students: An argument for the studio / workshop approach. *Journal of Planning Education and Research* 2(2): 122–129.

Lerner, J. (2015) *Urban Acupuncture*. Washington, DC: Island Press.

Lydon, M. and Garcia, A. (2015) *Tactical Urbanism: Short-Term Action for Long-Term Change*. Washington, DC: Island Press.

Oswalt, P. Overmeyer, K. and Misselwitz, P. (eds.) (2013) *Urban Catalyst: The Power of Temporary Use*. Berlin: DOM Publishers.

Portugali, J. (2011) *Complexity, Cognition and the City*. Berlin: Springer.

Risselada, M. and van den Heuvel, D. (eds.) (2005) Team 10, 1953–81: In Search of a Utopia of the Present. Rotterdam: NAi Publishers.

Rosa, M. L. and Weiland, U. (2013) *Handmade Urbanism: From Community Initiatives to Participatory Models*. Berlin: Jovis.

Rowe, C. and Koetter, F. (1978) *Collage City*. Cambridge, MA: MIT Press.

Webb, D. (2017) Tactical urbanism: Delineating a critical praxis. *Planning Theory & Practice* 19(1): 58–73.

Ziehl, M. and Osswald, S. (2012) *Second Hand Spaces: Recycling Sites Undergoing Urban Transformation*. Berlin: Jovis.

Web References

Boer, R. and Minkjan, M. (2016) Why the pop-up hype isn't going to save our cities. https://failedarchitecture.com/why-the-pop-up-hype-isnt-going-to-save-our-cities/.

MOMA Exhibition on tactical urbanism (2014) https://www.moma.org/calendar/exhibitions/1400?locale=en.

SOMA Mining Disaster (2014) https://en.wikipedia.org/wiki/Soma_mine_disaster.

Zeiger, M. (2011) The Interventionist's Toolkit: 1. *Places Journal*. https://placesjournal.org/article/the-interventionists-toolkit/?cn-reloaded=1#0.

17. Conclusion: nurturing new learning landscapes and pedagogies

Artur da Rosa Pires and Andrea I. Frank

INTRODUCTION

The overarching aim of this book was to facilitate and to advance the dialogue about contemporary challenges in planning education and associated pedagogical practices. At least from our editorial gaze this dialogue started with the making of the book. Throughout the writing process there ensued a lively exchange with different contributors, the publisher, and colleagues about the teaching case studies and the featured pedagogies. These conversations, then, triggered reflection and tracing of our own educational journeys. Just how much the university, educational paradigms, and curricula in terms of content and pedagogy have changed over our own working life is remarkable.

We wanted to articulate these trends and share the novel and innovative pedagogical practices in the planning education field. In order to enable readers to replicate and adapt ideas featured in the teaching cases, authors were asked to clarify many details on the mechanics of the delivery and to share their own deep reflections and learning. This process not only furthered the dialogue but helped to uncover connections and to make international cross-national references. We realized that despite the contextual nature of planning practice and therefore its teaching there are common, universal themes. The emerging picture, thus, has some coherent tones that resonate globally but there is also considerable contrast and diversity in the actual materialization of how these themes are enacted in instructions. In other words, the similarity – with in parts very different interpretation and materialization – is fascinating to ponder and provides much food for thought and mutual learning.

In this final chapter we do not intend to produce a short summary of each individual contribution, which to some extent was already provided in the Introduction, nor will we pinpoint the articulation between each of the individual initiatives described in the book and the conceptual debate on pedagogical change. This task has been accomplished by Lamb and Vodicka (Chapter 2) with remarkable accuracy. There is, however, room to sum up the 'aggregate' lessons that can be drawn from all the contributions to this book and that will be done in the following section of this chapter. It makes sense, thereafter, to set the overall debate within a brief historical perspective, and end with a forward-looking perspective by returning to the question of the kinds of transformative changes in planning education that may be desirable or indeed needed.

AGGREGATE LESSONS

It would certainly be very difficult, if not impossible, to do justice in a short summary to the richness, significance, deep thinking and agency embedded in the individual contributions to this book. It is, however, possible, in a gesture of due recognition of the value of individual *apports*, to highlight some major 'global' contributions. And there are, in our opinion, two main areas of note.

The first area concerns the emergence of a holistic though still evolving reference framework to understand and guide a transformation in planning education. Indeed, several chapters of this book provide a surprisingly coherent and broader picture of the forces driving change in planning education. This is of key importance not only for the full understanding of changes underway but also for anticipating the directions of change that are likely to structure the evolution of contemporary planning education.

The second area is related to a most valuable fine-grained analysis in the field of spatial planning of the practicalities of delivering pedagogical and educational change in the prosaic world of the contemporary academy. Herein we want to make the following observations. First, the accumulated experience from the teaching cases shows that these practicalities are very diverse in nature and cover a variety of issues some of which may, and indeed tend, not to be taken in due account when preparing pedagogical initiatives. Second, such practicalities should (i) not be seen as an afterthought and, (ii) if creatively incorporated in the design phase, they may have a decisive influence on the impact of the initiative.

The multiple insights within these two areas do deserve further and individual consideration and will now be elaborated in turn.

AN EMERGING REFERENCE FRAMEWORK FOR UNDERSTANDING TRANSFORMATIVE CHANGE IN PLANNING EDUCATION

Going beyond Disciplinary Boundaries

The world is changing profoundly and at such a pace, that both planning and planning education, fully entangled in such changes, are bound to change deeply as well. In other words, it is not so much a question of whether educators want to change but the way the contemporary world is being shaped will inevitably impact not only the very nature and role of planning but also of higher education and, as a result of both, planning education as well. A striking feature is that one needs to go beyond the disciplinary boundaries of planning in order to more fully understand the overall process of change in planning education. This fact is also rooted in the growing awareness about the specificity of the situation at the current historical moment, where the distinctiveness "is not change *per se* but its character, its intensity, its felt impact" (Barnett 2004, p. 248). In this context, we may paraphrase Barnett (Chapter 3), referring to the university and argue that "in the 21st century, *planning* is always in the making", since it is deeply entangled with the wider world that is changing in a way that is quite distinctive from other changes in the past. Indeed, many of the key characteristics of the contemporary process of change are challenging the nature, scope, and purpose of spatial planning, as profusely illustrated by the chapters of this book, from different angles and contextual situations. Such circumstances, per se, would certainly raise challenges to planning education, concerned as it is with the preparation of students to perform these evolutionary forms of planning. But additionally, such challenges are inherently intertwined with other challenges, namely those associated with prominent debates on how to educate students for the contemporary world and about the role, nature and purpose of the university. The views expressed in this book vary in the interpretations and recommendations regarding desirable future directions due to weighing differently incipient driving forces, yet, they all set the process of change in planning education within broader dynamics of global change and the higher education landscape. In other words, the debate on the future of planning education cannot be dissociated from, rather it should be articulated with other debates in spheres of change to which planning, and planning education are closely interlinked.

The Rise of Pedagogy as a Fundamental Dimension of Planning Education

The rise of pedagogy as a fundamental component of the change in planning education is another striking feature that emerges strongly from different contributions to this book and particularly from the educationalists' book chapters. For example, Lamb and Vodicka (Chapter 2), not only subscribe to a 'critical postmodern pedagogy' perspective but also underline the role of pedagogy in endowing students with key skills underpinning contemporary planning. For instance, critical reflexivity, seen as fundamental for "planners striving to create just places in complex settings" requires purposeful pedagogical approaches that help "the self … to consider itself as its own object", in order to develop awareness and adequately address their own preconceptions that may constrain their actions (e.g., Chapters 5, 6 or 11). In the other chapters of the book, planning educators promote different types of educational initiatives, from introducing new contents to support inter- and trans-disciplinary action (Chapter 10) or new forms of continuing and/or online education (Chapters 13–16). All of them converge on the value of purposeful pedagogical support to effectively implement those initiatives. It is perhaps noteworthy that this concern with the relevance of pedagogy in no way is exclusive to planning education. A powerful illustration of the growing recognition of the role of pedagogy can be drawn from the Aga Khan Academy, according to which "what students know is no longer the most important measure of the quality of education. The true test is the ability to engage with what they do not know and work out a solution" (Marques 2019). Barnett (Chapter 3) speculating about the role (and the challenges) of planning, reaches the conclusion that "both curricula and pedagogies have to be called upon to do justice to such a conception of planning studies". In other words, the evolving nature of planning will certainly have implications for planning approaches and methods but will also have a deep and multi-dimensional impact on how planners are trained and educated. In this sense, pedagogical issues, as well as content, come to the forefront of planning education in a way that has remained hitherto largely unnoticed if not ignored.

Facing the Prospect of In-Depth Changes in Planning Education

A further viewpoint that the educationalists bring into discussion is the need for considering profound pedagogical changes (throughout higher education not just in planning education). The irony is revealing with which Barnett (Chapter 3) refers to "the conventional tropes of curricula and pedagogy" that are likely to be found in future course documents but that fail do justice to the challenges ahead. Rather, Barnett emphasizes the dimension of 'becoming' in the learning process, where students "have to make themselves", by adopting values and making complex choices. The teaching case studies provide abundant illustrative material of these challenges. They are largely rooted in most useful insights on how the nature of 'planning spaces' is changing towards more multi-discursive and contested spaces. This situation requires, from the professional planner, greater sensitivity to otherness as well as the capacity to co-create 'blended' knowledge, framed within a purposeful sense of collective direction. Unquestionably, such requirement impacts strongly on the preparation of the (future) planner, demanding a more critical and humble approach to the role of scientific knowledge and, above all, the development of a critical appreciation of power structures and how they help to shape the relationship between science and society and impinge on the actions of the individual planner. Of course, there is room as well for incremental change, for enhancing the role of inter- and trans-disciplinary dimensions in planning education, for promoting communication and collaborative skills, together with creativity, in ways yet to be fully explored, as suggested and illustrated in several chapters of this book (e.g., Chapters 9 and 10). However, the whole range of educational challenges is broader and deeper, in the sense that the link between knowledge, society and context (see Kallus, Chapter 5) brings to the forefront the trans-formational dimension of education, where self-development, values, attitude and ethics, together with autonomous learning capacity, gain much greater prominence. This is aptly illustrated in Brück and Million's presentation of the Mikroakademie (Chapter 12), wherein for short workshops students assume the role of educator and co-construct new knowledge and learning with peers independently. This creates new responsibilities, insights and perspectives. As mentioned before, Lambert and Vodicka (Chapter 3) endorse the view of "understanding pedagogy as a deeply civic, political, and moral practice". This statement illustrates poignantly the depth of the challenges ahead. A question to be raised, now, is whether and how planners, the academy and planning educators are preparing to face these challenges.

Enlisting Planning (Education) in the Debate about the Contemporary University

There is an ongoing and increasingly rich debate about the challenges to the contemporary university and what the "University of the Future" (European Commission 2019) will look like. Some argue that the university either faces the challenge of contributing to address societal challenges or risks becoming irrelevant (Davey et al. 2018). Public expectations about the role of the univer-sity are changing, introducing in the higher education policy agenda the need to produce 'useful' knowledge, to better equip students with contemporary skills and competencies and to collaborate more closely with society and local communities. The framing of the debate is far from being a consensual one and many argue, in line with Lamb and Vodicka (Chapter 2), that the university should resist and counteract the dominant neoliberal narrative while making a commitment to inclusion and social justice. Several chapters of this book establish an explicit link to this debate, namely in what concerns pedagogical initiatives involving engagement with the community. What emerges strongly from reading these chapters is that there is (much) more to it than just the willingness to familiarize students with the requirements of planning practice. It may involve actively changing life circumstances through teaching and learning interventions including work with community members (e.g. see Chapters 7, 15 and 16). The sensitiveness to the place-specific socio-cultural dimension of public participation, the challenges of fully appreciating otherness, the labyrinths of power structures and dominant discourses as well as the (permanent) incompleteness of 'professional knowledge', to name just a few, do require careful pedagogical consideration and preparation that go beyond the mere good will. The point, however, is that if there is much to gain from knowing more about the hurdles associated with the ongoing debate it is also true that planning education is very well positioned, due its specific planning ethos of advocacy (Davidoff 1965), to enrich if not enlighten such debate. The challenge raised by Barnett (Chapter 3) is a testimony that planning education could and should be an active voice in the ongoing debate about the contemporary university.

THE PRACTICALITIES OF DELIVERING CHANGE

One of the aims of this book was to provide visibility to a lively landscape of innovative pedagogical initiatives, most often unconnected, quite diverse among themselves and taking place in a variety of spatial, socio-cultural, political and institutional contexts. A complementary aim was to focus on the hurdles of designing and delivering these initiatives, and to stimulate and help all those wishing to follow a similar path, even if in different contexts and with different objectives. Indeed, a key concern was to highlight the importance of paying attention to the practicalities of delivering a (pedagogical) initiative and to bear in mind the decisive influence that those practicalities may have in both the effectiveness and impact of the pedagogical activity. In other words, and as the planning community surely understands very well, implementation mechanisms should not be considered as an afterthought but rather be closely and simultaneously considered along and in tandem with the guiding (pedagogical) conceptual framework (see Morgan 2004, for an elaboration of this argument in policy making). The content of the contributions shows that this aim paid off very well and the aggregate learning is indeed extensive and deep.

The first key message concerns the (planning) educator and the range and diversity of challenges and demands to which s/he will be exposed when engaging in a different teaching-learning experience. Notwithstanding the planner-based motivations and the opportunities to learn something new while exploring emerging pedagogical avenues, the educator must develop an awareness of the broader demands of such initiatives, that go clearly beyond an almost inevitable increase in the teaching workload. The chapters in this book allow the reader to gain such a wider perspective. In addition to the need often felt of mobilizing and relying on the support of colleagues for specific tasks, it also means facing the burden and the uncertainty of securing additional resources, dealing with and being responsive to the expectations of other stakeholders, namely when it involves working with community, and caring for the well-being of students, if and when they are confronted with 'transformational' experiences (e.g., Chapters 5 and 6). It also means the possibility of exposure to situations that have not been experienced before by the educator and do require purposeful professional as well as pedagogical preparation. In order to have a structural educational impact, pedagogical innovation often requires reflexivity by the educator, who needs to be able to question his/her own assumptions, values and beliefs underlying teaching practice (see Lamb and Vodicka, Chapter 2, quoting John Smyth, 1989). In this, educators may have to face delicate dilemmas associated with the political dimension and even legitimacy of education oriented towards transformative practices and citizenry (e.g., Chapter 5). In a nutshell, not only are the delivery practicalities closely intertwined with the guiding pedagogical framework but also it is of fundamental importance to give due consideration to the wide range of responsibilities as well as the pedagogical underpinnings and the formative purpose the planning educator endorses and is willing to embrace.

A second message concerns a full appreciation of what is involved in preparing and delivering pedagogical initiatives *in addition* to the individual engagement of the planning educator. This is indeed a crucial point and twofold. First, as abundantly demonstrated in the chapters of this book, the design and implementation of pedagogical innovation involves a rich and diversified delivery landscape of stakeholders. This immediately points to the need for sensitiveness and empathy with the different stakeholders as well as for the capacity to engender and build alliances. Additionally, and second, it also points to the advantages of nurturing a supportive institutional framing, to avoid ephemeris and to effectively lay down the basis for structuring change in planning education.

Looking in more detail to the diversity of the delivery landscape, students come naturally to the forefront. A rather interesting perspective deserving attention, and explicitly addressed in several chapters in this book, is promoting *enthusiasm for planning* among students. One may be led to think that, consequently, the teaching-learning process is an easy ride for everyone. That is not necessarily the case, as Barnett (Chapter 3) warns that in some circumstances "students stand on a precipice and hurl themselves forward, not to their deaths but to their becoming". Caring for the well-being of students is of key importance in many situations. The point to be made, though, is the importance of students' motivation, the argument being that it is a bold assumption to think that all students will be (equally or easily) motivated to become involved in innovative pedagogical initiatives that may change significantly the nature of the learning process which they are used to either consciously or not. This is an important issue deserving attention at preparation, implementation and evaluation stages. Students exposed to a learning process of a different nature, for instance with greater emphasis on autonomous learning, will face the challenges of new routines and, most probably, more intense workloads.

The appreciation, understanding and acceptance of these challenges are of crucial importance for the smooth running and the success of the modules. The situation may be compounded if the initiative is an 'isolated' (i.e., very different) pedagogical experience compared to other courses in an educational programme. This may increase the difficulty for students to understand and accept the rationale and purpose of the initiative. Having to deal with voices of discontent, if not dissent, among students may jeopardize the very enthusiasm that the planning educator is aiming to create or strengthen among planning students.

The latter situation points to the importance of searching for, and trying to secure broader support within the institution, the school or the department, going beyond the access to (needed) material resources. Establishing or contributing to strengthening pedagogical and educational change within the institutional agenda may become a key ingredient for easing the way to successful individual initiatives in planning education. It is interesting to notice that several contributors refer to institutional identity and/or historical trajectories (e.g., Chapters 4 and 7) as a lever to engage in the respective initiatives. A possible alternative, which in fact is compatible with what was just said, is to build inter-institutional, often international networks to support individual initiatives and/or link such initiatives with the dominant but broader policy agenda of the university, as so well illustrated by Rafferty et al. (Chapter 8). More recently, educational and pedagogical issues are finding their way to the core of higher education policy agendas, leading many universities to create some sort of institution-wide pedagogical support service, and several programmes have also been established at national (e.g. AdvanceHE in the UK, https://www.advance-he.ac.uk/) and supranational scale (e.g. the European Universities Initiative, https://ec.europa.eu/education/events/european-universities-initiative_en), providing not only further support but also legitimacy (and guidance) to individual initiatives. This is a multifaceted valuable resource that planning education should not ignore.

A final mention goes to other, often non-academic stakeholders that do participate directly in the initiatives, specifically when they involve the community. Several of the chapters in this book draw attention either explicitly or implicitly to the heterogeneity of these stakeholder groups and the likely diversity of their views – sometimes even the inherent conflict of interests. The capacity to manage tensions and conflicts that may arise, and to guide students in such processes, can be quite challenging for the planning educator. Thus, the point raised by Grams (Chapter 14) regarding the advantage of having among the educators' team at least some members with prior professional experience is poignant. Moreover, managing expectations amongst stakeholders is also of importance and, as argued before, this task has to be started at the very stage of preparing the initiative. A related point that also emerges quite strongly is reciprocity – i.e., stakeholders should receive a 'reward' in whatever form in return for their engagement. Ethically, there is a need or even duty to share the benefits of the initiative, which cannot be measured only by students' learning or improved capacity to learn – and students must be made aware that they should be able to give back something to the community (e.g., Yonder et al., Chapter 4; also Angotti et al. 2011; Frank and Sieh 2016). In a nutshell, when preparing the ground for the initiative, one needs to go beyond the academy and, with stakeholders, one needs to clarify the potential, the hurdles and the limitations of the exercise, in order to enhance both the learning potential and the impact of the initiative.

ONGOING OR TRANSFORMATIVE CHANGE?

Historically, not only have planning education curricula changed but at a higher level also the concept of what it means to obtain a university degree. The relationship of the university with society and its economy has changed quite fundamentally over time. Barnett (Chapter 3, and 2011) as well as others (e.g., Fallis 2011; Moore 2019) have examined the different conceptions of universities in the past and present, and how they have re-invented their purpose and meaning throughout history. At this point it may be not entirely clear what model of a university will dominate or prevail in future, or whether there will be multiple models that coexist. However, overall there seems to be an understanding that a modern university does not stand apart or above society but "interpenetrates society, as society interpenetrates the university" (Barnett 2011, p. 453) and as such using its full range of resources to progress societal and individual well-being and sustainability.

Theories of change and transformation in society suggest that most substantial transformations derive from the convergence of multiple factors (WBGU 2011) and the co-evolution of different associated subsystems (Grin et al. 2010). Four main triggers or drivers of change have been identified: (a) technology, (b) crisis (e.g., war, economic crash), (c) knowledge, and (d) vision (new narratives such as communism; or collaboration/coalition etc). Major transformations typically take several decades such as the transition from the agricultural to industrial society (e.g., Osterhammel 2009) which was fuelled by an increasing use of fossil fuels, globalization of trade, and technological innovation and diffusion. Advances in technology, knowledge and new visions and narratives change values in society and bring about a change in lifestyles, socio-cultural conditions and power relations. A new transition or transformation is now urgently needed to shift societies to cleaner production, non-carbon renewable energy sources, and more equitable access to knowledge as well as wealth and resources (WBGU 2011).

This transformation necessarily requires a questioning of past and present values and beliefs. In the social sciences, and planning through which we organize our spatial environment, it means greater inclusivity, a relinquishing of the expert-knows-best approach to include different interests and knowledges to co-construct future shared visions of ways to live on the planet. As such, postmodern education for spatial planning includes social and cultural awareness, adaptability, creativity, collaborative ways of working and becoming global citizens with a shift to learner choice and autonomy (e.g., Lamb and Vodicka, Chapter 2). Interestingly, technological advances, such as digitalization – while offering an ever increasing access to knowledge resources around the world via the internet, networked databases, digital books and texts – have until recently remained at bay at the 'places of higher education' such as the universities and further education colleges. Yes, distance, online and blended learning have made some inroads but the majority of young adults have flocked to cities and campuses, taken up residence and studied by attending lectures and seminars, by conducting experiments in laboratories, and discussing ideas with peers and professors in the coffee houses, hallways of institutional buildings, bars and society halls. The importance of chance social interaction, of body language and intonation for learning and discourse has been newly highlighted in the debates that have ensued in the early summer of 2020 after institutions of higher learning (and much of the rest of the world of work) were forced to shut doors temporarily to move teaching and learning online within a week or two in order to help stem the spread of a global health pandemic.

The incident was a shock to the system, for certain, and caused great strains but also forced academic leaders to rethink university provision. As Sheppard (Chapter 13) has related, learning at a distance can create isolation – not just of the learner but also the teacher by the way; however, the case study also showed that there are ways to overcome such isolation at least in part with smart application of technology. This case study illustrates well that it matters a great deal how people are using the tools.

And so while many of us initially despaired – particularly when considering a necessity to 'interpenetrate society' (Barnett, Chapter 3) and co-learn with others to solve today's global and life threatening challenges and as it is attempted in the first set of teaching case studies – this crisis could also help with setting in train deep transformational change in the education of future planners. For example, can we use technology to create community and work with community even if we are not in the same room or space? While it is always great to visit a space, hear the sounds, and experience the different unpleasant or fragrant smells, perhaps our inability to visit places in person empowers the locals to tell us their stories with words and pictures through their eyes rather than ours. Possibly, this can create more authentic perspectives and accounts of local and stakeholder knowledges, and inclusivity that is at the same level – as there is no studied and external expert view available. Planners would then experience things through the eyes of residents (i.e., others). The greater use of online teaching might also provide greater regard to online degrees, and equality in the valuation of those teaching on distance learning degrees in comparison to those that customarily do not. The variety and choice for learners not able to join prestigious institutions for one or another reason may also become broadened with more provision offered in hybrid modes (online and in person) to ensure resilience against future shocks and issues. On the flipside, naturally there are many risks that come with transformations as well. Planning as well as other professions and academia need to help untangle the positives and the negatives.

FUTURE OUTLOOK

Editing this book has been in many ways at once unsettling and reassuring, confirming our expectations but also opening new windows and perspectives. Working with educationalists has been a challenge yet also highly rewarding and is something we believe will be of help to the planning education community in creating new and exciting future-fit learning landscapes.

This book continues and builds on previous research and explorations by other planning educators such as the innovative 'regional learning environment' developed to enhance collaboration skills for spatial planning students by Oonk (2016), the plea for integrating multiple knowledge types by Rooij and Frank (2016), or the interdisciplinary university–community partnerships to promote sustainability transitions of cities discussed by Schlossberg et al. (2018), and Wilson and Beatley's (2018) account of interdisciplinary university client projects involving planners. We also need to make the curriculum and our teaching more inclusive, decolonize the curriculum so to speak, and make sure the achievements of minorities are recognized in our historical reviews.

It is important to remember that transformations tend to be journeys which will not be completed overnight. It is also worth remembering that present teaching and pedagogies are not necessarily superfluous or entirely outdated. There may well be aspects of teaching that we want to keep alongside emerging new elements. This book with its collection of teaching case studies represents but one leg in a journey to fundamentally change the concept of higher education and as part of that the education for spatial planners in the 21st century. Pedagogies and aspects relevant to spatial planning – not covered in this volume – will need to be explored further – such as, for example, how to work more and better with other disciplines including the hard sciences as well as arts, media/communication or public health to name a few. This is part of the push beyond boundaries. There is a need to collaborate with natural and life sciences more in order to address issues of climate change, biodiversity loss and reframe the human–nature relationship in a mutually enhancing rather than destructive manner. In looking to transition cities as well as non-urban environments to become more ecologically sound and sustainable, we may have to glean from rapid development, testing and evaluation approaches as we can see them happening with the efforts to develop a vaccine for the COVID-19 virus that stifled economies, stopped normal schooling and almost overnight had major proportions of the world's population working and studying from their kitchen tables. Can new developments, building materials, insulation practices, and planning strategies be tested and monitored in different places in the world via living labs (see Evans et al. 2015), supported and evaluated by those studying and working – in similar ways as in the Residency Programme for early career urbanists and planners showcased by Refinetti Martins and Custódio de Oliveira (Chapter 15)?

There is one thing that seems clear if we do want to make progress which is that there need to be more forums to share and co-develop ideas and pedagogies. The effectiveness of such collaborative approaches in reviewing and developing teaching/instructional processes is powerfully demonstrated in the contribution by Rafferty et al. (Chapter 8). These debates and exchanges – while occasionally started in conversation over a coffee or dinner – often require more time than available during a chance meeting at a conference. We all have experienced the enthusiasm to implement something new after an event – but once back in the home environment best intentions are quickly stifled as we find ourselves mired in institutional inertia. There need to be appropriate training opportunities for educators and future educators. And, while in some countries opportunities for pedagogical advancement exist for academics working in higher education as well as for doctoral students, these are not consistently available throughout the world and not all of them suit the particular needs of specific disciplines. Finally, there also is a need to develop an evaluation framework to help monitor the effectiveness of various approaches in addressing specific learning activities. This is particularly important for engaged and action-based learning, that is interdisciplinary, and learner centred.

One idea to further promote such development activities has been to establish networks and workshops dedicated to pedagogical themes with regular multiday meetings which could provide the exposure to and training in new methods and approaches of teaching while also developing a support network to help facilitate change longer term across the programmes providing planning education. This network or networks can be platforms to share bottom-up ideas and support emergent changes, but they could also provide external evaluation and/or facilitate research activities and joint funding applications. They would help provide the upskilling of (future) educators that seems necessary if scholars are not to be overwhelmed with practicalities involved in introducing new pedagogies.

There is still much to be developed further, such as the promotion of inter- and trans-disciplinary pedagogies and learning and more flexible delivery of learning and teaching, asynchronous, and synchronous, online and face to face. How – if at all – can we teach design effectively and create experiential learning or interact with communities in meaningful ways without meeting in person? How can we appreciate and experience a global world without over-using resources in irresponsible ways? How can we develop the social and civic understanding, the emotional intelligence (Visser 2018) and dispo-sitions in future generations to cope with unknown futures and address moral dilemmas in an equitable manner?

We hope the readership will join us on our future journey and explorations.

REFERENCES

Angotti, T., Doble, C. and Horrigan, P. (eds.) (2011) *Service Learning in Design and Planning: Educating at the Boundaries*. New York: New Village Press.

Barnett, R. (2004) Learning for an unknown future. *Higher Education Research and Development* 23(3): 247–260.

Barnett, R. (2011) The coming of the ecological university. *Oxford Review of Education* 37(4): 439–455.

Davey, T., Meerman, A., Orazbayeva, B., Riedel, M., Galán-Muros, V., Plewa, C. and Eckert, N. (eds.) (2018) *The Future of Universities Thoughtbook*. Amsterdam: University Industry Innovation Network.

Davidoff, P. (1965) Advocacy and pluralism in planning. *Journal of the American Institute of Planners* 31(4): 331–338.

European Commission (EC) (2019) *European Universities Initiatives: Building the Universities of the Future*. https://ec.europa.eu/education/events/european-universities-initiative_en.

Evans, J., Jones, R., Karvonen, A. Millard, L. and Wendler, J. (2015) Living labs and co-production: University campuses as platforms for sustainability science. *Current Opinions in Environmental Sustainability* 16: 1–6.

Fallis, G. (2011) *Multiversities, Ideas and Democracy*. Toronto: University of Toronto Press.

Frank, A. I. and Sieh, L. (2016) Multiversity of the twenty-first century: Examining opportunities for integrating community engagement in planning curricula. *Planning Practice & Research* 31(5): 513–532.

Grin, J., Rotmans, J. and Schot, J. (2010) *Transitions to Sustainable Development. New Directions in the Study of Long-Term Transformative Change.* London: Routledge.

Marques, A. (2019) Rethinking the community with a pluralistic outlook: Bridging practice and knowledge in an uncertain world. Presented at the Aga Khan Foundation Research Summit, University of Aveiro, Portugal, 28–29 November.

Moore, J. C. (2019) *A Brief History of Universities*. Cham: Palgrave Macmillan.

Morgan, K. (2004) Sustainable regions: Governance, innovation and scale. *European Planning Studies* 12(6): 871–889.

Oonk, C. (2016) Educating collaborative planners: Strengthening evidence for the learning potential of multi-stakeholder regional learning environments. *Planning Practice & Research* 31(5): 533–551.

Osterhammel, J. (2009) *Die Verwandlung der Welt. Eine Geschichte des 19. Jahrhunderts.* München: Beck.

Rooij, R. and Frank, A. I. (2016) Educating spatial planners for the age of cocreation: The need to risk community, science and practice involvement in planning programmes and curricula. *Planning Practice and Research* 31(5): 473–485.

Schlossberg, M., Larco, N., Slotterback, C. S., Connerly, C. and Greco, M. (2018) Educational partnerships for innovation in communities (EPIC): Harnessing university resources to create change. In A. I. Frank and C. Silver (eds.), *Urban Planning Education: Beginnings, Global Movement and Future Prospects* (pp. 251–268). Cham: Springer.

Visser, J. (2018) The Anthropocene: A different learning landscape for a different world. Lecture delivered at the Universitas Nusa Cendana in Kupang, Indonesia 10 October.

WBGU (2011) *Welt im Wandel – Gesellschaftsvertrag fuer eine Grosse Transformation.* Berlin: Wissenschaftlicher Beirat der Bundesregierung Globale Umweltveränderungen (WBGU). https://www.wbgu.de/fileadmin/user_upload/wbgu/publikationen/hauptgutachten/hg2011/pdf/wbgu_jg2011.pdf.

Wilson, B. B. and Beatley, T. (2018) Educating code-switchers in a post-sustainability world. In A. I. Frank and C. Silver (eds.), *Urban Planning Education: Beginnings, Global Movement and Future Prospects* (pp. 307–322). Cham: Springer.

Index

action-oriented, action oriented 3–5, 16, 60, 221, 253
  see also pedagogy; pedagogies
advocacy, advocacy-oriented 58–60, 69, 80, 82, 120, 126–7, 253, 272
alumni 194, 215
animation techniques 100
Anthropocene 1
anthropological tools, anthropological methods, anthropologist 31, 79–80, 89
architecture and planning 30, 74–5, 78–80, 87, 89, 160, 176, 182, 239
architecture and urbanism 14, 108, 112–13, 116, 120, 131, 143, 146, 236–8, 240–42, 244, 247
Argyris, Chris 43
Association of European Schools of Planning (AESOP) 6
asynchronous 206, 209, 217, 219
audience 12, 15, 94, 98–101, 111, 114, 178, 180, 182, 186, 259
autonomous/ly 12, 27–9, 34, 112, 117, 157, 189, 271, 273
autonomy 10, 22, 26–9, 32, 34, 41, 101, 210, 259, 276

Bachelor, BSc, BA 6, 131, 145, 167, 177–9, 182, 186, 189, 193, 195–7
blended learning 13, 127, 205–6, 208, 276
Bologna Agreement 145
bottom-up 13–14, 77, 198, 200, 278
boundary/ies 30, 87, 130, 165
  disciplinary 11, 30, 121, 158, 268–9
  professional 198
boundary object 159
Brazil 10, 31, 108–9, 111–12, 117, 120, 236–7, 239–41, 245–6

certificate 193, 196, 207

challenges in contemporary planning education 6
civic commitment 99, 104
civic dimension 104, 135
civic engagement 10, 74, 77, 81, 104–5, 125–6, 129, 131, 135–6
civic responsibility 35, 52
clarification of problems and tasks 99, 221–33
class size 34, 61, 71, 207, 254
classroom-based 6, 10, 142
classroom, beyond the 9, 108–9, 121
classroom to coffee shop concept 213–18
co-design/ing 10, 16, 126–38, 184
co-learning 126, 128, 138, 192, 251, 264
collaboration/s 12–13, 16, 22, 26–7, 58, 60–67, 70, 76, 80, 94, 115, 127–30, 136, 152, 175, 185, 206, 209, 212, 226, 230, 246, 260–62, 275
communication skills 2, 151–2, 191–2, 198
communicative planning practices see planning practice/s
community-based client, community-based organization 57–9, 62–3, 70
community-engaged, community oriented 30–31, 58, 67, 74–8, 86, 88
community engagement, community involvement 8–9, 11, 57, 70, 77, 129, 138, 152, 262
community outreach, community–university outreach 9–10, 58, 108–23
community participation 28, 125, 129
conflict zone 75, 77, 81
context-based experiential learning 125
continuing education 13, 221–5, 229–33, 240
  see also further education